CW00421575

They Fought with Extraordinary Bravery

III German (Saxon) Army Corps in the Southern Netherlands, 1814

Geert Van Uythoven

Helion & Company

Helion & Company Limited
Unit 8 Amherst Business Centre
Budbrooke Road
Warwick
CV34 5WE
England
Tel. 01926 499619
Email: info@helion.co.uk
Website: www.helion.co.uk
Twitter: @helionbooks

Published by Helion & Company 2019
Designed and typeset by Farr Out Publications, Wokingham, Berkshire
Cover designed by Paul Hewitt, Battlefield Design (www.battlefield-design.co.uk)

Text © Geert Van Uythoven 2019
Illustrations as individually credited. Colour artwork by Christa Hook © Helion and Company 2019
Maps by George Anderson © Helion and Company 2019

Cover: The Saxon Hussars in the Combat of Sweweghem, 31 March 1814. Artwork by Christa Hook
(www.christahook.co.uk) © Helion and Co. 2019

Every reasonable effort has been made to trace copyright holders and to obtain their permission
for the use of copyright material. The author and publisher apologise for any errors or omissions in
this work, and would be grateful if notified of any corrections that should be incorporated in future
reprints or editions of this book.

ISBN 978-1-912866-65-6

British Library Cataloguing-in-Publication Data.
A catalogue record for this book is available from the British Library.

All rights reserved. No part of this publication may be reproduced, stored in a retrieval system, or
transmitted, in any form, or by any means, electronic, mechanical, photocopying, recording or
otherwise, without the express written consent of Helion & Company Limited.

For details of other military history titles published by Helion & Company Limited, contact the above
address, or visit our website: http://www.helion.co.uk

We always welcome receiving book proposals from prospective authors.

Contents

Introduction

One of the last encounters in the field that took place between the allies and the French in 1814, was the engagement near Courtray on 31 March between a French force, commanded by the able and experienced *Général de Division* Maison, and the Saxon *Generalleutnant* Johann Adolf *Freiherr* von Thielmann commanding a mixed allied force consisting in a part of Saxons who had defected to the allies in the midst of the Battle of Leipzig alongside raw Saxon Landwehr, just recruited, untrained in battle. The outcome was never in doubt, and if Thielmann had known the odds he was up against the engagement never would have taken place. Such, however, are the uncertainties of war!

Although an insignificant encounter in itself, with all eyes on France where Napoleon fought to retain his empire, it is still interesting to have a closer look at the events in Flanders during the first months of 1814. Not only because the encounter itself is the subject of a number of first-hand descriptions, describing how the newly enlisted German troops behaved in battle and how their mutual relations were (of which information is relatively scarce and many stories are being told, mostly not very positive), but also because the history of III German Corps, of which von Thielmann's force was a part, is relatively unknown and the subject of many prejudices. I will focus mainly on the actions of the III German Corps, therefore the French role will only be treated as far as necessary to paint a complete picture of the events that are described.

1

The Advance of the Army of the North

The Army of the North

The Battle of Leipzig, 16-19 October 1813, was a resounding victory over Napoleon by the combined allied armies. As a result the Saxon king tried to come to an agreement with the allies in an effort to save his kingdom. Instead he was taken prisoner, the Saxon kingdom for the time being governed by a Governor-General. The remnants of the French army slowly retreated back in the direction of France, leaving behind garrisons in various fortress cities. At Hanau, an Austro-Batavian army under *General der Kavallerie* von Wrede tried to block Napoleon's retreat but was soundly defeated, the French continuing their retreat and crossing the Rhine. The allies were slow in following up their victory, needing time to decide on a plan of operations on which everyone could agree and which would mean attacking the French Empire itself. At the end of November the armies were put in motion. The allies split up their forces: Blücher's Army of Silesia followed Napoleon to the Rhine; the main army marched through Switzerland to France, occupying the plateau of Langres; finally the Army of the North (Bernadotte) had to advance to the northeast to Hannover and Westphalia, to free these parts from the French. Of this army, *Generalleutnant* Friedrich Wilhelm Bülow's III Prussian Corps had to march to the Netherlands to free them from French rule, in cooperation with the Russian Cossack Corps of General-Major Tschernischew, later to be followed by the remainder of General of Cavalry Ferdinand von Wintzingerode's Russian corps.

The situation was somewhat confusing. There was no love between Bülow and Bernadotte, and the latter had his own agenda. Jean Baptiste Bernadotte was born in Pau, France, in 1763. Entering the French army in 1780, he rose through the ranks during the Revolutionary Wars and Napoleon's reign, and he finally became a French Marshal in 1804. The Swedish king having no heir, Bernadotte was elected Crown Prince by the Swedish *Riksdag* of the Estates in 1810 for having been kind to Swedish prisoners. On his adoption he assumed the name 'Karl Johan', but for convenience the name Bernadotte will be used throughout this book. In 1813 he sided with the

The Northern and Southern Netherlands in 1814

allies and received command of the Army of the North of about 130,000 men, consisting of a Swedish army of 30,000; Bülow's III Prussian corps and two Russian corps (Wintzingerode and Vorontsov). Not surprisingly, Bernadotte had his own agenda in favour of Swedish interests and turned his attention to Hamburg and Denmark whilst ordering Bülow to continue the advance to the Netherlands. Both made their own decisions: Bülow continued to send reports to Bernadotte and received various instructions from him, but acted as he saw fit without bothering too much.[1] Proceeded by Cossacks and with an advance guard under *Generalmajor* Friedrich Adolf von Oppen, Bülow marched west. On 17 November his headquarters were in Münster. Already days before, on 9 November 1813, bands of Russian Cossacks had crossed the border of the former Netherlands. They occupied Zwolle and Kampen, on the 15th they entered Groningen. *Generalleutnant* Karl Leopold von Borstell marched to Wesel with his 5th Division to cover Bülow's left flank and to blockade the French garrison.[2]

The Dutch rise against the French

Swiftly pushing forward and aided by the Dutch, about 250 Cossacks reached Amsterdam on 24 November. In order not to be cut off and with the Dutch population rising against French rule, the Governor-General of the Dutch departments, Anne Charles Lebrun, had already abandoned Amsterdam on 15 November and the French moved south leaving behind garrisons in fortress cities like Delfzijl, Naarden, Helder, and Arnhem. The Dutch leaders of the uprising judged the time was right and requested Prince Willem Frederik of Orange to return to the Netherlands to become the head of state. On 30 November 1813 he landed on the Dutch coast at Scheveningen, near The Hague, and was inaugurated as sovereign of the United Netherlands. The Netherlands declared themselves independent from France. Willem of Orange was followed by 250 British marines. Bülow, after having reached the Yssel River, captured the cities Doesburg and Zutphen (23 and 24 November). Then he turned his attention to the fortress-city of Arnhem, occupied by a strong French garrison. Possession of this city, as was still the case over a century later in 1944, was important to facilitate a swift crossing of the Rhine River, even more so with Wesel still occupied by the French. The defences of the city itself had been neglected and it was rightly assessed that the garrison of about 3,500 French was insufficient to defeat a full-scale attack. Therefore, Bülow decided not to besiege the city but to take it by storm, succeeding in capturing it on 30 November. The French *Maréchal* Macdonald retreated, occupying Nijmegen and Grave. In mid-December he was reinforced by the remains of *Général de Division* Molitor's division (1,500 men), which had left behind a garrison in 's Hertogenbosch.

1   Remark from *Major* von Reiche of Bülow's general staff, in Louis von Weltzien, *Memoiren des königlich preußischen Generals der Infanterie Ludwig von Reiche* (Leipzig: F.A. Brockhaus, 1857), Vol. 2, p.7.

2   Contemporary sources use the designation 'Brigade' as well as 'Division' for these formations in Bülow's Prussian III Corps. As these formations were in fact of division strength, I will use the designation 'Division'.

Entrance of General Bülow in Arnhem, 1813. (Rijksmuseum)

Parties of Cossacks made their way to the west, later followed by *Major* Friedrich August von Colomb's *Streifkorps* and regular Prussian and Russian units. Small parties of British marines and soldiers landed along the coast, the British commitment needed to strengthen their influence at the table deciding about the future of the Netherlands. On 3 December, Lieutenant Colonel James Campbell arrived with a marine battalion (500 men) which marched to The Hague. Next day, General Sir Thomas Graham was ordered to take command of the British force of 10,000 men which it had been decided to send to the Netherlands. On the 6th, the first regular army battalions arrived; two Guards battalions (1,500-1,700 men) which marched to Brielle.[3] This all gave the Dutch enough heart to rise en masse against French rule, forming small provisional units which gradually would take over blockading the fortresses still occupied by French garrisons. With the French field forces driven back south across the rivers Waal and Meuse, British attention immediately turned to the southern part of the Netherlands. Especially the French naval forces in Antwerp were important, as illustrated by the instructions that General Graham received:

It is now my duty to call your attention to another object in which the British interest are deeply involved. I mean the destruction of the naval armament at Antwerp. If at any time you should find it possible by marching suddenly on Antwerp to occupy such a position as would enable you to destroy the ships which it is understood are now laid up there, you would perform an essential service to your country. A lengthened operation for that purpose is neither compatible with the description of the force under your command nor with the service on which you are to be employed under my former instruction: but if in the course of your operations, it should be found practicable to bring down to your assistance a considerable force of the allied army, much facility might be devised from such

3   For a complete account about the British presence in the Netherlands see Andrew Bamford, *A Bold and Ambitious Enterprise – The British Army in the Low Countries, 1813-1814* (London: Frontline Books, 2013).

assistance. And you will not fail to give me the earliest information of what you may deem necessary for the purpose of undertaking an attack upon the place; — always bearing in mind that it is the destruction of the naval armament, not the capture of the citadel or town which should be the principal object of your exertions.[4]

The above explains why the British under General Graham did not participate in the common allied cause to defeat the French but focussed on a single goal during the following months.

The French were of course aware of the importance of Antwerp, and the experienced *Général de Division* Decaen was send here to take over command. Arriving in Antwerp on 5 December, Decaen found it without the necessary garrison: only about 3,000 to 4,000 National Guards were present, without proper uniforms and unarmed. To remedy this, he decided to evacuate Willemstad, Breda, Steenbergen, and Tholen to reinforce Antwerp with these garrisons which departed on 11 and 12 December. The evacuated positions were promptly occupied by Dutch provisional units supported by the British, while Major General George Cooke moved from Hellevoetsluis to Willemstad to occupy it with both Guards battalions. Together with Hellevoetsluis, Willemstad would become the depot for Graham's army, although supplying the troops was difficult because of the cold weather covering the rivers with ice. More evacuations followed, and slowly the French were pushed south out of Zeeland and Brabant by the Dutch provisional units, closely supported by British troops and the Cossacks. The only exception was the strong fortress-city Bergen op Zoom, which was occupied by a strong garrison, reinforced even more by retreating French troops.

After having captured Arnhem, further advance to the south of Bülow's Prussian III Corps was slow. In over five weeks he covered a distance of only 60 kilometres. Prussian troops blockaded Gorkum and Nijmegen, still occupied by strong French garrisons, while Bülow with his main force crossed the rivers Waal and Meuse at the Bommelerwaard on 15 December, close to 's Hertogenbosch which was also occupied by the French. With his Prussians having to blockade so many fortresses, the British still building up their forces and the Dutch still much under strength with untrained units, Macdonald with his French corps still between Nijmegen and Grave,and the news of substantial French troops gathering around Antwerp, Bülow halted his advance, to wait for the arrival of Wintzingerode's Russian corps as well as III German Corps which was planned to come up from Germany. Many Prussian historians and contemporaries explained this delay due to the apathy of the Dutch, perceived as not willing to fight for their country, The British would complain about this as well though, but it may well be possible that they were influenced by Bülow's opinion or just from hearsay. The facts show however that the Dutch were doing what they could to raise troops but that it was difficult. Contrary to for example the Prussians, the Dutch departments had year after year been drained of manpower by conscription; tens of

---

4   Quoted in English in G.J.W. Koolemans Beijnen et al., *Historisch Gedenkboek der Herstelling van Neêrlands Onafhankelijkheid in 1813*, Part I (Haarlem: De Erven F. Bohn, 1912-1913), p.150.

thousands had died in Spain and Russia. Now numerous units were raised and many enthusiastic volunteers flocked to form provisional units. They were however of all ages, untrained and without arms: the Prussians needed muskets themselves and were in no position to provide these for the Dutch. Fortunately, tens of thousands would be provided by the British. The Dutch were also in great need of experienced officers to lead these units. Despite this, the Prince of Orange and the provisional Dutch government took many measures to form a Dutch army as soon as possible. On 20 December the *Reglement van algemeene volkswapening* ('Regulation of general people's armament') was decreed, by which every defensible male between 17 and 50 years of age would have to be trained to form a *landstorm*. Out of this *landstorm*, a militia would be drawn of 16,000 infantry (20 battalions) and 4,000 artillery (four battalions). Beside the *landstorm* and militia, by decree of 9 January 1814 a standing army was to be raised consisting of 22 infantry battalions, four cavalry regiments, four foot artillery battalions, a horse artillery corps, pontoneers, sappers and miners, and a battalion of train soldiers. The nucleus of this standing army would consist of the provisional units of volunteers that had already been raised.

That the Dutch were indeed making efforts to raise a substantial army was confirmed by Lord Clancarty:

> On the ... want of military exertion in the Government, till your arrival here, although your cousin Yarmouth and other idle and unobserving travellers had spread reports in England that no exertions were making, I must confess I thought this charge extremely unjust.[5]

Clancarty then extensively illustrated the formation of the Dutch army. So it has to be doubted if the supposed lack of Dutch energy was the real reason for Bülow's inactiveness. Bülow himself explained his delay to the Prussian King as follows:

> If the action of the Russians and the English in my right flank works in a favourable way, I will try to get across the Waal. However, caution is necessary in this case, as there is no doubt that there is an increase in enemy forces. I believe that I cannot proceed sooner than until the Dutch have come so far with their armament that they can take over the observation and blockade of Gorkum, 's Hertogenbosch, and Breda. Of course, it is important to penetrate Brabant at this very moment, to incite the inhabitants there, and to take the fortresses there while they are probably incomplete equipped; but my present forces are not enough for such a success. Therefore, I ask for reinforcements, by relieving Brigade Borstell Brigade before Wesel and by returning the four battalions and six squadrons, which are still with the corps of Count Tauentzien. The Crown Prince of Sweden informed me that he wished General von Wintzingerode to march with 15,000 men from the Weser to the Yssel; but there this corps is of no use to me; but rather

---

5   Letter of 1 March 1814 from Lord Clancarty to Lord Castlereagh, in English in Dr. H.T. Colenbrander, *Gedenkstukken der Algemeene Geschiedenis van Nederland van 1795 tot 1840*, Vol. 7, *Vestiging van het Koninkrijk 1813-1815* ('s-Gravenhage: Martinus Nijhoff, 1914), pp.68-75.

by relieving Brigade Borstell before Wesel, whereby both corps remain united and can operate independently ... If nothing happens in my support, then the enemy finally has to learn my weakness. If severe frost sets in, the waters freeze, I shall not, at best, be able to maintain my extensive positions at the Waal and Meuse; especially when the enemy with superior forces passes the Waal between Nijmegen and Tiel. For such a crossing he still has all means in his hands. Now I am tied up at Gorkum. But if I am supported, I can attack Marshal Macdonald, cut off his connection with Wesel, and take possession of all of Brabant and Flanders.[6]

Maybe the best explanation for Bülow's delaying his advance south is given by Crusius: 'All too often his luck had to be attributed to his caution, and here in the midst of these abnormal circumstances of all kinds he is the least inclined to deviate'.[7]

Napoleon was furious when he heard of *Général de Division* Decaen's decision to evacuate the fortress-cities Willemstad, Steenbergen and Breda, and immediately gave counter-orders. 6,000 men, destined to reinforce the garrison of Mayence, were send to Antwerp instead. More reinforcements followed, raising French strength around Antwerp to 25-30,000. On 21 December, Decaen was replaced by *Général de Division* Nicolas Joseph Maison. On 19 December, *Général de Division* François Roguet marched to Breda to recapture it. With him he had a force of 7,000 to 9,000 with 30 guns, including a division of the Young Guard. A desperate defence by Dutch provisional troops, strongly supported by Colomb's *Streifkorps* and Cossacks on foot, prevented its capture and Roguet retreated to Hoogstraten when British and Prussians reinforcements closed in. This was the first real fight the Dutch raw soldiers and militia were in, proving that they were willing to fight for their country. On 26 December, von Borstell's 5th Division blockading Wesel was relieved by Wintzingerode and marched to re-join Bülow. On 6 January 1814, *Maréchal* Macdonald retreated with his corps of an estimated 7,000 men to Venlo, then further south along the river Meuse over Maastricht and Liège to join Napoleon. On the 13th, Wintzingerode crossed the Rhine at Dusseldorf and also marched south. Bülow had moved his headquarters to Breda on 1 January.

Antwerp

The famous *Général de Division* Lazare Nicolas Carnot was appointed governor of Antwerp. Arriving on 30 January he immediately started enhancing the defences and burned down the suburbs of the city:

> From Brussels is written on 7 March: ... The area around Antwerp suffered a lot. No tree is visible anymore. Everything that prevented a wide view for the

---

6   Letter of 18 December 1813 from Bülow to the King of Prussia, quoted in Karl Rudolf von Ollech, *Carl Friedrich Wilhelm von Reyher. General der Kavallerie und Chef des Generalstabes der Armee. Ein Beitrag zur Geschichte der Armee mit Bezug auf die Befreiungskriege von 1813, 1814 und 1815* (Berlin: Ernst Siegfried Mittler und Sohn, 1869), Vol. 2, pp.336, 339-340.

7   A. Crusius, *Der Winterfeldzug in Holland, Brabant und Flandern, eine Episode aus dem Befreiungskriege 1813 und 1814* (Luxemburg: B. Bückt, 1865), p.93.

besieged has disappeared. Thus they have torn down most of the houses of St. Willibrord and Borgerhout. The beautiful country houses are burned down. From the villages, which were not occupied by the Allies, the besieged brought so far much cattle into the fortress. All beggars and people who cannot feed themselves are driven out of the city. The same is the case with the nuns.[8]

Beside its garrison of about 10,000, mostly raw troops, the city was protected by the French I Corps under *Général de Division* Maison. In 1813 after the Battle of Leipzig, the remnants of the original I Corps had been captured in Dresden. A new I Corps, sometimes designated with (bis) was ordered to be raised from the numerous depots that garrisoned the fortresses in the Southern Netherlands and northern France, to be augmented with conscripts. To garrison the fortresses the depots would be replaced with additional conscripts, *douaniers* and marines. Maison arrived in Antwerp on 25 December. He received command of the 24e Division Militaire, in addition of a young guard cavalry division (Lefebvre-Desnoettes) and two young guard infantry divisions (Barrois and Roguet). He would be subordinate to *Maréchal* Macdonald, who stood at the Rhine between Coblenz and Arnhem with the remains of XI Corps and II Cavalry Corps. I Corps would have three divisions, but, so as to give Antwerp a strong enough garrison, Maison had to add 7,000 men to the garrison instead of to his corps. There would be more delay as the depots, which expected 16,000 conscripts, on 28 December had only received 6,500.[9]

Maison initially deployed his troops in front of Antwerp, adding a substantial part of the garrison to his field army. His right wing of 5,000 men under *Général de Brigade* Antoine Aymard was at Hoogstraten. The centre, also 5,000 men, was at Wuustwezel. The left wing of 1,000 men was at Lier, while Maison himself commanded a reserve of 3,000 men near Brasschaat. Bülow had managed to concentrate about 12,000 men near Breda, the remainder of his army corps still necessary to blockade the various French-occupied fortresses, although they were gradually relieved by the Dutch. Despite being outnumbered and the British still unable to participate in the attack, Bülow decided to attack the French centre at Hoogstraten on 11 January. He managed to force back the French, unexpectedly assisted by the British who also attacked. However, during the following night the French deployed in a new position close to Antwerp and Bülow retreated back to Breda, leaving Von Borstell's 5th Division around Hoogstraten as an advanced guard. The British also retreated over Roosendaal and Steenbergen and blockaded Bergen op Zoom. On the 13th the allies attacked again, driving the French back to Antwerp. However they again retreated to their starting positions. It is unclear why Bülow had decided to execute these attacks as he had achieved nothing, his force much too weak to undertake a serious effort to capture Antwerp.[10]

---

8   *Allgemeine Zeitung*, 18 March 1814.

9   Jean Joseph Robert Calmon-Maison, 'Le Général Maison et le 1er Corps de la Grande Armée', in *Revue des Deux Mondes* (Paris: Bureau de La Revue des Deux Mondes , 1914), Vol.19, pp.168-169.

10   Andrew Bamford gives in his book an extensive explanation why these battles and the one on 1 February 1814 in front of Antwerp took place. I tend to follow the simpler

Wintzingerode was expected to join Bülow and to take over command in this area, but instead he followed Macdonald's French army corps over Aachen, Liège (22 January) and Namur to Soissons, entering French territory. Macdonald's retreat to France, and the direction which Wintzingerode took with his corps, uncovered *Général de Division* Maison's flank, also leaving the French northern border virtually unprotected. This gave Maison two options: to remain at Antwerp to be shut up with his whole army, or to march with I Corps to a more central position in order to protect northern France. He opted for the latter, still leaving behind a strong garrison in Antwerp but marching away with 4,000 men of *Général de Division* Pierre Barrois' division and 800 cavalry commanded by *Général de Division* Bertrand Pierre Castex. Initially he marched to a new position behind the river Dyle, between Louvain and Mechelen. Already 30 January he retreated further south to Halle, close to Brussels, to be in a better position to protect the French northern frontier. His presence, however, did not prevent *Major* Karl Ludwig Hellwig from occupying Brussels, an open city without defence works, with his *Streifcorps* and Cossacks (1 February). On 4 February Borstell's 5th Division arrived in this city as well. Maison continued his retreat to Tournay, his retreat giving Bülow more freedom, used to order *Oberst* Karl Friedrich von Hobe to capture 's Hertogenbosch by a *coup de main*, in which he succeeded with active aid of the Dutch citizens. This remarkable success earned Von Hobe, who would distinguish himself again during this campaign, the *Orden Pour le Mérite mit Eichenlaub*. In addition, Gorkum and its garrison of 4,000 French surrendered, removing yet another threat. These successes, combined with Dutch provisional units gradually taking over the blockade of remaining French-held fortresses, enabled Bülow to bring his depleted corps up to strength again.

In the meantime Bülow had received news which he did not take lightly. After finally having succeeded in freeing himself from Bernadotte, he was ordered to place himself under the orders of the commander of the newly raised III German Corps, the Duke of Saxe-Weimar, who would soon arrive in the southern Netherlands. Bülow was enraged and tried everything to avoid having to follow the orders of the Duke. While he still had time, he concluded an agreement with the British General Graham for yet another attack on Antwerp for the reasons explained by a member of his general staff:

> The intention to seize the French fleet lying in the basin of Antwerp and the important naval arsenal located there may have been an excellent motive. If the destruction of the ships was in the English interest, the Prussian was the appealing part of the prize money to be claimed, in the case of success, not an indifferent object.[11]

Although it is difficult to ascertain what exactly led up to the attack, what is known is that the Duke of Saxe-Weimar had travelled ahead of III German

---

explanations given by various Prussian/German sources. This subject is however beyond the scope of this book, for an excellent description of these battles see also Bamford, *A Bold and Ambitious Enterprise*, chapters V-VII.

11 Weltzien, *Memoiren*, pp.56-57.

Corps, and on 27 January he spoke with Graham. In a letter of that same date, Clancarty wrote to Castlereagh:

> I should rather think that, from his rank in the service, the Duke of Saxe Weimar supersedes Bülow in the command: if so, this is to be regretted, as the latter is an excellent officer, and perfectly acquainted with his ground.[12]

British fears soon became reality. On 30 January Graham met Bülow, learning that Bülow as well as the Duke were opposed to an attack on Antwerp and preferred an advance to Brussels. According to Major General Herbert Taylor, he and Lieutenant Colonel James Carmichael Smyth were sent to Bülow to try to bring him round to execute the attack on Antwerp:

> Colonel Smyth and I got to West Malle between 12 and 1, and were immediately admitted to General Bülow, who, to our surprise, proposed as a matter of course, the very measure to which we were instructed to press him, viz. that we should at once make the attempt in question in combination with the greater part of the Prussian corps, while General Borstell moved on and occupied Malines; the latter was to drive the French from Lier this day. General Bülow meant to move to Wynegem to-morrow, and have a principal advance post at Schoeten, and he wished Sir Thomas to move on Brachschoten with advanced posts at Donk and Eeckeren. On the following day we should move on Merxem the Prussians on Deurne, Berchem, etc. and we should lose no time in establishing mortar batteries, for which purpose our heavy artillery must immediately be brought up close on the rear of our columns. General Bülow partly let the cat out of the bag by lamenting that the Saxon troops were not come up and that he was thus prevented pushing the grand operation on Valenciennes, etc. Before we left him the Duke of Saxe Weimar came into his room.[13]

So, despite the initial objections, on 1 February the attack took place and the French troops were pushed back inside Antwerp. During the night of 2 to 3 February batteries were built and for three days the allies bombarded the fortress, their shots directed mainly at the French fleet, but with only minor results. Bülow thus had fought a third needless battle achieving nothing. On 6 February Graham and Bülow stopped their joined efforts and again withdrew their troops.

---

12 Letter of 27 January 1814 from Lord Clancarty to Lord Castlereagh, in English in Colenbrander, *Gedenkstukken*, pp.36-37.

13 Ernest Taylor (ed.), *The Taylor Papers, being a Record of Certain Reminiscences, Letters and Journals in the Life of Lieut.-Gen. Sir Herbert Taylor G.C.B., G.C.H.* (New York, Bombay & Calcutta: Longmans, Green, and Co., 1913), pp.132-133.

2

The Duke of Saxe-Weimar, Bernadotte, and Bülow

The Duke of Saxe-Weimar

In agreement with the Frankfurter Conference Protocol of 24 November 1813, III German Corps would be raised, to be used for 'common operations in the north'. It would consist of units mainly from the Saxon Kingdom, to which units of the Saxon Duchies Gotha and Weimar, the Principality of Schwarzburg, and the Anhalt Duchies were added. Care was needed to find an appropriate commander for this corps. The French retreat, which saw its former allies now fighting for the allied cause, had left a political vacuum in Germany. It must be realised there was no German Empire, no German Confederation, nor a German emperor. As a result every German commander had to be decided on separately, and in many cases the more or less 'neutral' Russian Emperor Alexander appointed Germans to Russian officer rank and as such they received a command in the allied armies. The same happened with the commander of III German Corps: the ruling Herzog Karl August von Sachsen-Weimar-Eisenach (Duke of Saxe-Weimar) was appointed as a Russian general of cavalry and received command of III German Corps.

The Duke of Saxe-Weimar was, understandably, not without combat experience. As a volunteer he had accompanied in 1787 the Duke of Brunswick during his invasion of Holland. In 1788 he had entered Prussian service as a *Generalmajor* of cavalry and became *chef* of a cuirassier regiment, participating in the Rhine campaigns against France in 1792 and 1793. Promoted *General der Kavallerie* he commanded the Prussian advance guard in 1806. After the crushing defeat at Jena-Auerstadt, in order to prevent his removal from his duchy of Weimar by Napoleon, he changed sides and joined the Confederation of the Rhine. After the Battle of Leipzig he again changed sides like so many and joined the allies, entering military service again. The Duke of Saxe-Weimar is described as follows:

> A prince with a patriotic attitude, inspired by the best intentions, warm-hearted, enthusiastic and open-minded, with a strong sense of self-esteem, spirited even passionate, and when excited of reckless harshness; as a result, his actions could

seem unpredictable, though his nature in itself was transparent and without reserve.[1]

The Duke received the difficult task to operate in the Southern Netherlands in co-operation with Bernadotte's Army of the North, General Graham's British army, and the raw Dutch and Belgian units as soon as they were ready to take the field.

Karl August von Sachsen-Weimar-Eisenach. (Rijksmuseum)

Who commands who?

The presence of various armies and nationalities just mentioned, combined with the unique backgrounds of the units making up III German Corps, were already enough challenge for any commander. The constant changing chain of command the Duke found himself in, combined with constant direct interference of the allied sovereigns, made the situation even worse. To be able to understand the complexity of the situation in the Southern Netherlands and the difficult situation the Duke of Saxe-Weimar would find himself in, we have to take a closer look at the relations between the Duke, Bernadotte, and Bülow. With Bernadotte still far away and not really controlling the situation in the southern Netherlands, initially, the Duke believed he would be under the command of Bülow. Bülow commanded III Prussian Corps and was already a distinguished commander: in the army since 1768, in 1813 victorious at the battles of Luckau, Großbeeren, and Dennewitz, defeating the famous Marshal Ney in this last battle which would bring him an earldom with the honorary name 'von Dennewitz'. As described in the previous chapter, his army corps liberated the Northern Netherlands from French rule, although his exploits here were not very sensational contrary to what often is stated. It would take some time before Bülow learned that the Duke of Saxe-Weimar would have command of III German Corps as it was communicated initially that *Generalleutnant* Johann Adolf von Thielmann would have command. As late as 14 January Bülow still writing to the Prince of Orange: 'From the approach of General Thielmann I have no specific information.'[2] The Prince of Orange wrote to Bülow on the 23rd: 'Moreover, You will already know that the Duke of Weimar and the Saxon troops arrived at Arnhem on the 20th of this month.'[3] The Duke of Saxe-Weimar had been senior to Bülow during their mutual previous Prussian service, nevertheless the Duke was prepared to serve under the command of Bülow, writing to him on 16 January from Lippstadt:

Excellency. My pleasure in joining and working with the Prussians and my old acquaintance is so great that I am in a hurry to eliminate any unpleasant impression. As for command, in this war my principle is that the General, who

1   Generalleutnant A. v. Janson, 'Der Herzog Karl August von Sachsen-Weimar und der Kronprinz Karl Johann von Schweden während des Feldzuges 1814 in den Niederlanden', in *Deutsche Rundschau*, Vol. CXXVIII (Berlin: Gebrüder Paetel, 1906) pp.40-41.
2   Letter of 14 January 1814 from Bülow to the Prince of Orange, in German in Colenbrander, *Gedenkstukken*, pp.457-458.
3   Letter of 23 January 1814 from the Prince of Orange to Bülow, in German in Colenbrander, *Gedenkstukken*, p.468.

has done most in the field since the beginning of 1813, has the command over those troops of another power who join him and should lead them. Since you have now distinguished yourself gloriously and I meanwhile sat at home, I am under your orders.[4]

However, within 24 hours the question of command would become the complete opposite. In the early morning of 17 January the Duke received a letter dated the 8th from General Volkonsky, Chief of the General Staff of the Russian Emperor Alexander. This letter stated that it was proposed to Bernadotte that the Duke of Saxe-Weimar would take over command of all troops present in the Netherlands on his arrival. Initially another Russian general, Wintzingerode, also commanding an army corps in Bernadotte's Army of the North, would have to resume overall command in this area on his arrival as the most senior general. This was according to Bernadotte's wishes, but not Bülow's, who was not prepared to be subordinate to Wintzingerode. Letters were sent back and forth to the headquarters of the allied sovereigns, not without result: Wintzingerode would receive new marching orders to remove him from the scene.[5] Apparently the Russian Emperor was also not pleased with Wintzingerode's hesitant way of warfare and for not attacking Macdonald's army corps before him. However, it also seems there were concerns about the relationship between Bülow and Wintzingerode.

At the same time, a second letter was received from Volkonsky. This letter contained a plan of operations devised by Bülow end December and approved by the Emperor:

With the arrival of General Wintzingerode near Dusseldorf and the English corps of General Graham at Willemstad, our forces in this area are growing in such a way that it seems important to undertake a powerful operation in order to conquer a large part of Belgium. To this end, I have submitted to General Wintzingerode an operational plan for consideration which, with the assistance of General Graham, will produce desirable results. The Russian Army Corps is expected on 6 January at Dusseldorf. If it crosses the Rhine, it would be able to take the direction of Jülich and Maastricht from there. Since these two places, according to all the news, should not be in any shape of defence, there is no doubt that General Wintzingerode will seize both fortresses. By such a movement the enemy, which makes front against Holland, is taken in his right flank, and Marshal Macdonald, if he should still stand at Cleve, would be compelled to retreat instantly. The enemy troops standing near Cologne are too weak to put obstacles in the way of General Wintzingerode. From Maastricht the general has the choice to assist us on the right or left bank of the Demer, as circumstances require (for example via Hasselt, Diest and Mechelen, line north of Brussels), in the direction of Antwerp.

    The possession of Heusden, Geertruidenberg, and Breda enables us to begin strong offensive operations on the lower Meuse and to proceed against Antwerp, thus supporting the advance of General Wintzingerode. While 's

---

4   Quoted in Ollech, *Carl Friederich Wilhelm von Reyher*, p.333; Janson, 'Der Herzog Karl August', p.44.

5   Ollech, *Carl Friederich Wilhelm von Reyher*, p.332.

Hertogenbosch and Grave remain masked, I shall have a part of my corps marched from Heusden to Brussels, and with the bulk I will move to Antwerp. General Graham will make a strong contribution to this operation from Willemstad, and while he is observing Bergen op Zoom, he will also proceed against Antwerp, where I shall arrive with him at the same time and attack this place. Should the enemy confront us in the open field, this case would be all the more desirable. Having become masters of the terrain between the Meuse, the Scheldt, and the Demer by these combined operations, we will be able to continue operations against the borders of Old France. The forthcoming reinforcement by the Saxon Army Corps will greatly facilitate the feasibility of this operational plan.[6]

In the letter it was further explained to the Duke that the troops in the Netherlands would form a detached army, still part of the Army of the North and still under the overall command of Bernadotte. This was: 'Except for the English, who are also here, waging war as on an island and having only the special purpose of destroying the French fleet in the port of Antwerp.'[7] So it was decided that for the short time it would take Bernadotte to arrive in the Netherlands, the Duke of Saxe-Weimar would resume overall command. His authority however was still very limited. In the first place because Bernadotte was still commander in chief, and the Duke was told by Emperor Alexander that he had to act in accordance to the arrangements of Bernadotte. Secondly because Bülow received also direct orders from the headquarters of the allied sovereigns as well as from the Prussian commander of the Army of Silesia operating in Northern France, *Generalfeldmarschall* Gebhard Leberecht von Blücher. Bülow of course acted if he was not under the Duke's command when it favoured him. Bernadotte's quick arrival with the bulk of the Army of the North was assumed, although this would in fact not happen. To understand this delay, it is also necessary to look at Bernadotte, as his behaviour had a huge impact on events. Bernadotte is described as follows:

An ever-posing Gascogner, who spoke with emphasis, and was fond of playing the great general, he sought to promote his ambitions rather by intrigue than deeds; under the mask of benevolence and disinterestedness, he did not reject any chance, completely unconcerned about their origin; The man, well-endowed with intelligence, became cocky and fought for the trust of all because he strove to keep it at the same time with all parties. The fact that he nevertheless consistently and successfully sought the interest of Sweden and later performed well as ruler for the peaceful development of his adoptive fatherland proves that he possessed a number of good qualities that proved their value when he was in calm waters. That was by no means the case at the time we are talking about. Rather, the situation had already become very complicated for him at the end of 1813. He rightly felt responsible for Sweden's future and recognized it as his duty to secure Norway for his new homeland, which was promised to him by the treaty of Petersburg and during the assembly at Åbo in 1812, as a substitute

---

6   Plan of operations from Bülow, send to Emperor Alexander on 30 December 1813, in Ollech, *Carl Friederich Wilhelm von Reyher*, pp.343-344.

7   Janson, 'Der Herzog Karl August', p.45.

for Finland which was ceded to Russia in 1809. To render this country, Denmark had to be forced by war. In addition to these specific Swedish goal, Karl Johann, in his capacity as commander of the 'Northern Army', was to keep track of the interests of his allies in the fight against his old compatriots, the French. Surely in itself it was no dishonour that it would be difficult for him to cross the borders of his old homeland as an enemy. He knew how to obscure his delaying tendency as if he had only the best for his allies in mind while at the same time satisfying his natural aversion to decisive acts of war.[8]

So Bernadotte had a very difficult time. Even more, he had ambitions to become the new Emperor of France, replacing Napoleon! *Oberstleutnant* Graf Ludwig Ernst von Kalckreuth, who was the Prussian liaison officer with Bernadotte and apparently held confidential conversations with him, among other things stated that: 'The Crown Prince by the way promised me – that if he would become Emperor of France – I should receive a principality from him, and then he would request Your Royal Majesty to appoint me ambassador to him.'[9] It was all wishful thinking from Bernadotte though, not the least because the influential Austrian Foreign Minister Klemens von Metternich was totally opposed to the idea, stating: 'I do not want to sacrifice one man to put Bernadotte on the French throne!'[10] Nevertheless, for some time Bernadotte was supported by the Russian Emperor, who rather saw Bernadotte as his ally on the French throne then as his unpredictable neighbour. However, after the Prussians received guarantees that Austria would not object against the Prussian acquirement of Saxon territory, the Russian Emperor found himself isolated and Bernadotte could forget his ambitions.[11] For the moment, though, all this was still in the near future. For now it was believed that Bernadotte would arrive himself in the Netherlands soon, on Kalckreuth writing on 13 January to the Chief of General Staff of the Prussian III Corps, *Generalmajor* Leopold Hermann von Boyen, that Bernadotte would make peace with Denmark on

Bernadotte as Crown Prince of Sweden. Coloured engraving by Heath after Gilberg. (Anne S.K. Brown Collection)

---

8 Janson, 'Der Herzog Karl August', p.41.
9 Letter from Von Kalckreuth to the Prussian King in *preußisches Geheimes Staatsarchiv*, quoted in Janson, 'Der Herzog Karl August', p.42.
10 Quoted in Janson, 'Der Herzog Karl August', p.43.
11 Adelbert Wahl, *Geschichte des Europaïschen Staatensystems im Zeitalter der Französischen Revolution und der der Freiheitskriege (1789-1815)* (München & Berlin: R. Oldenbourg, 1912) pp.238-239.

the 13th of 14th and would depart for the Netherlands in about eight days, joined by a corps of 10,000 Danes.

For the Duke of Saxe-Weimar there was no doubt who would be his superior, as he wrote to Bernadotte on 17 January: 'Since all troops united in the north are under the command of Your Royal Highness, given the marching direction that my corps is taking, it will give me the advantage of being under your command as well, and I await with impatience either your arrival or your instructions.'[12]

Back to the Duke of Saxe-Weimar and Bülow: it appears that the Monarchs indeed expected the Duke's overall command as a short intermezzo and that the Prussian King Friedrich Wilhelm neglected giving Bülow a formal order. The Duke, sensing the danger, wrote urgently to the Prussian King on 29 January:

> I regard this directive of His Majesty the Emperor of Russia as a means of bringing unity between the army commanders and unity into the operations through my intervention, and will only in this regard use my rights as Commander in Chief. Meanwhile, General Bülow has received no orders from Your Majesty to stand under my command. I leave it up to Your discretion as to whether such is required, as well as I dare to request that you will inform me about this matter.[13]

The Prussian King indeed gave such orders to Bülow (7 February), placing him under the Duke's command. But there are indications that the king did so grudgingly and for unexplained reasons, the written orders did reach Bülow only at 17 March! Not surprisingly, on receiving the news he was infuriated and disappointed. Nevertheless, it seems that Bülow was not angry at the Duke for this decision, as the Duke wrote to his wife:

> It's up to me to put Wintzingerode in motion and obedience for I shall be ashamed to remove the glory of Bulow ... and the brave men of the Russian army, like Czernichef, Benkendorf, etc. who are ours ... . Bülow has just written to me, that he is delighted to have me for his chef, because he is set free from the Royal Prince of Sweden, which he abhors and declares for a counterfeiter, and by that I will be the cement between him and Wintzingerode who is also of this kind.[14]

Having orchestrated the attack on Antwerp as described in the previous chapter, after its failure Bülow only wanted one thing: to leave this sideshow and to join Blücher's Army of Silesia. After having reached an agreement with the Duke of Saxe-Weimar about his departure he left mid-February. Against his will but forced by the Duke, he had to leave behind Borstell's 5th Division. It is even stated that the Duke at one moment threatened Borstell that he would be arrested if he dared to march off with Bülow, but no evidence for this assertion was found. It is understandable that the Duke wanted to retain

---

12 Quoted in Janson, 'Der Herzog Karl August', p.45.
13 Quoted in Janson, 'Der Herzog Karl August', p.46.
14 Letter of 23 January from the Duke of Saxe-Weimar to his wife, quoted in Hermann Freihernn von Egloffstein, *Carl August im niederländische Feldzug 1814* (Weimar: Verlag der Goethe-Gesellschaft, 1927), pp.15, 116-119.

this experienced division, as at this moment it was far from clear to him what he was up against. All he knew was that there still were substantial French forces along the French northern border, as well as in Maubeuge, Antwerp and a series of fortresses in the Netherlands. The only forces he had were his own – still very depleted – III German Corps and the collection of ramshackle 'Belgian' units, not counting the British which were not under his command and were only focussing on Antwerp. More bad news was to follow. General von Wintzingerode was expected to arrive in the Netherlands as well, but after the Duke of Saxe-Weimar had been chosen as commander of the forces in the southern Netherlands instead of him, he was ordered to marched his army to France. So hope was set on the one remaining form of support, the arrival of Bernadotte with the remainder of the Army of the North. After what has already been explained about Bernadotte, it cannot come as a real surprise that this also would not be so obvious.

On 31 January, Bernadotte had send a letter to the Duke of Saxe-Weimar ordering him to march III German Corps to Düsseldorf. However, receiving this order on 9 February, the Duke himself was already in Brussels, his corps in the Southern Netherlands as well! On that same day, the 9th, Bernadotte wrote to the Duke that he had victoriously ended the war with Denmark and was marching to the Rhine immediately. In fact, peace had already been signed in Kiel on 14 January, with Denmark ceding Norway to Sweden in return for Swedish Pomerania, and Helgoland to Great Britain. Indeed, after some delay the Russian army corps of Vorontsov, Stroganov, and Tettenborn marched south, although directly to France to join Wintzingerode. In mid-February, *Generalleutnant* Ludwig Georg von Wallmoden's Russo-German Legion marched over Düsseldorf to the Netherlands. The Swedish army however marched with extreme slowness to Liège. The promised Danish corps never materialised and Bernadotte remained idle. Then followed another twist of fate. On 24 February, Blücher's Army of Silesia (for the second time) split off from the main allied army. On the 28th, Blücher was informed that he would be reinforced with Bülow's and Wintzingerode's army corps and that he had to march to Paris. He was also to recieve command of the Duke of Saxe-Weimar's III German Corps. Apparently the allied sovereigns were done with Bernadotte and his inactivity. Although Bernadotte felt insulted for losing the greater part of his Army of the North, he just had one reason more to remain passive. The Duke of Saxe-Weimar was informed by Emperor Alexander of this change, at the same moment receiving a letter from Blücher:

> Most serene duke, gracious duke and lord, to be united with Your Highness for such a great object makes me feel indescribably happy, especially since the united monarchs have put their great confidence on our operations. The admiration that I feel for Your Highness, is in line with the unlimited attachment in which I remain.
>
> Your Highness most faithful and humble servant Blücher.
>
> The Graf Nostitz will report to Your Highness about my march to and crossing of the Marne.[15]

---

15   Quoted in Janson, 'Der Herzog Karl August', p.48.

Taken from the tone of this letter, one could even believe that Blücher was subordinate to the Duke of Saxe-Weimar, which of course was not the case. However, as their relationship was good it seems that the Duke had one problem less to cope with. Not surprisingly regarding the difficult political manoeuvres that took place amongst the allies, this proved again to be wishful thinking. About the same time the above letter was received by the Duke, he received an order from Blücher to hold the fortresses in northern France still occupied by the French under close observation, at the same time concentrating III German Corps in such a position that it would be close to Blücher's army, enabling him to join him when a battle was close at hand. This all until Bernadotte should arrive: thereafter Bernadotte would have to complete the conquest of Holland and Flanders with the remainder of the Army of the North: his Swedish army and Wallmoden's corps, augmented with Hanoverian and Dutch units. Unfortunately for the Duke, the Emperor Alexander's letter also contained a direction and emphasized the importance of holding on to the Southern Netherlands! With the Russian Emperor directly interfering with the Duke's task, the need for Bernadotte to arrive and take over the Duke of Saxe-Weimar's role in the Southern Netherlands became highly important.

Yet still, Bernadotte would not stir and remained where he was, writing from Liège on 5 March to the Duke, on his request to send troops to Mechelen to hold Antwerp under observation:

> In view of my distance from the scene of operations on which Blücher commands, I have acknowledged the urgency of this measure, which has my consent. I only expect the concentration of the Swedish Army to advance and take over command again of the corps which I have been temporarily deprived of.[16]

With events unfolding in France, the Duke of Saxe-Weimar received urgent messages from Blücher. On 8 March, the Duke was ordered to try to capture Maubeuge, or, if this proved to be impossible, to blockade it closely, so that its garrison could not pose a threat to Blücher's army. The following night at midnight, after the first day of the battle of Laon, Blücher again ordered the capture of Maubeuge immediately, and for the Duke to march with III German Corps on the 15th to join him as surely the Swedes would have arrived by now. Yet still, Bernadotte did not stir, writing to the Duke on the 17th that he was still waiting for a reply from the allied sovereigns, to his question when he would receive command again of the three corps which had been taken away from him (i.e. Bülow, Wintzingerode and the Duke of Saxe-Weimar's III German Corps). Finally, on 23 March, under the pretext of inspecting the artillery in Verviers, Bernadotte went to the headquarters of the allied sovereigns in person, to promote his personal interests and those of Sweden in person. The Duke already for a long time had had no illusions about Bernadotte, writing to Blücher on 29 March: 'The army of the Crown Prince of Sweden is still standing in Liège and there is no likelihood that it will leave so soon. His Royal Highness has left the army

---

16   Letter from Bernadotte tot the Duke of Saxe-Weimar, quoted in Janson, 'Der Herzog Karl August', p.49.

and is said to have travelled to the Great Headquarters.'[17] Despite all this, the Duke of Saxe-Weimar still tried to execute his orders, blockading Maubeuge with insufficient forces, but this had to be changed in close observation when, despite the Duke's objections, Borstell marched off to join Bülow with his 5th Division. His problems came to an abrupt end when Napoleon abdicated, when the Bourbon restoration put an end to Bernadotte's dreams of the French throne.

---

17   Quoted in Janson, 'Der Herzog Karl August', p.51.

3

The creation of III German Corps

Leipzig: the defection of the Saxons

Before looking at the creation of III German Corps, it is necessary to have a look at what, regarding the Saxons, happened during the Battle of Leipzig, the 'Battle of the Nations' which was fought 16-19 October 1813. After the debacle of Russia in 1812 and the disastrous French retreat, Napoleon frantically raised troops to continue the war against the Russians, who were joined by the Prussians and later also the Swedes and Austrians. Napoleon's German allies also had to deliver contingents of troops which were incorporated in the French army. This included the army of the Kingdom of Saxony whose king, Frederick Augustus I, was one of Napoleon's staunchest allies. Initially, the Saxons formed a corps consisting of two divisions – a total of 9,000 men, 2,230 horses and 30 guns – which was part of VII Corps commanded by *Général de Division* Reynier. Soon both divisions were merged into a single division, consisting of two infantry brigades and a light cavalry brigade (7,846 men). In addition, a battalion of the Saxon Grenadiergarde served with Napoleon's Guards. At the same time, reliability of the German contingents, including the Saxons, became doubtful: allied proclamations did their work and the German contingents started to lose more and more men through desertion. For example, on 23 September eight officers and 300 men of the Saxon battalion 'König' defected to the Swedes near Oranienbaum. From then on, the Saxons were not allowed to do outpost duty anymore.

After a series of battles and combats all armies converged on Leipzig. On 16 October the battle started and ended indecisive with both sides remaining in their positions. On the second day of the battle, Reynier's VII Corps also arrived on the battlefield. On the 18th, VII Corps was deployed near Paunsdorf. That same morning, Reynier told the commander of the Saxon Division, *Generalleutnant* von Zeschau, that Napoleon did not trust the Saxons anymore and that the division would receive orders to march to Torgau. Almost immediately, these orders could not be followed because of the advance of the allied Army of the North. The allies attacked fiercely all along the line, cutting off the troops in Taucha village and taking prisoner the Saxon battalion 'Prinz Friedrich' positioned here. The attacks threatened the left flank of Marshall Ney's army corps and Reynier was forced to deploy the Saxon division to protect it. At that moment the Saxon units defected *en masse* to the Allies: the light cavalry brigade first, almost immediately followed by Württemberg cavalry, and then by the Saxon infantry and artillery. Only about 700 men remained with *Generalleutnant* von Zeschau, who in person went to Leipzig to inform his King about the situation. The defected Saxons withdrew behind the allied lines to prevent them being captured and shot at by the French, concentrating near Engelsdorf. *Generalmajor* von Ryssel, the senior officer, also stated that the Saxon King, Frederick Augustus I, had to be consulted first to decide about the deployment of the Saxons. Only a single horse artillery battery (*Hauptmann* Birnbaum) saw action on the allied side at Leipzig, supporting a Cossack regiment.

Unfortunately for *Generalmajor* von Ryssel, the allies treated the Saxon King as their prisoner for supporting Napoleon so long and transported him to Berlin. This left the Saxon troops in the dark about their destiny. Saxony was placed under a General Government, with Generalleutnant Nikolai Grigorjewitsch Repnin appointed Governor-General of the Saxon Kingdom, who on his turn on 28 October appointed General-Lieutenant Johann Adolf von Thielmann (a Saxon in Russian service) as commander in chief of the Saxon army.[1] Already two days earlier, it was decreed that all Saxon military personnel, not already part of the units that had joined the allies, had to report to the General Intendant *Oberstleutnant* von Ryssel in Leipzig.[2] The Saxon troops, except for the Saxon Light Cavalry Brigade which was initially attached to Blücher's Army of Silesia, were send to the region between Eilenburg and Wurzen, to reorganise and at the same time to protect Leipzig against an attack from the French garrison still in Torgau. On the 30th they were actively engaged in the blockade of this fortress-city. In this role they remained for 14 days before they were relieved, pushing back several sorties, suffering about 80 dead or wounded. With their cockade changed from white to green, yellow, and black,[3] on 12 December, although having received orders to march to Hildesheim to join Bernadotte's Army of the North, their destination was changed as they would be used to create the *3. Deutschen Armeekorps* (III German Corps).

Creation of III German Corps

In agreement with the Frankfurt Conference Protocol of 24 November 1813, the German states that had abandoned Napoleon's cause and his Confederation of the Rhine, had to raise eight German army corps with a total strength of 145,000 line troops, augmented with the same amount of

---

1   Publicandum of 28 October 1813 in *General-Gouvernements-Blatt für Sachsen* (Leipzig: Redaction des General-Gouvernements-Blatts für Sachsen, 1813), Vol. 1, p.6.

2   Patent No. 5 of 26 October 1813 in *General-Gouvernements-Blatt*, p.5.

3   Publicandum of 12 November 1813 in *General-Gouvernements-Blatt*, p.24, confirmed by Repnin by Publicandum of 14 November 1813 in *General-Gouvernements-Blatt*, p.33; Order of the day of 12 November 1813 from *Generalleutnant* von Thielmann, in Johannes Anton Larraß, *Geschichte des Königlich Sächsischen 6. Infanterie-Regiments Nr. 105 und seine Vorgeschichte 1701 bis 1887* (Straßburg i.E.: H.L. Kayser, 1887), p.523.

Landwehr.[4] III German Corps would be raised with a strength of 24,250 regulars made up of the following contingents:

- Kingdom of Saxony: 20,000 men
- Saxon Duchies (Gotha-Altenburg and Weimar): 2,800 men
- Anhalt Duchies (-Bernburg, -Dessau and -Köthen): 800 men
- Principality of Schwarzburg: 650 men

These regulars would be augmented with an equal number of Landwehr, to be used for 'common operations in the north'. Initially the core of this corps was formed by the Saxons, to which units from the smaller contingents would be added. As the intense fighting of the 1813 spring and autumn campaigns had taken a heavy toll on the regular units, provisional units and regiments were formed from the remains of the existing units, to be augmented with recovered men and released prisoners of war. The following regular Saxon units were formed:

- Provisorisches Garde-Regiment (3 battalions, 4 companies each). The first battalion, the 'Gardebataillon', was formed from the former Leib-Grenadier-Garde-Bataillon (872); 'II. Grenadier-Bataillon' from the Regiment 'König'; and III. Grenadier-Bataillon from the grenadiers that remained of all the infantry regiments, as well as the remains of Grenadier Bataillon 'Von Spiegel'.
- II. and III./1. Provisorischen Linien-Regiment (4 companies each). Formed mainly from the men of the Regiment 'Prinz Anton'.
- II. and III./2. Provisorischen Linien-Regiment (4 companies each). Formed from the remains of the Regiment 'Prinz Maximilian' and those of the disbanded regiments 'Rechten' and 'von Steindel'.
- A Jäger Bataillon (4 companies).
- I. and II./1. Leichten Infanterie-/Schützen-Regiment (4 companies each). I. Bataillon formed from the Leichten Infanterie-Regiment 'von Le Coq'; II. Bataillon formed from a veteran cadre, recovered men, and former prisoners of war.
- II./2. Leichten Infanterie-/Schützen-Regiment (4 companies). Formed from the Leichten Infanterie-Regiment 'von Sahr'.
- A Kürassier-Regiment was formed from the Leibkürassier-Garde and the Kürassier-Regiment 'von Zastrow' (3 weak squadrons initially).
- The Uhlanen-Regiment was re-formed (3 weak squadrons initially).
- The Husaren-Regiment was re-formed (reduced from 8 to 5 squadrons, 3 weak squadrons initially).
- Two foot artillery batteries (6x 6-pdr or 12-pdr cannon, 2x 8-pdr howitzers).
- Two horse artillery batteries (4x 6-pdr cannon, 2x 8-pdr howitzers).
- A sapper company and a bridge train.

---

4   For the protocol: (Karl von Damitz), *Geschichte des Feldzuges von 1814 in dem östlichen und nördlichen Frankreich bis zur Einnahme von Paris* (Berlin, Posen und Bromberg: Ernst Siegfried Mittler, 1842-1843), Vol. 1, pp.535-540.

This brought III German Corps almost immediately up to a strength of about 9,000 men of all arms and 1,600 horses, although the units itself were still much under strength. These troops marched to Querfurth in Thüringen, arriving on 18 December. The Duke of Saxe-Weimar, appointed commander of the corps, was told that his corps would have to be ready to march the end of December, its Landwehr twelve days later. In agreement with the results of an allied conference, *Generalleutnant* von Thielmann was assigned to raise additional Saxon troops to join the fight against Napoleon. Thielmann's character, combined with his behaviour in Torgau some months earlier (which is beyond the scope of this book) meant that he was not loved by his fellow officers nor by the men. Despite this, he was able to re-form a Saxon army in a very short time. According to the initial design of the allies, Saxony would have to bring a total of 34,000 combatants into the field. So, with about 25,000 men short, there was more than enough work to do for Thielmann. For this purpose he returned to Dresden, in order to take command, to raise and commence training of additional Saxon units which were to join III German Corps as soon as they were ready to take the field. Regarding the regular troops, the following units had to be raised:

- I./1. Provisorischen Linien-Regiment (from recovered men, former prisoners of war and recruits).
- I./2. Provisorischen Linien-Regiment (from the musketeers of the Regiment 'Max' having been taken prisoner at Lüneburg and Luckau, augmented with recovered men, former prisoners of war and recruits).
- I./2. Leichten Infanterie-Regiment (from former prisoners of war).
- Additional cavalry squadrons, to bring the cavalry regiments up to their full complement (an additional 4th squadron for each regiment, and also a 5th squadron for the hussars).
- Additional men to complete the artillery batteries.

Beside these, as soon as possible a 3. Provisorischen Linien-Regiment had to be formed. In addition, by conscription a Landwehr (militia) had to be raised, out of the male population between 18 and 45 years of age, and units of volunteers. The Landwehr would consist of the following units, while wealthy conscripts and volunteers had the chance to serve in special units:

- Seven regiments of Saxon Landwehr of three battalions each, with each a reserve depot of a half battalion. The Saxon regions would raise these battalions with a nominal strength of 19 officers and 810 men.[5]
- A Banner der Freiwilligen Sachsen of 98 officers, 2,800 others and 955 horses.[6] Raised from the wealthy and educated families of Saxony. It would form a light infantry regiment of two battalions (*Fußjäger*), each battalion consisting of four *Schützen* ('marksman')

---

5   Patent No. 29 of 16 November 1813 in *General-Gouvernements-Blatt*, pp.34-40. See Appendix V for details of the organisation of the Saxon Landwehr.
6   Patent No. 21 of 31 October 1813 in *General-Gouvernements-Blatt*, pp.18-21.

companies and a fifth company of *Scharfschützen* ('sharpshooters'); two hussar squadrons; three squadrons of *Reitender Jäger* ('chasseurs a cheval') and a sapper company. To this Banner, a line foot artillery company (6x 6-pdr or 12-pdr cannon, 2x 8-pdr howitzers) was to have been added but this never happened.

- Two Landwehr cavalry squadrons formed of wealthy conscripts, who would have to pay for their equipment themselves and would be attached to the Banner with the name of Land(wehr)dragoner.

Generalleutnant von Thielmann was supported by *Generalmajor* Carl Adolf von Carlowitz who was tasked with raising the Banner, and *Generalmajor* Johann Justus Vieth tasked with raising the Landwehr. Thielmann himself was ordered to join the Duke of Saxe-Weimar at the front, to march on 15 January with reinforcements for the existing units as well as nine additional infantry battalions. When all planned units would have been raised, the order of battle of III German Corps would be as given in Appendix VII, although this organisation would never be fully completed. Raising these troops met with numerous problems. The regular provisional Saxon units fairly quickly regained strength by absorbing Saxon soldiers released from hospital and prisoners of the 1812 and 1813 campaigns:

> True respect deserves the speed and perfection with which the Saxon line troops, which had suffered so terrible, have been supplemented in such a short time since the battle of Leipzig, and have been raised to the highest possible number, without needing a new levy of recruits. Seven excellent served batteries are again able to maintain the ancient fame of the Saxon artillery. The cavalry exists, except for the depots, of 3,900 horses only. But these are exquisite and the troopers are full of their former courage. Saxons are still returning from captivity from the rearmost Russian provinces. The brigade captured under General von Klengel at Kobryn is marching again, against France.[7]

Those of 1812 consisting of former prisoners of war released by the Russians, including those of Klengel's brigade, amounted to only 2,000 as many had perished. In addition, all Saxon deserters were pardoned on the condition that they returned to their units.[8] Bringing up to strength the Landwehr proved to be more difficult, Saxony lacking the manpower. From March 1812 until 19 October 1813, the Kingdom of Saxony had to deliver 50,000 men to support Napoleon. On the latter date, only 7,000 of these remained, to which about 3,000 men would be added returning from Russian imprisonment. The country already suffered from lack of labourers, was riddled with diseases and epidemics, and its inhabitants were finally very impoverished. Yet another problem became arming the seven Saxon Landwehr regiments. Initially all French muskets found on the battlefield of Leipzig, in addition those of the French garrison that had surrendered at Dresden, were issued, but these were not enough. A report states: 'It is totally unclear, were we should find the arms for the 5th and 6th [Landwehr]

---

7   *Allgemeine Zeitung*, Beilage, 2 March 1814.
8   Patent No. 15 of 3 November 1813 in *General-Gouvernements-Blatt*, p.12.

Regiments, as the 3rd and 4th Regiments are still without muskets yet, and the 2nd Regiment had to give up those they had for completing arming the 1st Regiment.[9] Several decrees were issued by the Governor-General Repnin for individuals possessing muskets and military equipment to give these up, even receiving payment for them:

> Patent relating to the purchase of weapons and other military effects to be effected for the Saxon troops corps within Saxony: After the General Government of the Kingdom of Saxony had convinced itself that the Saxon Line Army, the Banner der Freiwilligen, and the Landwehr could not obtain the necessities for their equipment within a short time, than that if the General Intendant of the Saxon Army, *Generalmajor* von Ryssel is allowed to buy weapons and all other military effects individually; this mandate has only been given to the mentioned General Intendant, the purchase of these pieces within Saxony ... to be carried on until the Saxon troops destined for the Third German Army Corps, including the Banner and the Landwehr, are fully equipped.[10]

Not surprisingly many muskets were of bad quality, worn out or completely useless. Although this problem would be solved later, it again was the cause for more delay. To raise morale all volunteers, including those of the Saxon Banner, as well as all men who would distinguish themselves during the upcoming campaign, were authorized to wear a distinctive cross of green cloth in the shape of a crucifix on the left breast.[11] Despite al problems and setbacks the Saxon army quickly regained shape. On 25 November 1813, 1,100 men had joined the Saxon Banner; on 1 March 1814 both *Landdragoner* squadrons were ready to march (twelve officers with 200 dragoons); the conscripts willingly joining the Landwehr as well. Although at the end of 1814, Saxony would have again about 40,000 men under arms, their training took time. The campaign progressed too quick for all these troops to be ready in time and many would not see any action at all, while others found themselves marching straight into battle on their arrival. In addition, there was a great lack of the necessary money for equipment and other expenses, as well as muskets and cartridges and not to speak about uniforms and other equipment items. For example, the Uhlanen-Regiment was to receive a completely different uniform, but it was impossible to provide these in time before their departure. As a result the initial three squadrons marched in their old uniform, while the 4th squadron as well as aditional troopers joining later wore the new uniform.[12] Cartridges were a problem as well. When orders were received for the first contingent of III

---

9   Report quoted in Ludwig Ferdinand Bucher, *Der Feldzug des dritten deutschen Armee-Corps in Flandern, im Befreiungskriege des Jahres 1814* (Leipzig: Hermann Costenoble, 1854), pp.34-35.

10 Patent No. 73 of 10 February 1814 in *General-Gouvernements-Blatt*, p.199.

11 Patent No. 33 of 17 November 1813 in *General-Gouvernements-Blatt*, p.45; Patent No. 55 of 12 December 1813 in *General-Gouvernements-Blatt*, p.97; Patent No. 81 of 12 March 1814 in *General-Gouvernements-Blatt*, p.257; Letter of 16 March 1814 from *Generalmajor* von Vieth in *General-Gouvernements-Blatt*, pp.261-262.

12 Von Oppel, *Sammlung von Beiträgen zur Geschichte des Königl. Sächs. 1. Leichten Reiter-Regiments vacant Prinz Clemens. Zusammengetragen von dem Rittmeister und Adjutant von Oppel im Jahre 1829* (Freiberg: Gerlach'schen Buckdruckerei, 1857), p.84.

German Corps to march, the Duke of Saxe-Weimar went to Dresden, where the French just had capitulated, in person. Here he managed to lay his hands on 72 cartridges and a pair of shoes for every soldier.[13] The exception to the above were the volunteers of the Banner, who were equipped carefully and even luxuriously. Finally, it had been decreed on 30 November that all officer appointments in III German Corps, as well as promotions, would be made by the Russian Emperor Alexander himself.[14]

In the Saxon Duchies (Gotha-Altenburg and Weimar) efforts were also made to form the troops as soon as possible. These duchies had to raise twice as much troops as they had done as Napoleon's ally for the Confederation of the Rhine. Gotha-Altenburg would raise a line infantry battalion (6 companies) and a Landwehr battalion (5 companies), a volunteer foot *jäger* company and a volunteer horse *jäger* company. Weimar would raise a Landwehr battalion and also a volunteer foot *jäger* company, as well as a volunteer horse *jäger* company. Both volunteer horse *jäger* companies would be combined in a single squadron. Until January 1814 governed by the Russians, Repnin had assigned a Saxon officer to raise Landwehr in Altenburg aided by officers returning from Russian imprisonment.

On 21 December, a conference was held between the Governor-General of the Saxon Kingdom, Repnin, the Duke of Saxe-Weimar and his chief of staff *Generalmajor* Justus Philipp von Wolzogen, *Generalleutnant* von Thielmann and other Saxon senior officers. At this conference everything necessary was arranged for the formation of III German Corps, including the allotment of 100,000 Thaler. After this conference the Duke of Saxe-Weimar himself left on the 28th for his own duchy, to mobilise and organise his own contingent which, with those of the other duchies and those of Schwarzburg, would be combined into an 'Anhalt-Thuringian Brigade' or Division, to be commanded by *Generalmajor* Prinz Paul von Württemberg, a protégé from Emperor Alexander. It would however take time to equip these units and to bring them up to strength. This did not prevent the first formed Saxon units of III German Corps, 8,620 men with 2,163 horses to which the 743 men strong Bataillon Füsiliere des Herzogs zu Sachsen-Weimar was added, to leave for the front on 3 January 1814 in three columns. The Duke of Saxe-Weimar himself joined his army corps at Cassel which was assigned as the concentration point of all units destined to join III German Corps.[15] Destination would be the Southern Netherlands, nowadays Belgium. This left Thielmann with the cadres of six battalions, five cavalry squadrons, and the crews of three artillery batteries. When their formation was complete, additional troops combined in contingents would depart as soon as they were ready. About a month later, on 8 February *Generalmajor* Prinz Paul von Württemberg departed from Cassel with the Anhalt-Thuringian Division, while *Generalleutnant* von Thielmann crossed the Saxon border the day before with additional Saxon troops. During his march he would be joined by additional units of the Anhalt-Thuringian Division.

---

13 R. Starkloff, *Das Leben des Herzogs Bernhard von Sachsen-Weimar-Eisenach, Königlich niederländischer General der Infanterie* (Gotha: E.F. Thienemann, 1865), Vol. 1, p.134.

14 Publicandum of 30 November 1813 in *General-Gouvernements-Blatt*, p.56.

15 For the strength and composition of III German Corps on 3 January see Appendix I.

The march to the southern Netherlands

The troops with which the Duke of Saxe-Weimar departed were for the greater part experienced, having seen fighting as French allies during 1813, a substantial part even veterans with many years of battle experience. The newly raised battalions and squadrons which would reinforce him later were mainly composed out of newly levied, raw and young soldiers and Landwehr. This explains the different steadiness and behaviour under fire, as will be illustrated later. The troops marched west through cold winter weather on frozen roads, taking up cantonments around Lippstadt on 14 January 1814. Arriving here the Duke temporarily halted his corps, ordering his General-Adjutant, *Oberst* Friedrich Caspar von Geismar, to reconnoitre in the direction of Düsseldorf to find out how the war situation was. Arriving here, Geismar encountered Wintzingerode who requested that the Duke would join him and take over the blockade of Wesel, enabling Wintzingerode to march to the southern Netherlands by way of Jülich and Maastricht. The Duke of Saxe-Weimar hesitated, as he believed his corps at the moment much too weak for this task, in addition to lacking heavy artillery and cartridges. Great was his relief when, on the 14th, a letter was received from Bülow stating that the Russian Emperor Alexander had ordered that III German Corps would have to join his III Prussian Corps in the Netherlands. The Duke wrote to his wife:

> So here I am, saved from Wintzingerode, who passed the Rhine at Dusseldorf yesterday and marches to Liège; I march straight into Holland, where I will recuperate my troops, *vivrai à Gogo* [living gorgeous and happy], and do not put at great risk the nucleus of the army which I have to command. I will send an officer to the Prince of Orange tomorrow, and if I have only a few days leave, then I will probably go to The Hague to negotiate the necessary money, the weapons, the ammunition and the clothes; eating myself oysters and codfish. I admit this is a nice change of fortune.[16]

The above letter is of interest, as it illustrates that III German Corps was still lacking arms and ammunition among many other necessities. Indeed, the troops were still badly equipped: the muskets were of different pattern, many worn out or even unusable. Worst was the clothing, especially the infantry having no winter clothing. It seems from the above letter that the Duke was convinced that the Netherlands could supply him with everything that his troops would need, forgetting that this country was building an army of its own, needing the same equipment. The fact that the Duke was lacking the necessary equipment had also been noticed by the British, already taking in account that they would have to support the Duke as well:

> I have written to Liverpool privately to notify the arrival at no distant period of the Duke of Saxe-Weimar, with 9,000 men, who would possibly be in a very unequipped state, and have forwarded the private letters of the Duke addressed to the Prince of Orange, noticing his various wants, in order that Government may

---

16 Letter of 15 January from the Duke of Saxe-Weimar to his wife, in Egloffstein, *Carl August*, pp.8-9, 113.

decide whether some of these may not be supplied from England, rather than leave 9,000 men in an inefficient state in this quarter. To-day I hear that the Duke has arrived at Arnheim, his troops at Zwoll.[17]

By return mail, the Duke of Saxe-Weimar send a letter to General Volkonsky, chief of staff of Emperor Alexander, stating that he would march to Holland. He was happy to join Bülow and ready to serve under his command. However, as already has been described in the previous chapter, next day the Russian Emperor had changed roles giving the Duke command over Bülow. Yet this did not change the situation the Duke's own corps was in, the lack of money was very urgent in order to be able to buy the necessary equipment still lacking, as the 100,000 thalers that had been allocated on 21 December had been exhausted. Efforts to requisition the necessary equipment in Münster failed. Therefore, he asked the Russian Emperor for a credit of 100,000 ducats. The lack of money and the great urgency is also illustrated by the fact that the Saxon troops had received no pay at all since 20 November 1813. On the advice of his chief of staff he also wrote to Prince Willem of Orange for money, and on the 21st, when the Duke was in Arnhem, he was answered that the prince would help him out with 100,000 Dutch guilders.[18]

On the 18th, the Duke of Saxe-Weimar left Lippstadt for the Netherlands, accompanied by his chief of staff *Generalmajor* von Wolzogen, *Oberstleutnant* von Lindenau and his chef of the quartermaster staff *Oberstleutnant* Ernst Ludwig von Aster. By way of Münster, Doesburg and Bommel, they arrived in Breda on 24 January. At Bommel, the Duke was joined by the 21-year-old son of the sovereign of the United Netherlands, Prince Willem Frederik George Lodewijk of Orange. *Oberstleutnant* von Aster was send back to speed up the advance of the Saxons as much as possible. From Breda, the Duke moved his headquarters to Schilde, just west of Antwerp. The troops of III German Corps continued their march through bitter cold weather under the command of *Generalleutnant* Karl Christian Le Coq, taking their route over Münster, entering Dutch territory. On 24 January they were at Borculo, where news came that the Rhine could not be crossed at Arnhem:

> Since the day before yesterday we have arrived here in Borkelo a few miles from Doesburg in the area of the Yssel and cannot go to Arnhem because of the swollen water and strong ice, to where our Serene Duke already preceded us on the 18th, and awaiting for the train today. Since it is not to be hoped that the water will fall quickly, we will have no choice but to take a long detour perhaps over Zwolle to Arnhem. At the same time we are not far from Deventer, which fortress is still occupied by the French and is blockaded by Russians … The current strong cold has plagued us very much, and here on Dutch soil you will not find a warm room.

17 Letter of 23 January from Lord Clancarthy in The Hague to Lord Castlereach, in Charles William Vane, Marquess of Londonderry (ed.), *Correspondence, despatches, and Other Papers, of Viscount Castlereach, Second Marquess of Londonderry* (London: John Murray, 1853), Vol.IX, pp.188-189.

18 Egloffstein, *Carl August*, pp.11-12. The Duke's intendant, *Hauptmann* von Nostitz, was on 3 February ordered to go to Breda to receive the money from the Dutch governor, first of all paying the arrears of the Saxon troops for the months November and December.

His Highness Prince Bernard came to us on the 16th in Lippstadt, and will march with the Saxon Guard the same road we will take.[19]

So III German Corps had to make a long detour and indeed crossed the river Yssel north of Zwolle, marching further over Kampen, Utrecht and Tiel. They passed the Rhine on 2 February, cantoning near Breda from 5 to 7 February.

The Provisional Government of the Southern Netherlands

Not surprisingly, news of the allied advance through the Northern Netherlands and the uprising there, found quickly its way to the French in the south, for example illustrated by a letter of 20 November 1813 from the prefect of the Dyle Department:

> I cannot conceal from you that our public spirit, far from improving, seems, for a few days, to have gone from bad to worse ... The insurrection that broke out in Holland is an example and a dangerous neighbour for a country that is not French (it must be admitted), and where it may be lacking only leaders for the revolt to break out. The banks of the Rhine, which have been reunited since the Revolution, are, it is said, still completely German, especially Aachen ... Of five hundred conscripts lately en route from the district of Brussels alone, two hundred and ninety-four have already been reported to me as deserters en route ... It is very necessary for this part of Belgium that the force arrives to impose on turbulent spirits ... The cross-roads and the woods are filled with fugitive conscripts; and the detachments sent to stop the principal issues can not suffice to stop this prodigious desertion ... This part of Belgium might need to be guarded against herself as well as against the enemy, if it approached, and if the rumours relating to Holland continue to be so alarming.[20]

After Bülow and Graham's fruitless attack and subsequent bombardment of Antwerp, Bülow retreated back to Lier. Next day, on 7 February, the Duke of Saxe-Weimar entered Brussels, accompanied by Bülow and Prince Willem of Orange. Since his arrival in the Southern Netherlands the Duke reported nearly daily to the Emperor Alexander, about the situation and his decisions, as well as the results of Bülow's fighting around Antwerp. The same information can be found in the correspondence with his wife, giving us a good insight in the situation the Duke found himself in:

> Here I am since yesterday noon. The bombardment of the fleet in the Antwerp Basin has damaged some vessels and many houses and that is the result. The English have remained in the vicinity, and we have also left some to observe the garrison which is 7-8,000 strong and commanded by the famous Carnot. To approach the city we had to take two very strong positions. General Bülow chose for his troops

---

19 Letter of 26 January 1814 from private secretary Vogel to privy councillor von Voigt, in Egloffstein, *Carl August*, pp.119-120.

20 Letter of 20 November 1813 from *Comte* d'Houdetot, Prefect of the Dyle Department, to Réal, *directeur du 1er arrondissement de la police générale*, in Prosper Poullet, *La Belgique et la Chute de Napoleon 1er* (Bruxelles: Société Belge de Librairie, 1895), p.29.

that of Deurne and General Th. Graham that of Merxem. We took advantage of a day before the English, successful, although the position was very strong and well guarded, but the bravery of the Prussian troops surpassed everything; they fought with prodigious courage. The fight lasted 6 hours, and we lost between 5-600 men dead or wounded. The loss of the enemy must have been very considerable. The English had a better game, their fight lasted only a few minutes; they lost, including the bombardment, 150-200 men. Two Dutch canons of iron, which had their carriage destroyed, were lost and some officers. We have more enemy in front of us than just the garrison of the fortress. *Général de Division* Maison, who alone fought the campaign still with 7 to 8,000 men, had withdrawn and scattered his troops across various places. Gorkum capitulated, surrendering on the 20th of this month. The famous senator Rampon commanded it, he is a prisoner of war with the garrison, 4,000 men strong. Bois le Duc has been assaulted by the Prussians, the places still in the hands of the French begin to diminish. In Holland they still have Deventer, Den Helder, Delfzijl, Coevorden. We leave it to the Dutch to take these places to stimulate them to speed up their armament: they are slow in doing something, making us lose patience. Wintzingerode makes a lot of progress and must be today near Philippeville. Müffling wrote to me that he thought the whole thing would be over soon. The Saxons and Bernhard will join me in a few days; broken dams and overflows severely halted the march of these troops; they were able to cross the Yssel at Kampen, and marched over Utrecht; Bernhard was in Amsterdam for a moment … Everything falls to me here and the Corps to reorganize Belgium; it is a hard task, but I must do it because this country forms our region, and must feed us; it is so unorganized that no penny enters the coffers. The Mayor of this place, the Duke of Ursel, is very suspicious; he is a narrow-minded man, without character, and very hated and despised. By doing nothing, he does a lot of harm. They treat me with great distinction, and they flatter me from all sides. The Duke of Clarence arrived today; he comes from my house, of all the sons of the English family he looks the most like his father.[21]

Bülow had been more than busy with his military task. So when the Duke of Saxe-Weimar arrived, one of the most urgent projects he had to take care of was setting up some kind of government and structure to be able to utilise the sources of the country itself, in manpower, supplies as well as money and to maintain order. On his arrival one of the first things he did was, together with Bülow, to issue a proclamation to the inhabitants of the Southern Netherlands, urging them to join the cause, to fight against the tyrant Napoleon and for their freedom. Beyond the scope of this book, it will suffice here to state that this proclamation fed hope to many for an independent Belgium. The Southern Netherlands had been part of France; before that they had formed the Austrian Netherlands. Although there were plans and Prince Willem of Orange had ambitions, it was by no means decided yet that the Southern Netherlands would become part of a United Netherlands. Nevertheless, it was necessary to create a central government

---

21 Letter of 8 February 1814 from the Duke of Saxe-Weimar to his wife, in Egloffstein, *Carl August*, pp.128-129. The Bernhard mentioned here is *Oberst* Prinz Karl Bernhard von Sachsen-Weimar-Eisenach, the son of the Duke of Saxe-Weimar, who received command of the three battalions of the Saxon Provisorisches Garde-Regiment.

to fill the vacuum left by the French, to form armed units to help in defeating Napoleon and to organize provisioning for the Allied troops present, etc. The Duke of Saxe-Weimar wanted to copy the structure designed by Freiherr Heinrich Friedrich vom Stein for the liberated German territories united under a *Generalgouvernement*, for which it was necessary to involve representatives of the southern departments. This proved to be impossible though, because of the bad roads, French troops still present in several fortresses and so forth. Therefore, on 12 February the Duke summoned the heads of the 32 most respectable families in Brussels. Twenty-four appeared, and during the meeting a provisional government was appointed which came into office on 15 February 1814.

Responsible for the military administration became the Prussian *Generalmajor* Heinrich Christoph Reichsgraf von Lottum, commander of the Brandenburgischen Dragoner-Regiment in Bülow's III Prussian Corps, also appointed governor of Brussels. Responsible for the civil administration became Daniel Heinrich Delius. Frédéric Auguste, Duc de Beaufort became governor-general. His deputy *jonkheer* ('squire') Eugène de Robiano was also one of the three members of the board of directors. Then there were four general secretaries: for military preparations; for police and home affairs; finance; and finally justice and clergy. The existing regions of the Southern Netherlands remained the same, as well as the existing prefectures (now called intendancies). All officials retained their previous positions, including those of French origin, although they had to swear an oath for faithfulness and obedience to the allies.[22]

The change in government was not immediately recognised and even caused a riot in Brussels which was quickly suppressed:

> The mob from some of the quarters of our city gathered on the marketplace on the morning of the 21st and showed vicious sentiments, because a change had been made in the appointment of public officials, and people chosen whose worth and loyalty, their love for the people and the good cause in the first moments were not yet recognized. Count v. Lottum, military governor of Belgium, maintained public order through his wise arrangements. The garrison, consisting of Prussian troops, showed that with serenity and steadfastness it kept the enemies of the peace in check just as they managed to defeat the enemies of their king managed by the shedding of their blood for the just cause of the fatherland. The Civil Guard has fully supported it; one could not show more zeal and more citizenry. So that the same performances will not be repeated, the General announced the following proclamation ... [23]

22 Professor Dr. Otto Cartellieri, 'Karl August von Sachsen-Weimar in Belgien – die Anfänge der provisorischen Regierung im Jahre 1814', in *Die Grenzboten, Zeitschrift für Politik, Literatur und Kunst*, Vol. 76, 1st quarter (Berlin: Verlag der Grenzboten G.m.b.h.) pp.93-94; *Journal Officiel du Gouvernement de la Belgique* (Bruxelles: Chez Weissenbruch, 1814), Vol.1, pp.6-8, 15-16; Docteur Coremans, *Éphémérides Belges de 1814 (Février-Juillet), D'après les Archives du Gouvernement provisoire de Cette Époque* (Bruxelles: M. Hayez, 1847), pp.17-18.

23 *Allgemeine Zeitung*, 6 March 1814.

There also remained a pro-French party in Brussels, openly led by the mayor of Brussels, the Duc d'Ursel. So another measure of strength came soon, when d'Ursel sent a message to the Duc de Beaufort, about Blücher's defeat by the French at Vauchamps (14 February) stating that the French would be in Brussels again soon and that De Beaufort would be shot for joining the allies. De Beaufort in fear went to the Duke of Saxe-Weimar, asking if it was true what d'Ursel had said. The Duke acted immediately, ordering *Oberstleutnant* Lindenau to arrest d'Ursel for siding with the French and spreading false rumours. As a prisoner of state d'Ursel was sent to Münster. In his place, Baron van der Linden d'Hooghvorst was appointed mayor of Brussels. These abrupt measures effectively diminished pro-French influence in Brussels, as well as strengthening the position of the provisional government in the Southern Netherlands. In addition, it was ordered to destroy all telegraphs in the southern Netherlands as well all in French territory that could be reached, as it was believed that the Duc d'Ursel had communicated with the French by this means.[24]

Raising units in the Southern Netherlands

As in the former Dutch Republic, also in the Southern Netherlands units were to be formed. There would be three ways that units were raised. First those that were organized by the Dutch. The first effort to raise a unit composed entirely from men from the Southern Netherlands in Dutch service dates from 16 December 1813, *Major* de Perez raising the Bataljon Jagers van Perez in Breda. In February 1814, the Dutch Sovereign Prince Willem of Orange had authorised *Colonel* de Constant-Rebecque to raise the Régiment de Wallons Liégeois or 'Regiment Luikerwalen' (two battalions) to garrison Liège. Already on 3 March, Constant-Rebecque handed over command to *Colonel* Michel van der Maesen because of other duties. Secondly, units were raised from volunteers native in the parts of the country on the right bank of the Meuse, occupied by Prussia. Finally, units raised by the provisional government formed by the Duke of Saxe-Weimar. The first unit would be a cavalry regiment consisting of chevaux-légers, the Duke on 13 February authorizing *Colonel* Comte Charles-Albert van der Burch to raise this regiment in Brussels and having the right to choose the officers himself. By proclamation of 4 March 1814,[25] it was announced that four infantry regiments would be raised, together forming the *Légion Belge*, to which the regiment chevaux-légers and an artillery battery would be added, the Legion to be commanded by the Austrian *Feldmarschalleutnant* Graf Murray de Melgum:[26]

- 1er Régiment 'de Brabant' in Brussels. This regiment was formed around the nucleus of volunteers already enlisted by *Capitaine* Marbais du Graty, who on 23 February on his own initiative had started recruiting an infantry unit. He completed the 1st

---

24 Alfred Freiherrn von Wolzogen, *Memoiren des königlich preußischen Generals der Infanterie, Ludwig Freiherrn von Wolzogen* (Leipzig: Otto Wigand, 1851), pp.247-250.
25 Proclamation of 4 March 1814, in *Journal Officiel*, pp.42-43.
26 Order of the day of the *Légion Belge* of 18 March 1814, in *Journal Officiel*, p.107.

company and would later become commander of the 1st battalion. Commander of the regiment was *Colonel* Baron de Poederlé, but as he was general secretary for military preparations as well, *Lieutenant-Colonel* Rouchet held command. In the beginning of April, the 1st battalion of the regiment counted 600 men in six companies;

- 2e Régiment 'de Flandre' in Ghent. Its commander was *Colonel* de Polis. Aided by a few officers he started forming the 1st battalion, which was interrupted by the French attack on Ghent (26 March) where they captured part of the battalion, including its colonel;
- 3e Régiment 'de Hainaut' in Namur. On 1 March, *Colonel* N. Du Pont was appointed by the Duke of Saxe-Weimar to raise and command this regiment. Although according to the proclamation it would be raised in Mons but in reality it was Namur;
- 4e Régiment 'de Namur' in Namur (according to the proclamation). At the beginning of March, *Colonel* Marquis de Trazegnies d'Ittre was charged raising this regiment. Starting recruitment at Mons, on 23 March the regiment was ordered to garrison Tournay where its nucleus would participate in the defence of this city on 31 March.

More units would be raised in the Southern Netherlands. When *Major* Graf Hermann Ludwig von Pückler-Muskau arrived in Bruges (see Chapter 4), he started raising the 1er Régiment d'Infanterie Légère. The nucleus was formed of volunteers raised in Flanders by *Lieutenant-Colonel* Chevalier Desnoyers. On 21 March, the Duke appointed *Lieutenant-Général* Comte de Murray as commander. Prince E. d'Arenberg became colonel-commander of the regiment. At the beginning of April, a former Austrian captain M. Graux raised, in the environs of Chimay, a battalion of six companies with the name 'Chasseurs de Le Loup', the name in remembrance of a former corps in Austrian service of the same name. The battalion was sent to Bruges and absorbed into the 1er Régiment d'Infanterie Légère. By decree of 1 March, the Duke of Saxe-Weimar appointed Prince F. De Croy as colonel commander of a hussar regiment. Initially raised at Tervuren near Brussels, it transferred to Ath later.

In the beginning of March, organisation of a 'Belgian' artillery corps started in Brussels. *Generalmajor* von Lottum defined its strength at four foot artillery batteries and two horse artillery batteries. A 'Belgian' 9-pdr battery, armed with British 9-pdr cannon, would join III German Corps and take an active part in the fighting, distinguishing itself at Tournay, as will be described further on. The remainder of the corps stayed in Brussels under the command of *Colonel* d'Aman de Schwanberg, *Major* van der Smissen acting as lieutenant-colonel. Finally a gendarmerie was raised. The gendarmerie was created by decree of 27 February under the name of 'Corps de la Maréchaussée', consisting of one company in each of the six departments. On 26 March the company of the Dyle was complete, it would take until 5 May until all six companies had reached full strength, although half of the necessary horses were still lacking. Total strength was 490 gendarmes; 314 on foot and 176 mounted.[27]

Although the British supplied an enormous number of muskets, cannon, and other equipment for these units as well as those in the northern Netherlands, weapons and cartridges were still in short supply, and many men had to be armed with home-made pikes, doing duty in their own civilian clothing. It would take much time to form an effective army and although on 22 April the *Légion Belge* had a paper strength of 20,883, *Major* Graf Einsiedel reported: 'Effectively however, only 3.961 men and 337 horses are already present, and only few of them are equipped with mounts and equipment … Today was the first revue, namely of the *Chasseurs Belges*, under the command of Prince Ernst von Ahremberg. Most of them were not yet with mounts and equipment.'[28] As a result their contribution to support III German Corps would only be minor.

---

27 Decree of 2 March 1814, in *Journal Officiel*, pp.9-13.
28 Report of 22 April 1814 from *Major* Graf Einsiedel to *Generalmajor* von Wolzogen, in Egloffstein, *Carl August*, p.216.

4

First Blood: February 1814

Organising and deploying the military forces

Finally, III German Corps had arrived in the southern Netherlands, the soldiers having suffered much from their long march through very bad and freezing weather. They received a few days of hard needed rest:

> We passed the waters of the Rhine, the Lek, Waal and Meuse on foot over the ice. Our Serene Duke is here since the 8th and is very well received by the citizens. Today his Highness Prince Bernhard arrived here with the Saxon Guard, we will stay here for a few days to give rest to those troops. Antwerp is out of sight and we will probably turn more to the interior of France. The money spent has since been bearable, wagon repairs and horses the most, the major detour from Münster to Zwolle and Kampen and via Utrecht has required much repair of harnesses.[1]

So there were successes: The Duke of Saxe-Weimar had been well received in Brussels; it proved to be relatively easy to form a provisional government for the Southern Netherlands; and despite the bad weather III German Corps had arrived on the scene. However, then there came a serious setback: Bülow decided to leave for France with his army corps. He strongly –and of course rightly – believed that the final decision would fall in France, and therefore it was expedient to concentrate as many troops as possible for the final battle against Napoleon. In addition, Bülow could argue that he was following orders joining Blücher's Army of Silesia. On the other hand, there were also orders to liberate and protect the Netherlands, aiding them in their armament and to expedite their support to the common cause. With the British still building up their army; Wintzingerode not showing up with his army corps, and Bernadotte also nowhere to be seen; with the local forces in the Southern Netherlands still having to be formed and those in the Northern Netherlands occupied blockading the various fortresses still occupied by the French; with the fortresses Bergen-op-Zoom, Antwerp, and Maubeuge occupied with strong French garrisons and *Général de Division* Maison close by with a weak but still substantial army corps, the Duke of Saxe-Weimar's still very weak III German Corps would be unable to fulfil this task on its

---

1   Letter of 11 February 1814 from private secretary Vogel to privy councillor von Voigt, in Egloffstein, *Carl August*, p.131.

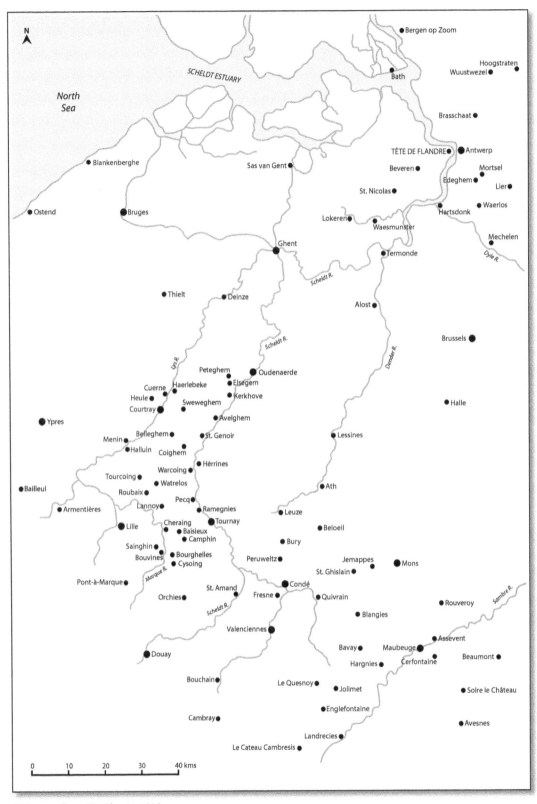

III German Corps War Theatre 1814

own. In addition, the idea of having to hand over command to the Duke seems also to have influenced Bülow's decision. It can be imagined that a heated discussion took place between the Duke and Bülow, and it was finally agreed that, in preparation for joining Blücher in France, Bülow would shift his troops south.

On 15 February Bülow moved his headquarters and the bulk of his army to Mons, while *Generalleutnant* von Borstell's 5th Division moved to Ath. The partaking in the blockade of Antwerp, about which Bülow had come to an agreement with the British General Graham before the Duke had arrived, was taken over by units from III German Corps, commanded by *Generalmajor* Heinrich Adolph von Gablenz. Colonel Bikhalov's Cossack Regiment with a strength of five squadrons, which was attached to III German Corps, was sent to Ghent to take over command from the departing Prussians, arriving there on the 14th. This was not a regular Cossack regiment but had been raised from volunteers in 1812 during Napoleon's advance into Russia. Its colonel, Vasiliy Andreyevich Bikhalov I, was about 80 years old, having a long white beard. He was analphabetic and spoke no foreign languages, so to aid him he was always accompanied by a Polish Jew who was his secretary and chief of staff as well as his interpreter. Bikhalov treated the citizens of Ghent at will and indulged himself and his officers with extensive dinners at the expense of the city treasury. Not surprisingly, his volunteer Cossacks surrendered themselves to excesses; theft, robbery and even rape were the order of the day.[2] *Major* Hellwig's *Streifcorps*, part of Bülow's III Prussian Corps, also remained under the Duke's orders: 'Since His Highness still wishes to have a cavalry regiment, so may Borstell leave the corps of Hellwig on his departure and place it entirely under the orders of His Highness.'[3] This *Streifcorps* was composed of German volunteers and had already fought the French since the beginning of 1813. Experienced as they were, they were a welcome addition to III German Corps.

However, news then arrived about the series of defeats that had been suffered by the allies in the battles of Champaubert, Montmirail, Etoges, and Vauchamps (10-14 February) which took away any reason to delay Bülow's departure to join Blücher's Army of Silesia any longer. Marching in the direction of Rheims, Bülow sent a letter to the Duke of Saxe-Weimar on the 17th, informing him about his departure and 'requesting' taking over the observation of the French-held fortresses along the border, as well as guarding against *Général de Division* Maison's army corps. The Duke of Saxe-Weimar replied: 'By the state of things described to me by your Excellency, I cannot help but agree that you march in the name of God.' He added that, because of the small force that he had under his command, it was self-evident that Borstell's 5th Division would have to remain, and, further,

---

2   Roger van Aerde, 'Kozakken te Gent – De Geschiedenis van Peetje Kozak', in *Ghendtsche Tydinghen*, Vol. 11, Nr. 6 (Gent: Heemkundige en Historische Kring Gent v.z.w., 1982), pp.300-301.

3   Quoted in Hans Fabricius, 'Der Parteigänger Friedrich von Hellwig und seine Streifzüge, im kriegsgeschichtlichen Zusammenhange betrachtet. Ein Beitrag zur Geschichte des kleinen Krieges in den Jahren 1792 bis 1814', in *Jahrbücher für die deutsche Armee und Marine* (Berlin: Verlag von A. Bath, 1896), p.174. See Appendix II for the composition of *Major* Hellwig's *Streifcorps*.

that *Generalmajor* von Gablenz, blockading Antwerp, would be ordered to send part of his troops south. The Duke further added: 'And if I have only a reasonable amount of troops appropriate to the circumstances, then the Division Borstell should follow you immediately ... No one can take a more active part in the good cause in general, and especially in the one that your Excellency is going to participate, I wish you good luck.'[4] The Duke of Saxe-Weimar further added that, when possible under the circumstances, he would attack Maison's army corps with Borstell's 5th Division and his Saxons in order to remove that threat.

Bülow received this letter on his march to France. Enraged, as now he had set himself the task to come to Blücher's aid with his entire army corps, he demanded from the Duke to send him Borstell's 5th Division immediately, at the same time ordering Borstell to march without delay. This obliged the Duke to reply by return mail:

> Your Excellency treats me like Charles Jean [Bernadotte], but forget that this Royal Highness would do nothing while he had many troops, and I would not like to be prostituted because, with all the so-called Supreme Command, I have almost no troops, and your Excellency wants to deprive myself of the troops which I most needed to cover my honour, and for the solid purposes of the great and general objective. I wish you much luck in Paris, but we do not want to be deprived of Belgium for the time being. Enclosed, you receive an order to Gen. Lt. Von Borstell ... Putting aside all ambition, I expected much of your Excellency's old friendship, out of the active display of mine that I publicly paid homage to your rare merit. In those mismatches of the service, I represent Gen. Lt. von Borstell entirely and I will publicly confess, if it should come to accountability, that it was **I** [sic!] who prevented it, that he did not follow your orders at that moment ... From this moment on, I ask your Excellency to regard the Gen. Lt. von Borstell, with his Division, as my property: to your king, who, as your Excellency knows is very close to me, and personally owes me some consideration; to the Russian Emperor, whose relationship to me your Excellency know of, even with the Emperor of Austria, and on top of that, by the judgment of the whole German nation, I represent your Excellency and the Gen. Lt. von Borstell, if I keep the latter with his division with me, until I will be so reinforced from Saxony, that I can yield the Prussian troops to your Excellency again.[5]

At the same time, he wrote a clear order to *Generalleutnant* von Borstell, ordering him to remain under his orders despite Bülow's direct order to him:

> General Lieutenant von Bülow completely misinterpreted my writing dated February 17, from Brussels, believing that I could already do without the division under your Excellencies orders. But as I do not want, that from this misunderstanding shall arise a disadvantage for the good cause, which will necessarily be the case, when by the departure of your division, Belgium and

---

4   Letter of 17 February from the Duke of Saxe-Weimar to Bülow, in Egloffstein, *Carl August*, pp.29-30.
5   Letter of 19 February 1814, Ath, from the Duke of Saxe-Weimar to Bülow, in Ollech, *Carl Friederich Wilhelm von Reyher*, p.354; Egloffstein, *Carl August*, pp.31-32.

Holland will be surrendered, I command your Excellency to remain in this area as long as I consider it necessary. I will inform General Bülow of my decision. Enclosing this order to you, whereby you will be relieved from all responsibility.[6]

Still, Bülow refused to yield, and tried to compromise with the Duke, offering him three of Von Borstell's infantry battalions, two squadrons of dragoons and *Major* Hellwig's *Streifcorps*. At the same time, he sent marching orders to Von Borstell for Laon, including the route he had to take. Again the Duke of Saxe-Weimar repeated his decision to Bülow, as well as to Borstell, on 23 February.[7] He also wrote about his decision to the Prussian King Friedrich Wilhelm, pointing out that at that moment III German Corps counted only about 8,000 men, lacking in cavalry and artillery. Out of these he also had to provide a blockading corps for Antwerp because of the agreement that Bülow had made with General Graham.[8] However, the Duke did act to support Bülow's march into France, providing indirect support. On 14 February, *Oberst* von Geismar received command of a *Streifcorps*, formed of II. Squadron of the Uhlanen-Regiment (*Major* von Berge), a squadron of the Husaren-Regiment (*Major* von Fabrice) and the Chernozubov Regiment of Don Cossacks (*Chernozubov IV Donskoi Kazachii Polk* – 540 men). Total strength was about 800 horse. Geismar was ordered to march with his *Streifcorps* into French Flanders, to draw as much attention as possible to himself, to support popular uprisings, disrupt communications, and so forth. He was also to distract French attention from Bülow's advance.[9] This task was ably executed. On the 15th Geismar captured Courtray. Advancing between Lille and Ypres to Hazebrouck, on the 17th he captured Cassel. On the 19th he raided Saint-Pol-sur-Ternoise, capturing Doullens on the 20th (its citadel two days later), defeated a 1,000 men strong column coming from Arras, and finally on the 26th joined Bülow near La Fère. Further exploits of Geismar are beyond the scope of this work.[10]

In the meantime, the expected reinforcements from Saxony were delayed. *Generalleutnant* von Thielmann had promised the Duke of Saxe-Weimar, by report of 2 January 1814, to reinforce him with 18 battalions, four cavalry squadrons and 14 guns, marching om 1 February. On 17 January however, Thielmann informed the Duke that he was not able to leave for at least another 10 days, and four battalions short. The Duke was particularly disappointed that no men of the volunteer *Banner der Freiwilligen Sachsen* would be present, apparently having in mind the volunteer units which proved to be a powerful addition to the Prussian army and badly needing the additional cavalry. In fact, no men of the Banner would ever join III German Corps,

6   Letter of 19 February 1814, Ath, from the Duke of Saxe-Weimar to Von Borstell, in Egloffstein, *Carl August*, p.135.

7   Letters of 23 February 1814, Ath, from the Duke of Saxe-Weimar to Bülow and Von Borstell, in Egloffstein, *Carl August*, pp.32-33, 135-136.

8   Returns of III German Corps of 15 February: Combatants; officers 258, others 8,323; horses 2,037; non-combatants 367, horses 61: Egloffstein, *Carl August*, pp.33, 215.

9   Von Wolzogen, *Memoiren*, p.250.

10 For more information about Geismar's exploits, see Major Joh. Bapt. Schels, 'Des Oberst Baron Geismar Streifzug in Belgien und Frankreich; im Februar und März 1814', in Oestreichische militärische Zeitschrift, Vol. 4 (Wien: Anton Strauß's sel. Witwe, 1838), pp.115-135.

as, for reasons beyond the scope of this book, the Banner was honoured by being attached to the Russian Imperial Guard and would leave for the Russian army instead![11]

Generalleutnant von Thielmann though did his best to join the Duke as soon as possible with the available troops, force marching his command to the Low Countries: on 18 February he arrived in Paderborn, on the 26th he reached Cologne. 'Thielmann finally arrived as well, but very cheap [weak]', wrote the Duke to his wife.[12] This remark is understandable, as from the expected 10,000 men, only about 8,000 would arrive, including reinforcements for the units already present. These had only few cartridges with them and many of the muskets had to be repaired at Liège before they could be used, delaying their arrival even more. Finally, on 12 March, Thielmann would arrive in Brussels.

Another problem was the support and supplies from Saxony that the Duke desperately needed to be able to do battle with his troops. The units that arrived were, as already described, lacking a lot, even arriving without cartridges. Saxony was still suffering much from the miseries of the late war on its territory, lack of labour force, and contagious diseases. On top of this the country suffered much from requisitions made by the allies; at one hand treating Saxony as an occupied enemy country, on the other hand expecting enormous exertions for the war effort. Especially the Russian General-Government demanded much, the Duke writing to his wife:

> In all the organization in Saxony is and will be the most miserable. Our friend Repnin hears nothing, and all who surround him are under the slightest pretext of being skilled. The Russians, a force of disorder, ruin Saxony completely and without aim. 12,000 *Capucins* of the Russian Landwehr under the command of that beast Gourief garrison Dresden ... They absorb the Mark [currency] of the country, which was to serve to maintain and raise the army.[13]

The Saxons that had arrived in the Southern Netherlands lacked a lot. Many had no greatcoats or were even wearing summer clothing, so not surprisingly there were many sick. For these, initially a small military hospital was established in Breda, followed by a bigger one in Louvain. Likewise, as the quality of the horses was bad and many were worn out; a depot was established in Breda, moved to Brussels later on, to let the horses recover and to receive and train fresh delivered horses. One of the biggest problems that had to be solved was the lack of ammunition. Except for the French muskets that had been captured, there were simply no cartridges available for the calibre of muskets used by III German Corps and the arrival of the Main Artillery

---

11   Decree of 3 March 1814 from Emperor Alexander, in Patent No. 80 of 12 March 1814 in *General-Gouvernements-Blatt*, p.250. For more details of how and why the banner became part of the Russian Imperial Guard, see Heinrich Zschokke (ed.), 'Denkschrift über den sächsischen Banner', in *Ueberlieferungen zur Geschichte unserer Zeit* (Aarau: Heinrich Remigius Sauerländer, 1817), pp. 583-600.

12   Letter of 24 February 1814 from the Duke of Saxe-Weimar to his wife, in Egloffstein, *Carl August*, pp.61, 136-138.

13   Letters of 24 February and 13 March 1814 from the Duke of Saxe-Weimar to his wife, in Egloffstein, *Carl August*, pp.58, 136-138, 146-148.

Park was not expected before 25 March. What was available were 200,000 French cartridges that had been left behind in the magazines of the cities of Hellevoetsluis, Delft, and Willemstad, as well as 150,000 British cartridges and 136 *Centner* of loose gunpowder. Again, the Duke of Saxe-Weimar contacted the Prince of Orange to help with this problem, who responded immediately. Experienced Dutch labourers were summoned from various cities to an ammunition laboratory in Breda, directed by *Premierleutnant* Hanmann, to change these cartridges into useful ones, by melting the balls and casting new ones of the right calibre, and by adding the right amount of gunpowder. The Duke was again very satisfied with this support, writing to his wife: 'The Prince of Orange has always supported me, both with money and ammunition. I owe him a lot, I lack everything; the English have infinite attention for me.'[14] With the latter remark, the Duke referred to the presence of Prince William Henry, Duke of Clarence, the future King William IV of England. Apparently on his own account, the Duke of Clarence had joined the British Army under Thomas Graham. After having been present at the 2nd combat of Merxem on 2 February, the Duke of Clarence had arrived in Brussels on the 8th. The next day, the Duke of Saxe-Weimar wrote to his wife: 'Imagine that the Duke of Clarence will campaign with us; it will be a great opportunity to put him at his ease', undoubtedly referring to his financial problems and the slander about him.[15]

The strategic situation

Very important for the French, as well as for the allies, was Antwerp. Antwerp was a strong fortress, possessing a huge harbour and numerous docks in which lay a huge number of French warships, posing a threat for Great Britain. In addition, when the allies would be able to take possession of Antwerp, logistics would become much easier; reasons for Napoleon to allot strong forces to the defence of this fortress-city. The garrison consisted of the cores of 55 battalions, totalling about 8,000 men. From these, the divisions of *Généraux de Division* Jean Jacques Ambert, Claude Carra Saint Cyr, and François Roch Ledru des Essarts were planned to be formed. An additional 7,000 men of *Général de Division* François Roguet's 1er Garde-Tirailleur-Division were present. The defence was led by the renowned *Général de Division* Lazare Nicolas Carnot, but rather surprisingly, and despite his theories, he never utilised more than about 4,000 men of these in his sorties. With the troops at his disposal he would have been able to create havoc for the allies, but now the results were only many dead and wounded on both sides, with no advantages gained. Although it must be said in his defence that quality of the French troops was very low. The allies were too weak to blockade Antwerp effectively. Beside Antwerp, the British also had to pay attention to another fortress-city just to the north, Bergen op Zoom. General

---

14 Letter of 13 March 1814 from the Duke of Saxe-Weimar to his wife, in Egloffstein, *Carl August*, pp.58, 146-148.

15 Letter of 9 March 1814 from the Duke of Saxe-Weimar to his wife, in Egloffstein, *Carl August*, pp.58, 129-130. For more information about the presence of the Duke of Clarence in the Low Countries, see Bamford, *A Bold and Ambitious Enterprise*, pp.116, 139-141.

Graham was obliged to try to capture Bergen op Zoom with a night-time surprise attack on 8 March, which however miserably failed.

Augmented with some Prussian, German and Russian units, forces at hand were still so few that and effective blockade was impossible, especially after Bülow had left for France. In fact, on the left bank of the Scheldt river there were virtually no allies present, except for some patrols of Cossacks, and there was virtually free communication possible between Antwerp and France. To make the situation even more precarious, to defend the northern border of France, the army corps of *Général de Division* Nicolas Joseph Maison was present. Maison received direct orders from Napoleon, who overestimated his strength and capabilities and ordering him to attack, Maison writing to the Minister of War: 'It is clear that the Emperor has to be completely deceived as to my strength and that of the enemy, for having given me this order'. Providing reports about the strength of his corps totalling, including gendarmes and artillery: 4,907 men, 1,730 horses and 20 guns. Maison added:

> I hope that His Majesty will see that with such small means, we cannot do better than to have the beginning of garrisons in the places to shut the gates, guard the armament and ammunition in these works for the moment, although they are partly armed, and prevent the inhabitants from opening them to the enemy to avoid a bombardment. I have no army, I never had one; I only brought to the places 2,200 men of the Division Barrois, 900 of the 12e Voltigeurs and a battalion of 500 men of the 72e. These 3,600 men assure the possession of Valenciennes and Lille; we cannot do without them. The rest of the infantry that there is are in the places, except for a battalion of the 25e at Landrecies and Quesnoy, these are not worth counting and cannot be put in the field. This is my alleged army.[16]

The real strength of Maison's troops is unclear, as there is also a letter from him, dated 19 February, in which he stateed his strength at 11,617. In addition, in Lille there were numerous depots of battalions allegedly numbering 19,780.[17] Forming these into battalions was problematic though, the commander of the 16e Division Militaire in Lille, *Général de Division* Antoine François Brenier de Montmorand, reporting to Maison that he was unable to raise the battalions previously announced as he had not received the conscripts intended for them.[18] What is also clear though is that Maison was short of field artillery, so in all engagements the French would only be able to deploy few guns. Although sources differ greatly, the French troops that garrisoned the various fortresses probably counted at Condé 6,000; Valenciennes 2,000; Le Quesnoy 600; Landrecies 6-700 and Maubeuge 1,000. These garrisons were being reinforcing by citizen gunners and militia. Maison himself was at Lille.

---

16   In addition, Maison stated he had 800 cavalry. Letter of 19 February from Maison to the French Minister of War, in Le Commandant Weil, *La Campagne de 1814 d'Après les Documents des Archives Impériales et Royales de la Guerre à Vienne – La Cavalerie des Armées Alliées Pendant la Campagne de 1814* (Paris: Librarie Militaire de L. Baudoin, 1892), Vol. 2, pp.425-426.

17   Fabricius, 'Der Parteigänger', p.175.

18   Calmon-Maison, 'Le Général Maison', p.174.

Although many of these men were still raw and badly trained, many historians believe that a substantial part of these garrisons could have been used for field operations. Many allied officers including the Duke of Saxe-Weimar feared that if Maison had concentrated his forces, he would have been able to break through the allied line at any chosen point easily, and also could be a threat to especially Blücher's Army of Silesia, operating inside France. This explains the actions of the Duke of Saxe-Weimar when *Général de Division* Maison advanced, as will be described. Despite that, Maison, maybe in the dark about the weakness of the allies confronting him, let the golden opportunity pass to strike the moment just after Bülow had left with his army corps; the moment III German Corps was still much too weak for any effective defence. As reinforcements started to arrive the corps became stronger and stronger. Although raw for the greater part, the men were motivated to come to grips with the hated French, a fact making good on a lot of things.

On 20 February, the Duke of Saxe-Weimar had 15,000 infantry, 2,200 cavalry and 42 field guns at his disposal. Except for building up his army corps he had the following targets to meet:

- To hamper, or even prevent, any sorties from the garrison of Antwerp in the eastern direction (right bank of the Scheldt river);
- Protecting the Netherlands against any advance or attack from the French troops commanded by *Général de Division* Maison, and against sorties from the French garrisons of the fortresses Yper, Lille, Douay, Valenciennes, Condé, and Maubeuge;
- Protecting Brussels against a French recapture, which could have serious political consequences;
- Securing the roads, supply lines and communications of the army corps of Wintzingerode and Bülow Corps; through Mons and Beaumont to Avesnes;
- Raising and organising army units in the Southern Netherlands, at least four infantry regiments and a cavalry regiment with the necessary artillery.

To reach these goals, the Duke of Saxe-Weimar decided to make Mons and Tournay his main points of defence. Both cities had been fortresses in the past, and although neglected, part of their main defence works were still intact. Precautions were taken by strengthening these defence works and giving both cities enough protection against a *coup de main*. The artillery arm was ordered to prepare positions on the walls, to be able to deploy field artillery for the defence. *Hauptmann* Carl Moritz Birnbaum, commanding officer of the 1. 6-Pfünder Reitende Batterie, received orders to repair and strengthen the defence works of Mons. For this purpose, the inhabitants of the city and the neighbouring country were summoned to provide 1,200-1,500 labourers. The defence of Tournay was more precarious, as it was situated much closer to the French lines and a number of French-held fortresses. Sapper *Hauptmann* Johann Franz Plödterl of the Duke's General Staff was ordered to improve the defences as much as possible. Not surprisingly, in this area Borstell's Prussian 5th Division was positioned, its troops believed to be more reliable than most other units of III German Corps which had not yet seen battle against their former ally.[19]

Another point of concern was the terrain combined with the weather: the non-paved roads were muddy and very bad. Passage was difficult, especially for the artillery and train. The region was covered with small woods making the terrain unclear and enabling troops to hide themselves. Especially in the west near the Scheldt river, the terrain was hedged in all directions. It was intersected by ditches, channels and dams, the latter often alone forming the traffic routes through the damp lowlands. Therefore, a harsh winter in those areas is the most suitable season for military operations, while in thawing the country is almost completely inaccessible. In the first half of January 1814 dry cold prevailed, which was replaced by heavy snowfall and finally by rainy weather. All the roads were covered with snow, under which the ice made slippery surfaces so that it was only with great difficulty that horses could move. In February and March frost and rain alternated. This all made movement of troops and mutual support difficult. One should take in account these conditions to get a true picture of the tremendous difficulties of warfare in the Southern Netherlands during this winter campaign.

First engagements

The first engagement between elements of III German Corps and the French was the capture of the Sas-van-Gent fortress by Colonel Bikhalov's Cossacks. Although even the word 'engagement' could be an overstatement. Sas-van-Gent was only a small fortified city, lying at the mouth of the canal beneath Gent. Its armament consisted of five obsolete cannon and it was occupied by a French garrison, consisting of five officers and 161 others of the 65e Ligne, commanded by *Chef de Bataillon* Bout de Charlemont. On 17 February Bikhalov sent a letter to the commander of Sas-van-Gent, inviting him to surrender. Bout de Charlemont had no stomach for a fight, replying: 'That if Colonel Bikhalov would arrive with satisfactory forces before the place, authorized to sign a decent capitulation, he as commander in this case would be honoured to give the place into the hands of such a hero as the colonel.'[20] Receiving this answer, Bikhalov ordered pamphlets to be printed, according to Van Aerde with the text:

> The Colonel Count de Bikhalov, owner of the first regiment Don-Cossacks, informs the inhabitants of the city of Ghent that he goes to Sas-van-Gent tomorrow at seven o'clock in the morning to oblige the commander to capitulate or to become master of the place; he gives the assurance that this trip will not expose anyone to any danger and that the whole event may be regarded as a pleasure trip.[21]

---

19 For the composition and disposition of III German Corps on 20 February, see Appendix II.
20 Quoted in Van Aerde, *Kozakken te Gent*, p.301.
21 Translation byVan Aerde in Van Aerde, *Kozakken te Gent*, p.301.

On the 18th, Bikhalov departed for Sas-van-Gent at the head of 250 Cossacks. He was followed by two hundred Belgian sailors, about 1,000 farmers with all sorts of crude weapons, as well as many curious citizens. Arriving before Sas-van-Gent, the Cossacks circled the fortress while the French garrison fired some obligatory shots taking care to hit nothing. In the afternoon, the French commander Bout de Charlemont surrendered the place. Colonel Bikhalov did not hesitate to try to use his 'victory' in his advantage, writing to the Duke of Saxe-Weimar:

> Lord Count, I have received your letter with the greatest joy, from which I learn that you will have the goodness to report to his Majesty the Emperor Alexander and to the king, not only on my merits but also on my honour, since I have already from the year 1799 the same rank, so to say fifteen years, so I pray Lord Count not to forget me. I also have the honour to make you known and to recommend my courageous officers who have dared their lives under the walls of the Sas-van-Gent fortress and forced the French to surrender.[22]

Sas-van-Gent was of no real strategic importance and the French never tried to recapture it.

Another interesting, although small engagement, was the following reconnaissance. *Generalmajor* Gustav Xaver von Ryssel had been ordered to find out as much as possible about the French-held fortress city Maubeuge, and to reconnoitre the roads at the west side of it. One reconnaissance would have to be the old Roman road called 'Brunehaut', leading from Mons to Le Cateau Cambresis. This would be a difficult reconnaissance, as the road passed between four French-held fortresses: Valenciennes, Maubeuge, Le Quesnoy, and Landrecies. Von Ryssel chose *Premierleutnant* George August Graf zu Solms und Tecklenburg of the Saxon Kürassier-Regiment to lead a patrol of twenty of its cuirassiers. On 23 February the patrol left, arriving in Bavay without any incidents. Here it stayed for the night, resuming its march the next day. Arriving at the village Jolimet near Le Quesnoy, the patrol surprised a convoy of four wagons with infantry cover, on its way to fetch palisades and wood for this fortress. The escort took flight into thick brushwood and was not pursued. *Premierleutnant* Solms decided to take the wagons with him, presumably to test the quality of the road he was to reconnoitre. Continuing the march, half an hour before reaching Le Cateau Cambresis, a few escaped Spanish prisoners of war were encountered. These informed *Premierleutnant* Solms that a transport of about 100 Spanish prisoners, escorted by six mounted gendarmes, was on its way from Landrecies to Cambray. Taking with him 14 cuirassiers, Solms pursued and attacked the prisoner transport, defeating the escort and capturing two horses. He took the freed prisoners with him to Le Cateau Cambresis. Then the lieutenant made a mistake, undoubtedly because of his inexperience. Instead of returning by another road he took the same road back. Taking with him the freed Spaniards on the captured wagons, before he could reach Englefontaine he was informed by farmers that the French garrison of Le Quesnoy had prepared an ambush

---

22 Report of 28 February 1814 from Bikhalov to the Duke of Saxe-Weimar in Bucher, *Der Feldzug*, pp.319-320.

near Jolimet with a strong force of infantry. To evade this ambush he turned right, taking the road through the Forêt de Mormal to Hargnies. He reached Bavay at 1:00 a.m., the much slower Spaniards on their wagons not before 8:00 a.m. early on the 25th. After a short rest the march was resumed around 10:00 a.m., but already while leaving the city through the gate of Bavay they were attacked by a detachment of about a hundred chasseurs à cheval, coming from Maubeuge. Abandoning the freed Spaniards, *Premierleutnant* Solms cut his way through the chasseurs, losing one of his troopers who was taken prisoner. He was pursued as far as Blangies, but got away without further loss and returned to Mons via Jemappes.[23]

On 25 February more important operations took place. Allied occupation of the fortress-city of Maubeuge would greatly improve communications with Bülow and Wintzingerode. To determine if capturing this place would be possible, the Duke of Saxe-Weimar decided on a reconnaissance in force. *Oberst* Otto Victor I. Fürst von Schönburg had to maintain communications by occupying Quivrain with both squadrons of the Saxon Husaren-Regiment, supported by two infantry companies detached by *Generalleutnant* von Le Coq. *Generalmajor* von Ryssel left behind a small detachment at Mons, consisting of the 1. 12-Pfünder Fußbatterie (4 guns), and two companies of the I. Gardebataillon. During the evening of the 24th he marched to Maubeuge with all other troops at his disposal. In order to divide the attention of the French and to reconnoitre that fortress-city as well, at the same time *Generalleutnant* von Le Coq concentrated the troops under his command before Condé. On the 25th, *Generalmajor* von Ryssel demonstrated before Maubeuge in three columns with the following composition:

1st or Left Wing Column (right bank of the Sambre):
    Kürassier-Regiment (1 squadron)
    II./2. Leichten Regiment (1 company)
    1. 6-Pfünder Reitende Batterie (½ battery)
    II. and III./2. Provisorischen Linien-Regiment
    1. 12-Pfünder Fußbatterie (½ battery, 4 guns)
    Kürassier-Regiment (2 squadrons – deployed as reserve)
2nd or Centre Column (right bank of the Sambre):
    Pommersches Husaren-Regiment (Prussian, 1 squadron, *Rittmeister* von Raven)
    1. 6-Pfünder Reitende Batterie (½ battery)
    Füs/2. Reserve-Infanterie-Regiment (Prussian, 2 companies)
    II./2. Leichten Regiment (3 companies)
3rd or Right Wing Column (left bank of the Sambre)
    Pommersches Husaren-Regiment (Prussian, 1 squadron)
    Füs/2. Reserve-Infanterie-Regiment (Prussian, 2 companies)

The 3rd Column advanced against the eastern front of the fortress, reconnoitring from the direction of Assevent. The 2nd Column, commanded by *Oberstleutnant* Hans von Thümen (the Prussian commander of the

---

23 Georg von Schimpff, *Geschichte des Kgl. Sächs. Garde-Reiter-Regiments* (Dresden: Wilhelm Baensch Verlagshandlung, 1880), p. 358.

outposts of *Generalmajor* von Ryssel), took up position also on the right bank of the Sambre, close to the forest of Roussies and the windmill there. It regulated its further movement in accordance with the advance of the 1st Column. This column finally advanced via Cerfontaine and Ferrière la Grande, along the road of Beaumont, against the southern front of Maubeuge. It was led by the commander of artillery of III German Corps *Oberstleutnant* Gustav Ludwig Raabe, as well as the Chef of the General Quartermaster Staff, *Oberstleutnant* von Aster. Both officers quickly came to the conclusion that capturing the fortress without the use of proper siege batteries would be impossible. The French fired at the various columns with their fortress guns, but as these used all the cover they could find during their approach while observing the fortress no casualties were inflicted. At Condé however, serious fighting broke out. As we have seen, *Generalleutnant* von Le Coq had concentrated before Condé. He commanded the following units:

II. Grenadier-Bataillon
III. Grenadier-Bataillon
II. and III./1. Provisorischen Linien-Regiment
1. 6-Pfünder Fußbatterie (6 cannon, 2x 8-pdr howitzers, *Hauptmann* Rouvroy II.)
Pommersches Husaren-Regiment (Prussian, 1 squadron, *Major* von Arnim)

Leaving behind his artillery near Peruweltz, he advanced to Condé with the remainder of his force, marching through a forest and occupying Vieux Condé and the edge of the Forêt de Condé forest. In front of him was a plain, all the way to Condé. His left was linked on the inundated terrain near the fortress, in front of him was a row of houses along the road, named Maucoux. Vieux Condé itself was for the greater part within range of the fortress guns; the edge of the forest was out of range. During the advance some outlying piquets of enemy cavalry and infantry were pushed back and the Saxons fired at by the fortress guns, but after some time the firing slackened. After all firing had ceased. Le Coq used this lull to reconnoitre the defences of Condé. Under the pretension of sending a parlay to the commander of the fortress, *Général de Brigade* Etienne Jacques Travers, to demand the capitulation of the fortress, an engineer officer moving even further forward. The French were apparently not deceived or not in a mood to surrender, and the officer had to beat a hasty retreat with a bullet hole in his hat. However, by now *Generalleutnant* von Le Coq knew enough: capturing Condé would be very difficult (even more difficult then Maubeuge); two thirds of the surrounding countryside had been flooded, and the still dry land had been mined, making an approach very dangerous and difficult. Despite that he did not retreat yet.

After having remained for some time in the above position, a concentration of troops of all arms was observed on the other side of the fortress, near Fresne village. Later it became known that this was a force of about four thousand men drawn from Valenciennes and Bouchain, to support the supposedly threatened fortress, under *Général de Division* Carra St. Cyr. Around 3:00 a.m. these troops entered Condé, but immediately debouched on the other side again, attacking *Generalleutnant* von Le Coq. Le Coq estimated the French at three infantry battalions, a hundred cavalry, and a horse artillery battery of six guns, supported by the fortress artillery. The attack on Vieux Condé was defeated, the left wing however was pressed harder. The French sending forward swarms of skirmishers, both grenadier battalions placed here had to retreat to a more defensible position further back, receiving support of two guns of the 1. 6-Pfünder Fußbatterie arriving from Peruweltz. The young commander of the Saxon grenadiers, *Oberst Prinz Karl Bernhard von Sachsen-Weimar*, joined the skirmisher chain to earn the respect of the veterans under his command.[24] Le Coq would receive some support: to maintain communications with him during his reconnaissance, *Generalleutnant* von Borstell had pushed forward a detachment of a hundred infantry and a squadron of the Pommersches National-Kavallerie-Regiment. Of this detachment, a force of about 40 cavalry also joined the fighting, together with the Prussian hussars commanded by *Major* von Arnim. It suffered the loss of five wounded troopers and seven horses. In the evening, *Generalleutnant* von Le Coq pulled back his troops and the fighting ended. Allied losses were: II. Grenadier-Bataillon five dead, 18 wounded; III. Grenadier-Bataillon one dead, one wounded; 1. Provisorischen Linien-Regiment four dead, four wounded. The Prussian hussars suffered several wounded men and horses. It is unclear why *Generalleutnant* von Le Coq remained in his position after having completed his reconnaissance of the fortress, engaging in unnecessary fighting. According to some sources, he believed it would be a stain on his honour to retreat in the face of the enemy, after having taken the initiative to advance himself. Whatever was the case, his decision was paid with blood.

The detachment blockading Antwerp, commanded by *Generalmajor* von Gablenz, had to fend off several reconnaissances and sorties during this period.[25] One of the biggest sorties was executed on 27 February by four infantry battalions, 200 cavalry, and two guns, about 2,000 men (some sources add 200 cavalry), directed at the posts at Edeghem and Bouchout. Favoured by the accidented terrain, a French battalion managed to turn the position at Bouchout, which was only saved by the alertness of the Saxon *Oberstleutnant* von Niesemeuschel, and the good behaviour of the troops. When the French advanced, the commander of the Saxon piquets, *Major* Carl Anton von Beeren, pulled the piquets back on their supports. Then the *Jäger* and *Schützen*, led by *Leutnant* Johann Gottlob Freyer, engaged the French, delaying their advance long enough for the Allies to stage a counterattack against the French left flank. The French retreated, pursued

---

24 Starkloff, *Das Leben des Herzogs Bernhard*, p.144.

25 *Generalmajor* von Wolzogen (Chef of the General Staff of III German Corps) in his memoirs states the following about *Generalmajor* von Gablenz: 'As in the meanwhile one did not trust the inclination of this general – he formerly maintained close contact with many French generals – *Oberstleutnant* von Niesemeuschel (commander of the Saxon hussars), a completely reliable person, was ordered to observe von Gablenz closely. In addition von Gablenz received the Prussian *Hauptmann* von Pfuel as adjutant, who had received the same task.' (von Wolzogen, *Memoiren*, p.251). It is unclear why von Gablenz was singled out for this 'special treatment', as many of his fellow officers had maintained close personal contact with French generals as dedicated allies between the years 1806 and 1813. Bucher looks at this matter more closely (Bucher, *Der Feldzug*, pp.25-27).

by the Saxon uhlans, suffering some loss; according to the inhabitants, the French lost a colonel killed and a lancer officer wounded. A simultaneous feint attack on Edeghem was defeated by the Prussian *Oberstleutnant* von Reuß. When *Generalmajor* von Gablenz arrived from Lier with supports; a battalion of the 1. Leichten Regiment, ½ squadron of the Uhlanen-Regiment, and 2 guns of the 2. 6-Pfünder Reitende Batterie, fighting was already over. Allied losses were two wounded officers (*Major* von Beeren and *Leutnant* Freyer), six dead, ten wounded, and five men missing; all loss sustained by the Jäger Bataillon and the 1. Leichten Regiment.

On the right wing of III German Corps, on 23 February *Major* Hellwig had been ordered to advance from Courtray to Menin with his *Streifcorps*, reinforced with Prussian troops; both infantry battalions of the 2. Reserve-Infanterie-Regiment, and four guns (two cannon, two howitzers) of the 6-Pfünder Reitende Batterie No. 11. Arriving there, he was told about the pro-allied feelings of the citizens of the fortress-city Ypres, and leaving behind a small force at Menin he advanced to that place with the rest of his troops. *Général de Division* Maison also had received word about the inclination of the citizens, and had ordered *Général de Division* Jean Baptiste Solignac on the 23rd to march to Ypres immediately with a mobile column. Arriving here, he reinforced the garrison with a battalion to keep the citizens under control and left again.[26] So when Hellwig arrived before Ypres, the situation was completely different to what had been expected. In vain he threw a few shells into the city and summoned its capitulation. Too weak for a serious attack, Hellwig returned to Menin during the evening, learning that his posts remaining there had been under attack by French troops coming from Lille.

As described, *Général de Division* Maison had explained to Napoleon that he was much weaker then he believed. Nevertheless, Napoleon repeated his orders that Maison should go over to the offensive, so on the 24th Maison marched from Lille in two columns totalling about three thousand men to intercept Hellwig: *Général de Division* Barrois marched in the direction of Menin with four battalions, an artillery battery and some cavalry, while Maison marched west with the division of Ledru des Essarts. *Général de Division* Castex was ordered to reconnoitre in the direction of Tournay with his cavalry reinforced by some infantry. On the 24th, Maison occupied Armentières, continuing his march to Bailleul. By then, Hellwig was already making good his retreat, Maison also marching to Menin and joining Barrois. After a few hours rest, combined the French march continued to Courtray. Arriving before the city on the 26th at nightfall the French attached immediately, but without resisting Hellwig evacuated the city and retreated to Oudenaerde. The French marched no further, placing outposts at Haerlebeke, Sweweghem and Belleghem.

Général de Division Castex had, on the 25th, attacked the outposts of *Generalleutnant* von Borstell in front of Lille with a force consisting of 150 cavalry, supported by as many infantry. They were counterattacked and thrown back, subsequently pursued by a squadron of the Westpreußisches Uhlanen-Regiment led by *Major* von Beyer. The pursuit ended when the French fell back on a more substantial force near Bouvines. The Prussian

---

26 Calmon-Maison, 'Le Général Maison', pp.182-183.

cavalry had only a few wounded horses, the French however had several wounded, including a cavalry-sergeant who was taken prisoner together with his horse. Being questioned, the sergeant stated that he estimated the strength of *Général de Division* Maison's troops in and around Lille at 10-12,000 men, with cavalry consisting of 300 men of the 2e Régiment de Chevau-Légers Lanciers de la Garde, 400 men of 2e Régiment de Chasseurs à Cheval de la Garde and 84 Jeune Garde Mameluks. To prevent similar attacks on Bruges, a city which had shown its willingness to take up arms against the French, *Generalleutnant* von Borstell detached the Saxon *Major* Graf von Pückler-Muskau with 70 troopers of the Pommersches National-Kavallerie-Regiment (*Rittmeister* von Rottberg), and the authorization to raise the 1er Régiment d'Infanterie Légère. Because of these detachments and the continuous French probes, it became apparent that Borstell was too weak to defend himself much longer against such continuing attacks, and would have no chance against an attack in force. Therefore it was decided to shift the reserves to the right. The half 1. 12-Pfünder Fußbatterie (4 guns) and two companies of the I. Gardebataillon at Mons marched to Leuze, on their way in Ath joined by both remaining *companies* of the I. Gardebataillon. Both squadrons of the Husaren-Regiment under *Oberst Fürst* zu Schönburg, in Ath at that time, went to Beloeil and Bury. Finally, the II. and III. Grenadier-Bataillon, as well as six guns of the 1. 6-Pfünder Fußbatterie were directly placed under the orders of *Generalleutnant* von Borstell at Tournay.

News about *Général de Division* Maison's advance to Courtray reached Ghent on 27 February. The Cossack regiment still occupying this city, with its commander Colonel Bikhalov staying in Sas-van-Gent at the moment, panicked on receiving the news. The arrival of Bikhalov in the afternoon restored order again, however several Cossacks had used the chaos to plunder. To set an example, two Cossacks received 80 lashes, after having received these they thanked their commander for the light punishment![27] The combats and skirmishes that took place during these days, as well as reports about the strength and aggressiveness of the French, made it very clear to the Duke of Saxe-Weimar that it the French had more in mind then just passive defence. His weakness became apparent. So it was a great relief when on 24 February the Anhalt-Thuringian Division arrived in Brussels. This weak division was of only brigade strength at that moment, with about 3,300 men and 80 horses in all, consisting of the following units (strengths shown as officers/other ranks):

Division commander: *Generalmajor Prinz* Paul von Württemberg
Brigadier: *Oberst* von Egloffstein
Chef of Staff: *Major* von Koppenfels
　　Infanterie-Bataillon 'Gotha' (line infantry, *Oberst* von Münch) (19/895)
　　Infanterie-Bataillon 'Schwarzburg' (line infantry, *Major* Blumröder) (10/541)
　　Infanterie-Bataillon 'Anhalt-Bernburg' (2 line and 2 Landwehr companies, *Major* von Sonnenberg) (11/459)

27　Van Aerde, *Kozakken te Gent*, pp.302-304.

Landwehr-Bataillon 'Weimar' (*Major* von Wolfskeel) (6/540)

Landwehr-Bataillon 'Gotha' (*Major* von Kirchbach) (15/518)

Freiwillige Jäger zu Fuß Kompagnie 'Weimar' (*Major* von Seebach) (3/83)

Freiwillige Jäger zu Fuß Kompagnie 'Gotha' (*Leutnant* Funck) (3/83)[28]

Freiwillige Jäger zu Pferde 'Weimar' und 'Gotha' (*Rittmeister* von Werthern) (5/51)

The Bataillon Füsiliere des Herzogs zu Sachsen-Weimar belonged officially also to this division but was already present as it had marched with the Duke of Saxe-Weimar's first contingent. This Anhalt-Thuringian Division had suffered much over the last days, having been forced to march enormous distances every day to reach the frontline without any necessity; apparently an indication that its commander wanted his share of the glory. This was a task he had set for himself in which he would fail miserably, as we will see later. The only result of this kind of marching was the loss of 250 sick and stragglers. So, for the moment, the troops would form the reserve. The battalions had been formed out of strong men with good equipment, but armament was bad. In addition they were practically untrained, for the greater part led by young and inexperienced officers. The division was also without artillery. To remedy this deficit a provisional half foot battery which had been created a few days earlier, known as the 3. 6-Pfünder Fußbatterie (*Premierleutnant* Johann Baptista Hirsch) (1/57), was assigned to the division. This battery had been created using three French 6-pdr cannon which had been captured at Arnhem by Bülow when he advanced into the Netherlands. The commander of the artillery of the corps, *Oberstleutnant* Raabe, initially drew the crews and horses out of the other artillery companies and the 1. Reserve Park. These were later replaced by commandeered carpenters and infantrymen. The half battery was initially deployed in Mons, but was transferred to the Anhalt-Thuringian Division on its arrival. This division initially remained in Brussels, to guard the city against a French coup the main and to give it some hard-needed rest. This period of rest was also made to good use for the Infanterie-Bataillon 'Gotha'; this battalion especially was badly armed; the few muskets it had were of the worst quality. During its stay in Brussels the battalion was re-armed with British muskets, present in a depot here.[29] Although weak, the division still was a welcome addition to III German Corps.

---

28 The Freiwillige Jäger zu Fuß companies 'Weimar' and 'Gotha' were combined into a battalion commanded by *Major* von Seebach, to which later also the Freiwillige Jäger zu Fuß Kompagnie 'Schwarzburg' was added. This did not prevent the companies from still being deployed separately.

29 Bucher, *Der Feldzug*, p.59.

5

Courtray 1–13 March 1814

Blücher in command

On the all deciding Council of War between the allied sovereigns in Bar-sur-Aube, the decision of how to act was taken out of the Duke of Saxe-Weimar's hands. It was decided that Wintzingerode's army corps, Bülow's Prussian III Corps, and the Duke's III German Corps would unite with Blücher. The Emperor Alexander wrote to the Duke of Saxe-Weimar on that same day: 'Your Serene Highness is therefore invited to follow from now on the directions that Marshal Blücher will send to him, and one promises himself all the more success of this reunion as the personal relations which exist between Your Serene Highness and Marshal Blücher can only infinitely facilitate the course of operations which you will execute together.'[1] This was followed by a letter from Blücher, ordering the Duke of Saxe-Weimar: 'For the time being, and until the arrival of the Swedish troops, which would undertake the complete conquest of Holland and Flanders, to keep the fortresses under observation, but for this purpose to take up such a position that you will be as close as possible to this army, in order to march quickly to join when a battle is imminent.'[2] Bülow, also receiving the order to unite with Blücher, immediately used the opportunity, again ordering *Generalleutnant* von Borstell to join him immediately. On 4 March, Borstell wrote to the Duke:

> Your Highness, I have the honour of obediently handing over the letter of Lieutenant-General von Bülow, in which I receive the definite order to at once depart from here, to re-join the Army Corps. As a result of this order received, I immediately ordered the troops under my command to march in the direction of Mons tomorrow, to concentrate them there. Your Excellency will deign to inform me afterwards of your dispositions for the replacement of my troops.[3]

---

1 Letter of 25 February 1814 from the Russian Emperor Alexander to the Duke of Saxe-Weimar in Egloffstein, *Carl August*, pp.33-34.
2 Letter of 28 February 1814 from Blücher to the Duke of Saxe-Weimar in Egloffstein, *Carl August*, p.34.
3 Letter of 4 March 1814 from *Generalleutnant* von Borstell to the Duke of Saxe-Weimar, quoted in Ollech, *Carl Friederich Wilhelm von Reyher*, p.355.

The Duke of Saxe-Weimar immediately responded, writing to Von Borstell:

> Your Excellency will recall the order to march off your troops immediately, in view of the fact that I will not let your brigade go earlier until I have received orders to do so from Field-Marshal von Blücher. At this moment I am sending a Courier to the Field Marshal.[4]

Although the Duke of Saxe-Weimar was finally freed from Bernadotte, his situation was still precarious. He could not decide on abandoning the Northern as well as the Southern Netherlands. He explained himself in an extensive letter to Blücher, stating among other things: 'Just as the direction of the army is in the present situation, the retreat of your army, although you have already won a decisive victory, will infallibly go near this country.' Stating next that Blücher would thank him in such situation, however improbably it might be, for having preserved Belgium. As reason for remaining strictly on the defensive, he argued the presence of many French-held fortresses, with numerically superior troops – which, based on intelligence, could concentrate at certain points – preventing him to split up his own small corps to cover all points. Every offensive action would meet a fortress which could not be captured within 24 hours. Further. the Duke explained that, without Borstell's division, III German Corps would cease to be an independent corps, with only five cavalry squadrons and 12 infantry battalions of which only nine were reliable and with hardly any ammunition. Although he expected, on 10 March, the arrival in Brussels of *Generalleutnant* von Thielmann, with six Landwehr battalions and complements for his weak line battalions, his corps would not gain in quality by these additions, especially since Thielmann brought no ammunition with him, not even the usual 60 cartridges for each soldier. With these troops, the Duke had firstly to defend Tournay, 'A place of very great size – and 22,000 inhabitants, in which not a single fortress gun, but which place, after my abandonment, can easily be endowed by the French from their fortresses, and then it will be difficult to retake again.' The city of Mons was just as big, and was important ' … to cover the passage of the troops to the interior of France and, in case of misfortune, to take up in the retreating troops.' By occupying both places, as well as positioning troops at Lier, he covered the whole of Belgium and all its resources, except for Flanders. Without the presence of III German Corps, the enemy could undertake raids from there, which had until now been prevented by him. The Duke could however not guarantee, because of the weakness of his corps, that he would always succeed in doing that. His main goal was the capture of Maubeuge. As soon as received the necessary artillery from the British he would undertake the attack, although only when if Borstell's division was still be present. The Duke finished by stating that Blücher, based on the operations in France and the Duke's explanation of the situation, would be able to ascertain how III German Corps could be utilised in the most convenient way stating: 'I will willingly and unhesitatingly carry

---

4   Letter from the Duke of Saxe-Weimar to *Generalleutnant* von Borstell, quoted in Ollech, *Carl Friederich Wilhelm von Reyher*, p.355.

out all your orders, but I ask that you to take into account that my troops are not to be equated with your soldiers used to war.' Without Borstell's division, the Duke stated, he would probably already would have lost Belgium and retreated to Liège. He would obey to Blücher's decision, leaving it up to Blücher's discretion that Borstell would remain at least until Maubeuge had been captured. Until having received this decision, he would not allow his departure, as this would mean relinquishing the country: 'The name of the Allies, that of General Bülow, and my own are thereby put to the test in front of the whole world. Also, the English will probably embark then.'[5]

Of course, the arrival of Bernadotte's 30,000 Swedish troops could have made a huge difference. However as explained in Chapter 2, he would go no further than Liège, halting his Swedes there for nearly the whole remainder of the campaign. Time and again, the Duke of Saxe-Weimar would write urgent letters to Bernadotte, nearly begging him to send troops to come to the aid of his weak corps. By now, Bernadotte's replies can be guessed: that *Generalleutnant* von Thielmann had just arrived in Liège, who would continue his march to Brussels, enabling the Duke to reinforce the most urgent posts. The Duke was also fobbed off with the imminent arrival of *Generalleutnant* von Wallmoden's Russo-German Legion, which Bernadotte would assign to positions between Brussels and Mechelen.[6] Receiving this letter on 8 March, the next day the Duke again wrote to Bernadotte, repeating his previous request, especially requesting for the Saxon sappers that had been lent to the Swedes to be returned to him, as well as requesting Swedish artillery. In addition, he asked Bernadotte to state when he would relieve the Saxon and Prussian troops blockading Antwerp in Lier and Mechelen, and when Bernadotte would relieve III German Corps as a whole and take over the observation of the various fortresses. To emphasize this need, he reported about the French move against Courtray and Oudenaerde.[7] Clearly the Duke doubted if his urgent letter would have the intended effect, already that same evening writing another letter to Bernadotte, this time trying vulgar flattery:

> The high reputation which Your Royal Highness has acquired through long labours protected by the decrees of providence known to the common people as happiness, inspires brave men with absolute confidence in the person of Your Royal Highness, in his projects and in his cosmopolitanism … Your Royal Highness is intended to protect these beautiful countries that I have defended until now and that I have tried to reorganize as best as possible so that the will of the inhabitants can support itself. It is for Your Royal Highness now to consolidate the work which I have only been able to undertake, and to give to the brave inhabitants of Belgium the clarity of the views of Your Royal Highness. They will all be yours, dear cousin, if Your Royal Highness persists in the sense of His previous proclamations [that Bernadotte made to the French] and if it joins His Highness' will to the wishes of all those who expect a solid peace. Uncertainties in

---

5   Letter of 5 March 1814 from the Duke of Saxe-Weimar to Blücher, in Egloffstein, *Carl August*, pp.35-37.
6   Letter of 5 March 1814 from Bernadotte to the Duke of Saxe-Weimar, in Egloffstein, *Carl August*, p.39.
7   Letter of 9 March 1814 from the Duke of Saxe-Weimar to Bernadotte, in Egloffstein, *Carl August*, p.40. See below for more about this French advance.

this moment cause much harm but could be brief. It is up to Your Royal Highness to create events which will make his reputation more elevated and more immortal than that of conquerors of all ages.[8]

Despite the tone of his letters, the Duke made himself no illusions about Bernadotte, writing to his wife: 'I am always complimenting Charles Jean, who locks himself up … in Liège, who must relieve me and who has no desire to move … An Englishman said to me today, believe me, this Charles Jean is a Jacobin: and I think he is right, "it is fake money and a flat foot".'[9] Indeed, Bernadotte responded with countless evasive replies, stating that the combined army had already made movements which were still not announced openly; that he had sent out agents to ascertain the situation in order to deploy his troops the best possible way, and so forth. The only positive thing, although insignificant, was that the Saxon sappers borrowed by Bernadotte re-joined the Duke on 16 March.

The French Advance

The Duke of Saxe-Weimar decided that something had to be done against the French in Courtray (divisions of Barrios and Castex) as their presence there was a threat to his right flank, as well as to the allied troops blockading Antwerp. French possession of Courtray gave them the possibility of uniting the troops of *Général de Division* Maison with a substantial part of the garrison of Antwerp, which would give the French a local numerical superiority against everything the allies would be able to bring into the field in the Southern Netherlands. As a result, during the following days all actions, initiated by the allies as well as by the French, would focus on this fortress-city. *Generalleutnant* von Borstell received the task of recapturing Courtray. The day for the attack was initially fixed on 1 March. The Prussian *Oberst* von Hobe would lead the attack from the direction of Tournay with a combined Prussian-Saxon force, consisting of:

Saxons:
II. Grenadier-Bataillon
1. 6-Pfünder Fußbatterie (6 guns only, *Hauptmann* Rouvroy II.)[10]
Prussians:
Gren./1. Pommersches Infanterie-Regiment, plus Freiwillige Fußjäger-Detachement
2. Reserve-Infanterie-Regiment (2 battalions)
2. Churmärkisches Landwehr-Infanterie-Regiment (1 battalion)
Pommersches National-Kavallerie-Regiment (2 squadrons)
Westpreußisches Uhlanen-Regiment (1 squadron, *Major* von Schmeling)

---

8   Letter of 10 March 1814 from the Duke of Saxe-Weimar to Bernadotte, in Egloffstein, *Carl August*, pp.40-41.
9   Letter of 13 March 1814 from the Duke of Saxe-Weimar to his wife, in Egloffstein, *Carl August*, p.42.
10 Two cannon had been assigned to the 3. 6-Pfünder Fußbatterie.

6-Pfünder Reitende Batterie No. 11 (2 cannon, 2 howitzers, *Leutnant* Gille)

This attack would be executed simultaneously with a feint attack by *Major* Hellwig's *Streifcorps*, which would start from Oudenaerde. It would not come to this, however. Just before the attack should begin at 2:00 p.m., Maison debouched from Lille with a force of 1,500 infantry (including the 12e Voltigeurs summoned from Valenciennes), four guns and some cavalry. Divided in two columns and marching via Bouvines, the attack was directed against Borstell's outposts around Bourghelles, Baisieux, and Camphin. It was not possible to undertake the attack on Courtray while the outcome of the fighting was unclear, so *Oberst* von Hobe and *Major* Hellwig were both ordered to halt their advance and to maintain their previous positions. To the south of them a lively cavalry fight ensued. Although outnumbered, a squadron of the Westpreußisches Uhlanen-Regiment (*Leutnant* Tiszka) undauntedly engaged the cavalry leading the French advance, buying time for two infantry companies in Bourghelles to retreat to Froidemont safely. *Leutnant* Tiszka charged a squadron of the 2e Régiment de Chevau-Légers Lanciers de la Garde, defeating it. Cut off immediately by another squadron, he turned and charged again, breaking through the French troopers and reaching the safety of the 1st squadron of his regiment sent in support, suffering the loss of only three men and five horses. *Major* von Beyer, meanwhile, who commanded the forward posts, had deployed an infantry battalion on a height in front of Marquain and another one in front of Froidemont, occupying Lamain with skirmishers. Then he advanced with his cavalry (Westpreußisches Uhlanen-Regiment) on the left of Baisieux, threatening the French left flank, while making an effective use of an accompanying gun of the horse artillery. After a combat of three hours the French infantry abandoned Bourghelles and Camphin and returned to Lille.

The unexpected advance of the French from Lille made clear that precautionary measures had to be taken before the attack on Courtray could be executed. The allies had to hold an extensive defensive line, as well as blockading Antwerp. They were opposed by substantial French forces which were able to concentrate under cover of their own line of fortresses, attacking the allies with superior forces at any chosen point. There was only one way left for defence; holding the frontline with small outposts to give warning of any French offensive movements, supported by substantial forces composed of all arms further back, strong enough to engage the French and to buy time for more troops to arrive. Clearly French attention had shifted to the west flank of the Duke of Saxe-Weimar's front, possibly the beginning of undertakings related to Antwerp and its strong garrison. This was exactly where the allied attack on Courtray would take place. With such strong French forces in the area more, allied troops had to be shifted west. Therefore the attack had to be postponed to 2 March at 6:00 a.m. In the meanwhile, a hussar squadron placed in Bury (in front of Condé) was ordered to Warcoing, to maintain communications between Borstell's troops and *Colonel* von Hobe's attacking force. From Brussels, *Generalmajor* Prinz

Paul von Württemberg was ordered to Termonde (southwest of Antwerp) with the following units under his command:

Infanterie-Bataillon 'Gotha'
Infanterie-Bataillon 'Schwarzburg'
Freiwillige Jäger zu Fuß Kompagnie 'Weimar'
Freiwillige Jäger zu Fuß Kompagnie 'Gotha'
Brandenburgschen Dragoner-Regiment (Prussian, 3rd squadron)

Oberst von Egloffstein deployed at Alost with the following units:

Infanterie-Bataillon 'Anhalt-Bernburg' (also coming from Brussels)
Bataillon Füsiliere des Herzogs zu Sachsen-Weimar (coming from Enghien)
2. 6-Pfünder Reitende Batterie (2 guns, detached by *Generalmajor* von Gablenz)

Brussels remained occupied by the Landwehr-Bataillons 'Weimar' and 'Gotha', and the Freiwillige Jäger zu Pferde 'Weimar und Gotha'. At the affixed time on 2 March, *Oberst* von Hobe started his advance to Courtray. His force consisted of the units already listed earlier. An additional 50 hussars of *Major* Hellwig's *Streifcorps*, which had escorted both howitzers of the 6-Pfünder Reitende Batterie No. 11, attached themselves to this force, a small but welcome addition of experienced troopers. *Oberst* von Hobe formed an advance guard of the Gren./1. Pommersches Infanterie-Regiment, two 6-pdr cannon of the 6-Pfünder Reitende Batterie No. 11 and the 50 Hellwig's hussars (*Leutnant* von Zawadzky), led by *Major* von Romberg. The French *Général de Division* Barrois responded to the allied advance by sending a column to Sweweghem, while sending two infantry battalions to Belleghem. Around 9:00 a.m. the Allies encountered the first French troops, a cavalry vedette near Coighem, which was engaged by the 1st grenadier-company (*Leutnant* von Grumbkow) of the Gren./1. Pommersches Infanterie-Regiment and thrown back on two infantry battalions standing on the height near Belleghem, a village on the road from Courtray to Tournay. The 1st grenadier company was reinforced with the 3rd and half of the 2nd company led by *Hauptmann* von Schönebeck. *Major* von Romberg was ordered to drive the enemy out of Belleghem attacking them from the left, with three skirmisher *Züge* of the Gren./1. Pommersches Infanterie-Regiment, a *Zug* of its Freiwillige Fußjäger-Detachement (*Hauptmann* von Bessel) and 20 troopers of Hellwig's hussars (*Leutnant* von Guretzky). Supported by the fire of both of his guns and reinforced by two grenadier companies (led by *Hauptmann* von Tilly), *Major* von Romberg managed to capture Belleghem, pushing the French back in the direction of Courtray and taking five enemy horse prisoner. Both French infantry battalions were attacked next and quickly pushed of the height they were deployed on, after which the French retreated to Courtray.

The height gave a clear view of the terrain up to Courtray, as well as the French force deployed in front of this city, outnumbering Hobe's troops.

Therefore, Hobe decided to shift his troops to the right, hoping to be able to make progress on that side. Von Romberg was ordered to occupy the height while the remainder of *Oberst* von Hobe's force continued its march behind him, to the right in the direction of Sweweghem, a village on the road from Courtray to Oudenaerde. After that movement had been executed, *Major* von Romberg would have to serve as rearguard. While Von Romberg screened his movement this way, *Oberst* von Hobe formed a new advance guard, commanded by the Saxon *Major* Günther von Bünau, and continued his march to Sweweghem. *Major* Hellwig in the meantime had also started his advance from Oudenaerde, capturing Sweweghem around 10:00 a.m. without much trouble. He deployed his troops on the road to Courtray, skirmishing with the French, sending a squadron of his hussars (*Leutnant* Viebig) to Haerlebeke, on the road from Courtray to Ghent. *Oberst* von Hobe resumed the march again in the direction of Haerlebeke, again screening his movement, this time with *Major* Hellwig's troops.

Haerlebeke had already been captured by a surprise attack around noon, executed by 60 Cossacks of Colonel Bikhalov in cooperation with the mentioned squadron of *Major* Hellwig's hussars. They captured 17 men of the 2e Régiment de Chasseurs à Cheval de la Garde in the process. Around 3:00 p.m. *Oberst* von Hobe arrived. He occupied the village with the bulk of his force, detaching *Major* von Bünau to Cuerne village with 1½ infantry battalion, a cavalry squadron and two guns, to occupy the bridges across the Lys and the Heule. With *Oberst* von Hobe in Haerlebeke the left flank of the French force at Courtray was threatened. *Général de Division* Maison, knowing the numerical weakness of his opponent, reinforced the forward troops of Barrois' command and ordered him to attack. Their first attack was aimed at *Major* von Romberg, at that time still at Belleghem. He was forced back so quickly by the fiercely attacking French which deployed large amounts of skirmishers, that the three skirmisher *Züge* of the Gren./1. Pommersches Infanterie-Regiment and the *Zug* of its Freiwillige Fußjäger-Detachement under Hauptmann von Bessel and 20 of Hellwig's hussars were cut off. These had no other choice than to retreat via Coighem and even further to Warcoing, joining the Saxon hussar squadron positioned here. With the remainder of his force *Major* von Romberg decided to fall back on the main column, in the direction of Sweweghem. He was pursued by the French for a while, losing 10 men dead or wounded by their artillery fire.

Arriving at Sweweghem it turned out that *Major* Hellwig was also under attack from a French force consisting of three battalions supported by artillery; his troops were pushed back into the village itself and soon most of his *Fußjäger* were running out of cartridges. He had already been reinforced by Hobe with the *Schützen* of the 2. Reserve-Infanterie-Regiment (*Hauptmann* von Stülpnagel), but this was not enough to stop the French from penetrating into Sweweghem. Reinforced with the company Wiersbitzky of the Gren./1. Pommersches Infanterie-Regiment of *Major* von Romberg's infantry after their timely arrival, Hellwig managed to throw the French out of the village again and to hold on to Sweweghem until nightfall. With his infantry again completely out of cartridges he then retreated to Heestert, leaving a hussar picket behind. During the night, *Oberst* von Hobe reinforced him with an infantry company and a cavalry squadron, to protect his own left flank. *Major* von Romberg in the meanwhile had continued his march to Haerlebeke, arriving there at 6:00 p.m. Hellwig's losses were five dead and 18 wounded.

Oberst von Hobe planned to continue his advance to Courtray on 3 March. First he would occupy Menin with a battalion and two guns. After having achieved that, Courtray would be attacked from the directions of Haerlebeke and Sweweghem. However, it soon became clear that these goals would never be achieved. The French had received ample warning of the allied intentions by now and acted accordingly. Menin was occupied by a large French corps, which during the night had dispatched another thousand infantry (three battalions) and seven guns to reinforce the troops in and around Courtray, raising strength there to 4,000 men with eighteen guns. This made an attack on Courtray itself, which could only be executed by crossing an open plain for a thousand paces, totally impossible. Already early on that same day, all the infantry commanded by *Major* Hellwig completely ran out of ammunition again, after which at 8:00 a.m. Sweweghem was captured by the French. *Oberst* von Hobe had no other choice then to retreat. At daybreak his corps marched over Thielt to Deinze were he arrived at 4:00 p.m., on the 4th continuing the retreat and occupying Oudenaerde. *Major* von Bünau led the rearguard. The French occupied Cuerne but did not engage the allied rearguard. *Major* Hellwig, after his hussar picket had been forced to abandon Sweweghem around 8:00 a.m., had already retreated to Oudenaerde as well. On the 5th, *Generalleutnant* von Borstell ordered him to march to Deinze to cover the right flank and to give warning of a possible French advance to Ghent. For unknown reasons and contrary to his orders, Hellwig marched to Ghent instead, with only some cavalry outposts further forward.

With the French becoming more aggressive, the Duke of Saxe-Weimar decided to reorganise his troops to oppose the threat. He moved his headquarters further west from Ath to Tournay, taking with him the Saxon I. Gardebataillon and the half 1. 12-Pfünder Fußbatterie, which were at Leuze. *Generalmajor* Prinz Paul von Württemberg was ordered to march with three battalions (Infanterie-Bataillon 'Gotha', 'Schwarzburg', and 'Anhalt-Bernburg') of his Anhalt-Thuringian Division from Termonde to Ath on 4 March, and to continue to Tournay the next day. In addition, the Duke of Saxe-Weimar kept with him three battalions of the 3. Ostpreußische Landwehr Infanterie Regiment (*Major* Graf Karl Friedrich von Klinkowström) and its Fußjäger-Detachement belonging to Bülow's corps. These had arrived from Gorkum after the capitulation of this fortress and were now placed in Alost and Termonde. The Bataillon Füsiliere des Herzogs zu Sachsen-Weimar and both Freiwillige Jäger zu Fuß Kompagnien 'Weimar' and 'Gotha' were ordered to Mons and came under the command of *Generalmajor* von Ryssel.

Oudenaerde, 5 March

Having become bold by the ease with which the allies had been pushed back, as well as learning that Napoleon had forced the Army of Silesia back to Laon, *Général de Division* Maison decided to take the offensive. He was also forced to do so by the urging letters of Napoleon, ordering him to leave the fortresses, to join forces with the greater part of the garrison of Antwerp and to go over to the offensive. Maison had 5,400 infantry, 930 cavalry and 19 guns. *Général de Brigade* Raymond Pierre Penne was ordered to overpower Bikhalov in Ghent with about 700 men, mostly cavalry, and to occupy the city until *Général de Division* Roguet's division could arrive from Antwerp that evening. At the same time, Maison would attack Oudenaerde with his main force, consisting of Barrois's division leading the advance followed by Solignac's. This attack was to be a feint attack to make the allies worry about Brussels and to obscure his real objective. That this plan worked can be concluded from an article in the *Allgemeine Zeitung*, based on an official report of 15 March: 'Already in the first days of this month, Division General Maison had assembled all his available troops to invade Brabant. His plan was nothing less than link with the garrison of Antwerp and then joining forces with them to reach Brussels ... '.[11] *Général de Brigade* Penne however never made it to Ghent, and although reports do not mention his movements most probably he was recalled early to re-join Maison.

On the 5th the allied outposts at Avelghem were pushed back and at the same time *Major* Hellwig's outposts were forced out of Deinze and had to retreat to Ghent. Around 11:00 a.m. *Oberst* von Hobe's outposts near Kerkhove were thrown back and the French marched to Oudenaerde. Although their advance was slowed down by cavalry threatening to charge, the French arrived before the city around 3:00 p.m. Oudenaerde was more or less an open city without any effective defences. The city centre was surrounded by a medieval wall, but over time many suburbs had been built on the outside. *Oberst* von Hobe nevertheless decided to try to hold on to that place, concentrating his defence inside the inner city due to his lack of troops. Although this had the advantage that Hobe could concentrate his defence at the gates, the French were able to make use of the cover provided by the houses of the suburbs. Sending forward the three Prussian cavalry squadrons at his disposal to buy time for his preparations (two squadrons of the Pommersches National-Kavallerie-Regiment and a squadron of the Westpreußisches Uhlanen-Regiment), *Oberst* von Hobe positioned his troops as follows:

- On the windmill hill before the Beveren suburb to support the cavalry: a battalion of the 2. Churmärkisches Landwehr-Infanterie-Regiment and two cannon of the 6-Pfünder Reitende Batterie No. 11 (*Leutnant* Gille).
- To the left of the Courtray Gate, on the windmill hill: *Major* von Mirbach with I./2. Reserve-Infanterie-Regiment and both howitzers of the 6-Pfünder Reitende Batterie No. 11.
- At the Courtray Gate: *Major* von Bünau with two companies of the Saxon II. Grenadier-Bataillon and two companies of the battalion of the 2. Churmärkisches Landwehr-Infanterie-Regiment after they had retreated from the windmill hill before the Beveren suburb.

---

11 *Allgemeine Zeitung*, 25 March 1814.

- To the right of the Courtray Gate: two companies of the II. Grenadier-Bataillon, as well as two companies of the battalion of the 2. Churmärkisches Landwehr-Infanterie-Regiment after they had retreated from the windmill hill before the Beveren suburb, and four guns of the Saxon 1. 6-Pfünder Fußbatterie (*Hauptmann* Rouvroy II.).
- At the St.-Henry Gate: *Major* von Hövel with II./2. Reserve-Infanterie-Regiment and both remaining guns of the Saxon 1. 6-Pfünder Fußbatterie.
- Behind the Scheldt river as reserve: *Major* von Romberg with the Gren./1. Pommersches Infanterie-Regiment and both cannon of the 6-Pfünder Reitende Batterie No. 11, after they had retreated from the windmill hill before the Beveren suburb. Of these, the 1st grenadier company and the Freiwillige Fußjäger-Detachement stood at the Watergate; a grenadier company (Wiersbitzky) at the gate to Tournay, and both remaining grenadier companies at the bridge across the Scheldt.

After having pushed back the Prussian cavalry squadrons, *Général de Division* Maison deployed three battalions in column to both sides of the road with sections of two guns in the intervals. His cavalry held to the road, proceeded by a third section of two guns. In this formation the advance continued against the Prussians infantry on the windmill hill before the Beveren suburb. These held their position for a while, but when the French prepared to charge and the infantry columns closed in they were ordered to retreat to their assigned positions inside Oudenaerde itself. Advancing further, the French again deployed artillery at close range, starting to fire at the city with six cannon and four howitzers. The six allied guns around the Courtray Gate replied, firing canister, according to some sources with great effect. In the meantime, around 4:00 p.m., French skirmishers penetrated the suburbs engaging the allied skirmishers. Twice the French stormed the Courtray Gate with infantry masses, but both times the attacks were defeated by the infantry and the Saxon *Hauptmann* Rouvroy II., who had deployed his 1. 6-Pfünder Fußbatterie in the gate itself, receiving the French with canister. Around 8:00 p.m. darkness made an end to the fighting, but Maison continued to bombard the city, causing further casualties among the allied troops as well as the citizens and damaging many houses. *Oberst* von Hobe's situation was bad. The French had until now committed only small part of their available troops to the attacks and they still had not attacked the weakest point of the defences of the city, the St.-Henry Gate. When the French would manage to break through his defences the artillery would be lost. The allied infantry had expended much of their cartridges. Knowing that three battalions of the Anhalt-Thuringian Division were on their way to Ath, he dispatched an aide to find them and to bring them to Oudenaerde. These troops however were not where they were expected to be, so these would bring him no support for now.

After being informed that the French were crossing the Scheldt river upstream, threatening to cut him off, next morning at 4:00 a.m. still during darkness, *Oberst* von Hobe retreated across the Scheldt, leaving only an advance guard in the city on the other side of the river. At daybreak however his patrols found out that the French had retreated as well, returning to Courtray. *Oberst* von Hobe immediately launched his cavalry in pursuit, which managed to capture 24 prisoners before the pursuit ended near Avelghem. Allied losses were severe, not surprising because of the close-range fighting and intense artillery fire: in total one officer and 18 others dead, two officers and 68 others wounded. The II. Grenadier-Bataillon had lost eight wounded. French loss however was much heavier: according to intelligence received, the French retreated with 40 wagons loaded with wounded; they had left behind an additional 40 seriously wounded. These were taken into the city for treatment. Seventy French dead were buried and in all 40 French had been taken prisoner.

Courtray, 6 March

As soon as the attack on Oudenaerde was reported to the Duke of Saxe-Weimar, he ordered *Generalleutnant* von Borstell to execute a feint attack in the direction of Courtray to threaten the rear of the French force before Oudenaerde, so as to force it to retreat. The feint attack would be executed by the Prussian *Oberstleutnant* von Schon, with a force composed of the following units:

> Füs./1. Pommersches Infanterie-Regiment, plus Freiwillige Fußjäger-Detachement
> I./1. Pommersches Infanterie-Regiment, plus Freiwillige Fußjäger-Detachement
> III. Grenadier-Bataillon (Saxon)
> Husaren-Regiment (Saxon, 1 squadron, *Rittmeister* von Seebach)
> 6-Pfünder Fußbatterie No. 10 (4 guns, *Hauptmann* Magenhöfer)

Generalmajor Prinz Paul von Württemberg was ordered to deploy near Warcoing. His orders were to support *Oberstleutnant* von Schon, securing the right flank of his advance with patrols, as well as observing the road leading to Oudenaerde. He commanded the following units:

> Infanterie-Bataillon 'Anhalt-Bernburg'
> Infanterie-Bataillon 'Schwarzburg'
> Pommersches National-Kavallerie-Regiment (Prussian, 1 squadron)
> 6-Pfünder Fußbatterie No. 10 (Prussian, 4 guns)

Oberstleutnant von Schon started his advance on 6 March at 4:00 a.m., leaving his concentration point which was at Porte de Sept Fontaines before Tournay. His advance was detected by a French post near Avelghem, informing Maison. Maison immediately reacted to this threat to his line of retreat, detaching some cavalry squadrons and ordering the French troops that had been left in Courtray to prepare for defence. After having reached Warcoing, Schon continued his advance after safety precautions had been taken, especially in order to guard his flank. He detached a force to occupy

Belleghem, which was found unoccupied by the French. Positioning half of the III. Grenadier-Bataillon at the crossroads were the road to Sweweghem connected with the main road to Courtray, *Oberstleutnant* von Schon halted on the height in front of Courtray. *Rittmeister* Friedrich Thilo von Seebach advanced further with the Saxon hussar squadron and drove the enemy out of the suburbs, but, while penetrating into the city itself, arriving on the market place the hussars came under fire of a substantial French infantry force, after which the hussars hastily retreated again, falling back on Schon's main force. The allies maintained their position on the height for over an hour. Then *Oberstleutnant* von Schon was informed that *Generalmajor* Prinz Paul von Württemberg had abandoned his position at Warcoing and had followed him along the road. This made his own force vulnerable to a French attack from the direction of Avelghem against his flank and rear. In order not to expose his force to that risk, Schon ordered to prepare to retreat, believing that his demonstration should have served its purpose by now. At the same time, he urged *Generalmajor* Prinz Paul von Württemberg to return to Warcoing immediately and to resume his positions here, which he duly did. In the meanwhile, the French *Colonel* Louis Doguereau of the Artillerie à Cheval de la Garde had deployed four guns in front of Courtray, opening fire at *Oberstleutnant* von Schon's troops. Schon did not delay his presence any longer and resumed a slow retreat back to Warcoing to unite with Prinz Paul von Württemberg. Schon was followed by a weak French cavalry force, which stayed well out of range and did not hamper the retreat. When Maison and his troops retreating from Oudenaerde reached Sweweghem, he dispatched a small column to Belleghem to intercept the allies, but these had already passed this village. Maison concentrated his fatigued troops around Coighem where he remained for the night. Arriving back in Warcoing, *Oberstleutnant* von Schon found orders to remain here and make camp for the night, together with Prinz Paul von Württemberg. To cover all eventualities, he was reinforced by an additional infantry battalion.

Général de Division Maison estimated allied strength at around 5,000 at Oudenaerde and 4,000 at Tournay. He guessed correctly that the allies would try to capture Courtray. So next morning he prepared himself for defence. Belleghem was barricaded, the village occupied by *Général de Brigade* Penne with an infantry battalion, a hundred cavalry and three guns of the guard artillery; Sweweghem was occupied by *Général de Brigade* Charles Eugène Lalaing d'Audenarde with two infantry battalions, a squadron of the 2e Régiment de Chevau-Légers Lanciers de la Garde and three guns of the guard artillery; Haerlebeke was occupied by *Colonel* de Lastours, *chef d'escadron* of the above guard lancers, with an infantry battalion, a hundred cavalry and two guns. Cuerne and Heule were occupied by an infantry battalion, two guns and the remainder of the cavalry. The main French force remained in Courtray itself under *Généraux de Division* Barrois and Solignac, consisting of the remaining infantry of their divisions, 400 cavalry and 12 guns.

Despite the fact that the allies had not been able to capture Courtray, the intense fighting in this area had removed the direct threat to the other parts of the Duke of Saxe-Weimar's frontline, as Maison had concentrated his troops around Courtray. So the Duke decided to continue with his tactics and to undertake a second attack with even more troops. For this purpose, additional units were shifted west. In front of Lille and Condé only weak outposts remained, commanded by *Generalleutnant* von Le Coq. On 7 March he also received the fortress-city of Tournay under his command, which was occupied by *Major* Moritz Christoph von Brand with the following Saxon units:

II. and III./2. Provisorischen Linien-Regiment
1. 6-Pfünder Reitende Batterie (4 cannon, 2x 8-pdr howitzers)
3. 6-Pfünder Fußbatterie (3 French 6-pdr cannon)

The Duke of Saxe-Weimar himself arrived that same day at Warcoing, around 8:00 a.m. With him he brought the last troops that would take part in the attack. Order of battle for the attacking troops became as follows:

Commander in chief of the attack: *Generalleutnant* von Borstell
Erstes Treffen ('first line') (*Oberstleutnant* von Schon)
Füs. and I./1. Pommersches Infanterie-Regiment
III./2. Churmärkisches Landwehr-Infanterie-Regiment
1. Provisorischen Linien-Regiment (Saxon, 1½ battalion)[12]
Westpreußisches Uhlanen-Regiment (1 squadron)
Husaren-Regiment (Saxon, 1 squadron, *Rittmeister* von Seebach)
12-Pfünder Fußbatterie (Prussian ½ battery, 4 guns)
6-Pfünder Fußbatterie No. 10 (8 guns, *Hauptmann* Magenhöfer)
6-Pfünder Reitende Batterie No. 11 (2 guns)
Zweites Treffen ('second line') (*Generalmajor* Prinz Paul von Württemberg)
I. Gardebataillon
III. Grenadier-Bataillon
Infanterie-Bataillon 'Anhalt-Bernburg'
Infanterie-Bataillon 'Schwarzburg'
Pommersches National-Kavallerie-Regiment (1 squadron, *Major* von Waldow)
1. 12-Pfünder Fußbatterie (6 cannon, 2x 8-pdr howitzers, *Hauptmann* Rouvroy I.)
Right Flank Detachment (*Oberst* Fürst von Schönburg)
II./1. Pommersches Infanterie-Regiment (*Major* von Reitzenstein)
3 skirmisher *Züge* of the Gren./1. Pommersches Infanterie-Regiment and a *Zug* of its Freiwillige Fußjäger-Detachement (*Hauptmann* von Bessel)[13]
Husaren-Regiment (Saxon, 1 squadron)

The latter detachment had to maintain communications with Oudenaerde and to protect the right flank of the advancing main force, by taking up

---

12 The remaining half battalion of the 1. Provisorischen Linien-Regiment was still on outpost duty in front of Condé.

13 These were the *Züge* led by *Hauptmann* von Bessel, which had been cut off from their battalion at Belleghem on 3 March and had stood at Ramegnies until now.

positions near St. Genoir. At Hérrines a stone bridge crossed the Scheldt. As this was the vital crossing point in case of an allied retreat and with so many troops on the left bank of the river, a pontoon bridge was constructed here as well, to allow a timely retreat when necessary. To protect this pontoon bridge, the Infanterie-Bataillon 'Gotha' and two guns of the Saxon 1. 6-Pfünder Fußbatterie were assigned to its defence. *Oberst* von Hobe, still in Oudenaerde and in the meantime reinforced by three infantry battalions of the Anhalt-Thuringian Division, was to advance to Avelghem to demonstrate with a small part of his detachment in the direction of Courtray. With the remainder of his force he had to march to Hérrines as well to form a reserve. Finally, *Major* Hellwig, supported by 150 Cossacks of Colonel Bikhalow, would have to advance from Ghent to Haerlebeke. However, because Hellwig had gone to Ghent instead of Deinze contrary to his orders, these troops were too far away to coordinate with the main attacking force.

In this way, the allies started their advance. The main force followed the road to Courtray. Arriving at Coighem, however, *Generalleutnant* von Borstell received the order to halt his columns and only to reconnoitre further forward, because report had come in that *Oberst* von Hobe had been delayed. At the same time the Duke of Saxe-Weimar dispatched his ADC, the Saxon *Oberst* Adolf Gottlob von Ziegler, to Avelghem with the 3rd and 4th companies of the Saxon III. Grenadier-Bataillon (*Major* von Döring) and 40 Prussian Freiwillige Reitende Jäger of the Pommersches National-Kavallerie-Regiment (*Major* von Waldow), to establish contact with *Oberst* von Hobe's advancing column.

Sweweghem, 7 March

After halting his troops at Coighem, *Generalleutnant* von Borstell formed an advance guard commanded by *Major* von Schmeling out of the squadron of the Westpreußisches Uhlanen-Regiment, three companies of the Saxon 1. Provisorischen Linien-Regiment (*Major* Ludwig Wilhelm von Eychelberg) and both guns of the 6-Pfünder Reitende Batterie No. 11. Advancing along the road these troops first engaged a French outpost just past Coighem, which was thrown back easily. After advancing for another half hour they encountered a French battalion, positioned behind a barricade across the road. *Major* von Eychelberg ordered *Leutnant* von Linsingen with his company to storm the barricade, which was enough for the apparently raw French who fired a feeble volley and then threw away their muskets and ran to Belleghem as fast as they could. Many French were killed, eight were taken prisoner. Saxon losses were 16 wounded. The advance guard continued their advance. Arriving on a height in front of Belleghem a second French battalion was encountered, behind which the routed battalion had rallied. Both advanced, after which the allied advance guard retreated to Coighem without any further loss. *Oberst* von Ziegler arrived around 1:00 p.m. in Avelghem, his arrival coinciding with the arrival of *Oberst* von Hobe who reported that Sweweghem was occupied by a thousand infantry with four guns. The Duke of Saxe-Weimar ordered *Oberst* von Ziegler to take over command of Hobe's advance guard as well, consisting of the Pommersches National-Kavallerie-Regiment (2 squadrons), the Westpreußisches Uhlanen-

Regiment (1 squadron) and two guns of the 6-Pfünder Reitende Batterie No. 11 (*Leutnant* Gille). With this force, he would have to act offensively against Sweweghem. However, because of his apparent lack of infantry, *Oberst Fürst* von Schönburg was also ordered to join the attack with his detachment. *Oberst* von Hobe, without his advance guard, was ordered to continue his march to Coighem, to act as a reserve for the main force. Except for both battalions of the Prussian 2. Reserve-Infanterie-Regiment which would have to join the Erstes Treffen of *Oberstleutnant* von Schon. The late arrival of Hobe forced the Duke of Saxe-Weimar to postpone his attack on Courtray to the next day. It was clear that, in order to be able to attack this place, the occupation of Belleghem as well as Sweweghem was necessary. Therefore *Generalleutnant* von Borstell attacked Belleghem around 2:00 p.m. The barricade across the road mentioned before had been replaced and was again occupied by 200-300 French infantry. Borstell ordered *Major* von Cardell to turn the right flank of the French with 2½ Prussian battalions, causing the French to retreat. The allies advanced further and the French also abandoned their position in front of Belleghem and inside village itself, falling back on a strong supporting force on a height in front of Courtray. Here they were reinforced by *Général de Division* Maison himself who brought up three battalions of Solignac's division, 200 cavalry and a light artillery battery. More battalions of Solignac's division followed, as well as a brigade of Barrois' division. This forced Borstell to deploy his troops as well, on both sides of the road and advancing the four cannon of the Prussian 12-Pfünder Fußbatterie he opened fire, which was replied by the French with their lighter calibres, on both sides without much effect. Firing ceased when darkness fell.

In Sweweghem the French offered much more resistance against *Oberst* von Ziegler's attack. Von Ziegler sent one company of the III. Grenadier-Bataillon (*Premierleutnant* von Mandersloh) forward in skirmishing order to the left of the road, holding back his remaining company, the cavalry and artillery in reserve. French howitzers fired several shells at this reserve, but initially to short, then to far, without doing any damage at all. Then a strong French skirmisher line was send forward and the Saxon grenadiers had to fall back for the overwhelming French force they were up against, estimated by them at two thousand infantry, suffering several casualties, including *Premierleutnant* von Mandersloh who was wounded leading his company. Command of the company was taken over by *Feldwebel* Hirsch, who would be commissioned for his behaviour on this day. The arrival of *Oberst* Fürst von Schönburg around 5:00 p.m. enabled another attack at nightfall. The four skirmisher *Züge* of *Hauptmann* von Bessel deployed to the left in skirmish order, supported by the 5th company of the II./1. Pommersches Infanterie-Regiment. *Major* von Gayl prolonged this skirmisher line on the left with two skirmisher *Züge* of the same battalion. The remaining three companies of the II./1. Pommersches Infanterie-Regiment (6th, 7th and 8th companies), led by their battalion commander *Major* von Reitzenstein, were formed up in an attack column on the road in front of Sweweghem. Both companies of the Saxon grenadiers attacked on their right. The French skirmisher line was now engaged from two sides simultaneously and fell back into the village. Their artillery fired a few last shots in the falling darkness without any effect and then fell silent, bringing themselves in safely and deploying inside the village again, covering the barricades on the road. Next, the village itself was attacked. On the right, the Saxon grenadiers advanced, pushing back the French tirailleurs and starting to penetrate the village. On the left, *Major* von Gayl and *Hauptmann* von Bessel also made progress, forcing the tirailleurs out of the intersected terrain.

With the attack column of the three companies of the II./1. Pommersches Infanterie-Regiment formed, *Major* von Reitzenstein was ordered to attack to support the Saxons and charged frontally into the village with his weak Prussian force, the 6th and 8th companies in front with the 7th company in reserve. While this column broke through the first barricade, the horse of *Major* von Reitzenstein was shot, and he himself badly wounded by the fall. He had to hand over command to *Hauptmann* von Kuilenstierna. Under his command the attack continued, the Prussians breaking through several barricades but still making progress. The column followed the straight road, which ended at the churchyard surrounded by a low stone wall. French infantry lined this wall, receiving the Prussians at 'pistol shot range' with volley fire, inflicting heavy loss on the brave Prussians. Although darkness already fell, Kuilensterna decided to attack the churchyard. Ordering the 7th company forward as well, despite the losses inflicted the Prussians stormed over the wall, the French defenders breaking and trying to flee. The Prussians, embittered by their heavy loss, gave no pardon and killed many. The Saxon grenadiers, attacking the French in the flank and rear, also suffered severe loss but not as heavy as the Prussians. In this combined attack the Prussians and Saxons cleared the village from the French. Allied losses were heavy; both companies of the III. Grenadier-Bataillon lost a total of one officer and 25 others wounded, and two dead. The II./1. Pommersches Infanterie-Regiment paid a heavy price for their charge into the village: three officers and 80 others wounded, and 18 dead. French loss in killed and wounded was more severe and 30 prisoners had been taken.

That same evening, *Major* Hellwig attacked Haerlebeke as well as the French at Cuerne. Around midnight the French abandoned Haerlebeke, which was immediately occupied by Bikhalov's Cossacks. For the night the allies camped in the following positions: Belleghem and Sweweghem remained occupied and one infantry battalion was positioned at the crossroads were the road from Belleghem joined the main road to Courtray; both *Treffen* camped in the open, one on the left, and one on the right side of the road; the artillery was send back to the reserve in Coighem.

The allies were now in a good position to attack the French in Courtray on 8 March. The attack would be executed by *Generalleutnant* von Borstell and *Oberst* von Ziegler, reinforced by another three infantry battalions, a cavalry squadron and a half-battery from *Oberst* von Hobe. With the remainder of the reserve; three battalions, a cavalry squadron and a half-battery, Hobe would have to move to Roubaix to threaten the French line of retreat. The attack would not be necessary. Outnumbered, *Général de Division* Maison did not want to risk his army in defending a city which was of no strategic importance. During the night he retreated in the direction of Menin, taking up positions behind the Lys near Halluin just south of Menin, with his outposts just north of that place. On that same day he retreated further in the direction of Lille, abandoning Menin as well. It was not without reason that Maison had decided to retreat, as illustrated by a report with a strength list found on a captured courier from Maison to Napoleon. During the previous days of intense fighting, his corps had dwindled down to 5,278 men, 224 officers, 14 cannon, and five howitzers on the 15th, although that same report remarked: 'not counting the reinforcements, that he can pull himself out of the fortresses'.[14] However, despite an additional 6,600 men of the 16e Division Militaire having reached him over the next five days, Maison decided to divide 5,500 of these amongst the various fortresses to reinforce their garrisons of national guards, so that only 1,100 men remained. This left him with an army corps of 7,000 at the most, too small for another attack against the numerically superior enemy.[15] This was especially the case with the raw forces he had at his disposal, which although being mainly Young Guard units had not behaved very well during the previous engagements.

On the other hand, the allied troops, of which many soldiers were raw, had fought well, and in Borstell's after action report the bravery of the Saxon troops under his command is mentioned several times, for example the behaviour the 1. 6-Pfünder Fußbatterie (*Hauptmann* Rouvroy II) at the defence of Oudenaerde and the Saxon troops in the attack on Sweweghem.[16] Also the cooperation between the Saxon and Prussian troops is praised:

> The complete good agreement between the royal Prussian and Saxon troops pleases me from the heart. It is the surest proof that everyone has only the great sacred purpose in mind, that every German in the other recognizes his brother, who sacrifices his life and good and blood with joy for the preservation of the freedom of the general fatherland.[17]

Another matter was Hellwig's case, he having gone to Ghent instead of Deinze. As a result, *Generalleutnant* von Borstell accused Hellwig of insubordination:

> The Major von Hellwig received on the 4th in the afternoon from me the order to leave Oudenaerde on the 5th, and to go to Deinze with the bulk of his detachment, from there to observe the main road from Courtray to Ghent, and to maintain communications with Major Graf von Pückler in Bruges and Oberst von Hobe in Oudenaerde. Contrary to my orders, von Hellwig went to Ghent and placed only cavalry detachments in Deinze and on the road from Ghent to Oudenaerde. Oberst v. Hobe was attacked on that day, and his cavalry was held en échec by considerably superior enemy cavalry; had v. Hellwig been in Deinze, a movement from there into the left flank and back of the enemy had forced him to divide his forces, and the not very favourable position of Oberst v. Hobe in Oudenaerde had been improved; the too large distance of Major v. Hellwig standing in Ghent did

---

14   Bucher, *Der Feldzug*, p.155.
15   Letter of 22 March 1814 from the Blücher to the Duke of Saxe-Weimar, quoted in Egloffstein, *Carl August*, p.85; Calmon-Maison, 'Le Général Maison', p.194.
16   Report of 10 March 1814 from *Generalleutnant* von Borstell, in Von Wolzogen, *Memoiren*, pp.253-256; report from *Oberstlieutenant* Raabe in Bucher, *Der Feldzug*, pp.87, 321-322.
17   Daily order from the Duke of Saxe-Weimar, quoted in Bucher, *Der Feldzug*, pp.86-87.

'Het oplossen van de Rijnbond, 1813' (The Dissolving of the Confederation of the Rhine, 1813). (Rijksmuseum)

'Komst van de Souverein Vorst te Amsterdam, 1813' (The Arrival of the Sovereign Prince in Amsterdam, 1813). (Rijksmuseum)

Saxon Hussars, 1810-1813. Watercolor by Boisseller. (Anne S.K. Brown Collection)

French attack on the decayed fortress-city Oudenaerde, 5 March 1814. Twice the French stormed the Courtray gate with infantry masses, but both times the attacks were defeated by the infantry and the Saxon *Hauptmann* Rouvroy II., who had deployed his 1. 6-Pfünder Fußbatterie in the gate itself, receiving the French with canister. (Original artwork by Christa Hook (www.christahook.co.uk) © Helion and Co. 2019)

Combat of Sweweghem, 31 March, allied retreat & hussar counterattack. Von Brause's II. and III./1. Provisorischen Linien-Regiment
were much too experienced to panic in the situation they found themselves in. To oppose the numerous French tirailleurs, more
and more companies were dispersed as skirmishers, until seven companies had been deployed this way. Protected by these
skirmishers the Saxons slowly retreated. The French cavalry, including Imperial Guard Mamelukes, noticing the retrograde

...ovement, immediately tried to exploit the situation and charged into the skirmisher line, taking a number of them prisoner. A brave counterattack by a hussar squadron, led by *Major* von Taubenheim as well as the commander *Oberst* Fürst zu Schönburg in person, ...hrew back the French cavalry, freeing many prisoners. (Original artwork by Christa Hook (www.christahook.co.uk) © Helion and Co.)

Saxon Uhlans. Print after Knötel (New York Public Library, Vinkhuijzen Collection)

Saxon Infantry. Print after Knötel (New York Public Library, Vinkhuijzen Collection)

Saxon artillery officer. Coloured engraving after Sauerweid. (Anne S.K. Brown Collection)

Freiwillige Jäger zu Fuß Kompagnie 'Weimar'. (New York Public Library, Vinkhuijzen Collection)

not allow this movement and was therefore the reason that the enemy on the 6th could continue his retreat without being closely pursued by cavalry.

As a result of the operations on the 7th, I gave the order to Major von Hellwig to proceed on this day to Haerlebeke, at the same time to disturb communications of the enemy from the left bank of the Lys by a movement on Menin. The latter he did not at all, and the former he did not adequately with regards to the situation, by not accepting the invitation of the Cossack Oberst von Bikhalov to attack Haerlebeke, which was only weakly occupied by the enemy, but instead stood an hour backwards from this place; even on the 8th he remained in Haerlebeke, although he was again requested by Oberst von Bikhalov to proceed with him to Courtray, which had already been evacuated by the enemy; he sent only a patrol of 40 horses with the Cossacks, who told me the first news of the presence of Major von Hellwig at Haerlebeke, although I should have received this news the day before through patrols to be sent by him.[18]

In fact, Hellwig did attack Haerlebeke and finally occupied it so in this matter Borstell's statement is not correct. It is unknown what the result of these accusations was, although Hellwig would continue to serve with his *Streifcorps* during the whole campaign.

The Duke of Saxe-Weimar knew the responsibility he had, and after having captured Courtray he decided not to follow and attack *Général de Division* Maison's corps at Halluin in order not to weaken his defensive positions too much. Even more, he treated Courtray just as an outpost, having not enough troops to spare to provide it with a strong garrison. Already on 8 March he returned to Tournay with part of his corps present at Courtray, ordering *Generalleutnant* von Borstell to follow him with the remainder of the troops the next day. *Major* Hellwig was ordered to occupy Courtray, aided by 70 Cossacks who received orders to scout the terrain in front of Courtray and to give early warning of any French advance. Menin was also occupied by a Cossack outpost, but these were soon after driven away again by the French. To be able to support *Major* Hellwig in time when necessary, *Generalmajor* Prinz Paul von Württemberg occupied Warcoing and surroundings with five infantry battalions and three guns. All other allied troops returned to their original positions, with the only changes being that Borstell also had to occupy the outposts facing Condé, and that *Generalleutnant* von Le Coq had to send a Saxon grenadier battalion, and the 1. 12-pfünder Batterie (Saxon, half foot artillery battery) to Mons.

---

18 Letter of 10 March 1814 from *Generalleutnant* von Borstell to the Duke of Saxe-Weimar, in Fabricius, *Der Parteigänger*, p. 318.

6

The Siege of Maubeuge

Antwerp

While Maison engaged the bulk of III German Corps around Courtray, at other places along the frontline the French went over to the offensive. On 7 March 5,000 men of the Antwerp garrison marched from Tête de Flandres to Beveren and occupied Lokeren, St. Nicolas and Waesmünster with a force of about 1,800 Young Guards commanded by Général de Brigade Aymard, supported by cavalry and two field guns. At Waesmünster a picket of four Cossacks with their officer was surprised and taken prisoner. After the retreat of Maison from Courtray, and having made large requisitions on the left bank of the Scheldt, this force returned to Antwerp again on the 9th. For the same purpose, on the 7th the French made a sortie out of Valenciennes with eighty chevau-légers lanciers and chasseurs à cheval, making large requisitions in the city of Quivrain. On 8 March, from Maubeuge, the French attacked a Russian transport column which stayed for the night in Solre le Chateau with 150 infantry and horse, managing to force their way into the completely open town. The escort consisting of 60 Russian infantry and seven Prussian hussars fought well, however, and the French were defeated with some loss.

Informed about the strong sortie out of Antwerp, the Duke of Saxe-Weimar became concerned about a concentration of a substantial part of the garrison with *Général de Division* Maison's I Corps. Not only was Maison concentrating and strengthening his corps in the vicinity of Tourcoing, but when reinforced by several thousand men out of Antwerp he would be too strong for III German Corps to oppose effectively. The first measure taken was to send the brigadier of the Anhalt-Thüringian Division, *Oberst* von Egloffstein, to Oudenaerde with 1½ battalion of the 1. Provisorischen Linien-Regiment, the Infanterie-Bataillon 'Gotha', a half squadron of the Husaren-Regiment (*Rittmeister* von Seebach) and the 3. 6-Pfünder Fußbatterie (*Premierlieutenant* Hirsch), all Saxon troops. These troops had to act as an observation post, as support for *Major Graf* Pückler in Bruges, and to provide support for the posts in Alost and Termonde. Both latter posts had been, as described, occupied by the three battalions of the 3. Ostpreußische Landwehr Infanterie Regiment belonging to Bülow's corps. However, its commander, *Major* Graf von Klinkowström, after having received fresh orders from Bülow and without informing the Duke of Saxe-Weimar, had resumed his march to unite with Bülow's Prussian III Corps on the 9th, after Maison's retreat from Courtray. When the Duke learned about this, he ordered Klinkowström to return to his previous position immediately, threatening: 'Otherwise, I will arrest you and turn your regiment over to the command of another officer.'[1] After this threat, Klinkowström resumed his positions at Alost and Termonde again on the 11th, at the same time sending a complaint to Blücher about his treatment.

The incident was characteristic of the situation in III German Corps at this moment, as the intense fighting during the previous days, with raw and insufficient troops, lacking ammunition, had taken its toll of the men as well as their officers. Usually, information of this kind is not available, but in this case there exists a letter from private secretary Vogel writing about this matter:

> Our present existence was too restless and anxious; news of victories of the great army of the Allies, which we hoped for every hour, did not arrive. General Maison seemed to be watching us closely, wanting to keep us busy, and the strength of our corps was not strong enough in the beginning. Without ammunition and cannon, this made us very thoughtful and worried about our critical position between the fortresses. Minor discords among the generals, each one wishing to have troops, and we could spare no one, gave occasion to many difficulties, and upset the good humour of our gracious Duke.[2]

The presence of a strong French force near Tourcoing, close to the allied outposts, was a threat which could not be ignored. More incidents made the insecurity of the allied positions all too clear, again in the Antwerp region. There were numerous sorties made by the French garrison on the right bank of the Scheldt, to requisition all kinds of supplies, leading to daily skirmishes with *Generalmajor* von Gablenz' blockade corps. For example, on 12 March a patrol of Prussian *Uhlans* ran into a French detachment near Mortsel, forcing it back with some loss of dead and prisoners. Also 12 March, the advance of a detachment of 400 soldiers of the 55e Ligne coming from Nieuport led by *Général de Division* Morand, reinforced by the French garrison of Ostend, was enough to oblige *Major* Graf Pückler to abandon Bruges, which was promptly forced to pay contribution to the French for an amount of 80,000 francs. After the French had left, Pückler reoccupied Bruges again that same evening.

On 17 March around 6:00 a.m., the garrison of Antwerp made a number of simultaneous sorties against various allied outposts. The strongest attack was directed at Waerlos, executed by five battalions with six guns. The allied outposts were pushed back, joining the supports coming from Mechelen, led by *Generalmajor* von Gablenz in person. Waerlos was counterattacked by two companies of the 1. Leichten Infanterie-Regiment and a company of the Prussian 4. Reserve- or Elb-Infanterie-Regiment and the French

---

1   Letter of 10 March 1814 from the Duke of Saxe-Weimar to *Major* von Klinkowström, quoted in Egloffstein, *Carl August*, p.73.
2   Letter of 12 March 1814 from private secretary Vogel to privy councillor von Voigt, in Egloffstein, *Carl August*, pp.144-145.

were forced to abandon the place, leaving behind all their requisitions. Another attack was directed at Bouchout village, defended by the Prussian *Oberstleutnant* von Reuß with the 4. Reserve- or Elb-Infanterie-Regiment. After intensive fighting he repulsed the French attackers, who retreated to Mortsel. The outpost near Hartsdonk was also attacked, by 400 French with three cannon mounted on boats, and pushed back for some time before they could counterattack with their supports and reoccupy the post. On this day Gablenz lost one dead and 10 wounded; French losses were 10 dead and eight horses. Probably there were a number of wounded as well, but the French took these with them during their retreat.

Forced by circumstances, the Duke of Saxe-Weimar again decided that an effort had to be made to push the French further back to make a junction with troops from Antwerp more difficult. To reach that goal, *Generalleutnant* von Borstell would attack Roubaix during the night from 13 to 14 March with seven infantry battalions. To find out what Borstell would come up against, *Oberst* Fürst von Schönburg was ordered to execute a reconnaissance in force on the 13th. With 300 infantry, 60 cavalry and two guns he surprised the French outpost in Watrelos, which had a strength of about 200 infantry and 60 horse, taking 20 prisoners. Advancing further to Roubaix, he discovered that the 3,000 French here had been reinforced with an additional 3,000 men from Lille that evening. This numerical strength, combined with the bad state of the roads that had to be used and which had been barricaded by the French at many places as well, caused the Duke of Saxe-Weimar to call off the attack. So the situation remained unchanged for now, leaving the French still much room to manoeuvre.

Some days before, the garrison of Maubeuge had been able to ambush a transport of 500 French prisoners of war. This transport came from Bülow's III Prussian Corps and had left Laon on 7 March, escorted by the Freiwillige Fußjäger-Detachement of the 2. Ostpreußisches Grenadierbataillon and forty men of the 4. Reserve-Infanterie-Regiment, 150 men in all commanded by *Leutnant* Woldenscher. Arriving at the village of Rouveroy, the Prussian transport ran into a French ambush, which managed to set free all prisoners. Prussian losses were one *jäger* killed and 12 others taken prisoner.[3] This unfortunate incident enabled the commander of Maubeuge, *Colonel* Schouller, to reinforce his garrison with another 400 experienced soldiers.

On 13 March there was again a sortie from Maubeuge and also one from Philippeville; it is believed to attack another prisoner transport of 2,000 men coming from Beaumont. This time the French failed to free the prisoners, because of the strength of the escort and the fact that *Generalmajor* von Ryssel was just then demonstrating from Mons in front of Maubeuge. After these events, Bülow positioned a few battalions and cavalry along the road from Mons to Avesnes to prevent any further attacks. However, the tide was about to turn. Blücher's decisive victory over Napoleon at Laon (9 and 10 March) apparently had a demoralising effect on the French. The accumulation of forces near Lannoy and Roubaix ended and the French force became

---

3   Anton von Etzel, 'Das Kaiser Alexander Grenadier-Regiment', in *Zeitschrift für Kunst, Wissenschaft und Geschichte des Krieges*, Vol. 87 (Berlin: E.G. Mittler und Sohn, 1853), pp. 199-200.

weaker instead. This enabled the Duke of Saxe-Weimar to order *Oberst* von Egloffstein from Oudenaerde to Avelghem on 14 March, and to allow *Major* von Klinkowström finally to leave on 15 March for his original destination, Bülow's III Prussian Corps (although we will meet him again). In addition, III German Corps received substantial reinforcements again. On 12 March *Generalleutnant* von Thielmann arrived in Brussels with a column of about 8,000 men, consisting of the following units:

From the Anhalt-Thuringian Division:

Infanterie-Regiment 'Anhalt-Dessau-Köthen' (*Oberst* Hoppe), consisting of:
   Infanterie-Bataillon 'Anhalt-Dessau-Köthen' (line infantry) (16/576)
   Landwehr-Bataillon 'Anhalt-Dessau-Köthen' (Landwehr) (16/576)
   Freiwillige Jäger zu Fuß 'Anhalt' (volunteers, detachment) (1/41)
Landwehr-Bataillon 'Schwarzburg' (*Major* Münch) (12/450)[4]
Freiwillige Jäger zu Fuß 'Schwarzburg' (*Oberforstmeister* von Holleben) (4/154)

Saxon troops:

I./2. Provisorischen Linien-Regiment (13/520)
1. Landwehr-Infanterieregiment (*Oberstleutnant* von Arnsdorf), consisting of:
   I. (Dresdener) Bataillon (*Oberstleutnant* von der Mosel) (14/756)
   II. (1. Wittenberger) Bataillon (*Major* von François) (13/727)
   III. (1. Niederlausitzer) Bataillon (*Major* von Könneritz) (14/750)
2. Landwehr-Infanterieregiment (*Major* von Wolan), consisting of:
   I. (1. Thüringer) Bataillon (*Major* von Taucher) (11/733)
   II. (2. Thüringer) Bataillon (*Major* von Planitz) (13/732)
   III. (1. Voigtländer-Neustädter) Bataillon (*Major* von Römer) (16/746)
4th squadron of the Kürassier-Regiment (3/97)
March battalion with reinforcements for the grenadiers and line infantry
March battalion with reinforcements for the light infantry

Their arrival was welcome, although the quality of the troops as well as their armament left much to be desired. To remedy this, Thielmann had halted at Liège a few days to repair as many muskets as possible. Again, the contingent had no artillery with them. The newly raised line units and especially the Landwehr were virtually untrained, and with only few cartridges. As such, they were not trusted by the regular and more experienced units, as described in a letter from the military surgeon Dr Kiefer, also describing

---

4   The 4th company of the Landwehr-Bataillon 'Schwarzburg' consisted of volunteer foot *jäger*, led by *Oberforstmeister* von Holleben. It would operate separated from the battalion.

Caption *Generalleutnant*
Johann Adolf von
Thielemann (Österreichische
Nationalbibliothek)

the lack of reliable information coming from the armies in France and the rumours that circulated:

If only the devil [Napoleon] was luckily defeated! We do not have much news from the army because we get it from Paris via Frankfurt, but it is slow, and here so much bad news is made that we are in doubt. Today it is said: Napoleon has raised another 30,000 cavalry at Versailles, Franz [i.e. the Austrian emperor] has retired to Basle, etc. Our corps is in a bad state; three have deserted (that is, stayed behind in Louvain), admittedly the worst, of Gotha, but one must not even talk about it; our flag is placed here in the depot. We should, it is said, join a Saxon regiment; it seems that nobody wants us. I nearly regret it not to have joined Blücher, if other considerations did not prevent me. We, the Weimar employees, do not receive any pay against all promises, so they lack money. All our officers are no good, everything will fall apart if nothing happens.[5]

Of the troops arriving with Thielmann, the I./2. Provisorischen Linien-Regiment and the 2. Landwehr-Infanterieregiment were send to Mons; the Landwehr-Bataillon 'Schwarzburg' remained in Brussels; and Thielmann himself together with *Generalmajor* von Brause, with the remaining units, marched to Tournay where they arrived on the 15th. III German Corps had now a strength of 18,000 men, including 1,000 cavalry and 3½ artillery batteries. With Borstell's Prussian Division, *Major* Hellwig's Free Corps and Colonel Bikhalow's Cossack Regiment included, the Duke of Saxe-Weimar had 27,000 men, including 3,200 cavalry and 45 field guns at his disposal.[6]

Blücher's orders

On 12 March, the Duke of Saxe-Weimar received a letter from Blücher, informing him about the victory over Napoleon at Laon. Assuming that Bernadotte surely would have arrived at the latest on the 15th, he ordered the Duke to march to Maubeuge as soon as possible, to capture this fortress when possible. That done he was to march further south to Avesnes and from there to continue according to the circumstances. Bernadotte with his Swedish army had indeed arrived in the Southern Netherlands on 10 March. With 26 battalions, 32 squadrons and eight artillery batteries he commanded a substantial corps, however, as already explained, they remained idle. Moving into cantonments around Liège and Aachen, Bernadotte limited his action to observing the French-held fortresses Maastricht, Venlo, Grave, and Jülich. A second letter arrived on the 15th, making it mandatory for the

---

5   Letter of 5 March 1814 from Dr. Kiefer to his family, quoted in Egloffstein, *Carl August*, p.66.
6   Bucher, *Der Feldzug*, pp.101-102; Von Wolzogen, *Memoiren*, p.258; Crusius, *Der Winterfeldzug*, p.233.

Duke to follow Blücher's army to Laon as soon as he had arrived in Avesnes, were he would receive new orders.[7] After having received the second one, the Duke forwarded both letters to Bernadotte immediately, adding:

> Here is a despatch from Mr. Blucher, which contains very clear orders. He thinks I have already occupied the fortress of Maubeuge, without him being able to imagine that your Royal Highness has not yet occupied Brabant. He has sent to me an officer of the Prussian General Staff to hand me his orders and he chose a trusted officer so that there was someone who specifically inquired about the reasons that made me contravene his orders. From what this officer told me with his own mouth, the Austro-Russian army was near Paris on the eleventh. Your Royal Highness puts me in a very real embarrassment as long as You remain with your army out of commission, without relieving me from the position I hold against my heart, and against the orders of Mr. Blücher. It stops major operations by forcing me to disobey my chief. I dare to hope that your Royal Highness will, on the first day, be willing to operate in such a manner as to enable me to put myself in the position my duty demands, I beg you to instruct me of His Will at the very least.[8]

Generalfeldmarschall
Gebhard Leberecht von
Blücher. (Rijksmuseum)

Most probably, by now the Duke would make himself no illusions about Bernadotte, and the reply was as to be expected:

> I am pleased to instruct you, that I await an answer to general questions from the allied sovereigns before deciding upon my subsequent movements; Your corps and those of Generals Wintzingerode and Bulow, being so much by the treaties as by the verbal conventions of Leipzig at my disposal, I must desire to know the period to which they will return under my orders; I can only refer to all that I have written to you on this subject.[9]

The Duke replied the same day, again requesting to at least return his own sappers: 'Allow me, with regard to the detachment of Saxon Sappers who are still with your army, to let them depart and order them to attend at my headquarters, since they are indispensable to us.'[10] As described in the previous chapter, the Sappers had already been returned to the Duke, arriving with the III German Corps the day before. Replying to the Duke's plea, Bernadotte went even further, the Duke of Saxe-Weimar stating in a

---

7   Letters of 9 and 13 March 1814 from Blücher to the Duke of Saxe-Weimar, quoted in Egloffstein, *Carl August*, pp.43-44.
8   Letter of 15 March 1814 from the Duke of Saxe-Weimar to Bernadotte, in Egloffstein, *Carl August*, p.44.
9   Letter of 17 March 1814 from Bernadotte to the Duke of Saxe-Weimar, in Egloffstein, *Carl August*, p.45.
10   Letter of 17 March 1814 from the Duke of Saxe-Weimar to Bernadotte, in Egloffstein, *Carl August*, p.151.

letter to his wife that Bernadotte had proposed to him that the Duke would keep Belgium for himself, adding some additional Rhine provinces to form a nation with a population of five million. Bernadotte gave the Duke his word that if he would accept, he would march immediately![11] Not surprisingly the Duke did not reply to Bernadotte but instead forwarded it to Blücher. Blücher's *Generalquartiermeister* Müffling replied to the Duke:

> How fortunate that Your Ducal Highness knows the Crown Prince and cannot be caught in his nets … In the meantime, his inactivity keeps however Your Highness in the Netherlands and the German provinces. Yesterday a courier came from him with an absurd letter to the Field Marshal, in which our hero exposed himself greatly. If the Field Marshal approves the answer that I have formulated, his friendship with him will be forever destroyed, but he will also hear some truths that will taste bitter.[12]

Time and again, Blücher urged the Duke to undertake offensive action, against Maubeuge and *Général de Division* Maison, and not to fragment his troops in a cordon system. The Duke explained himself with arguments that have already been enumerated: that he had to cover Mons and Belgium to enable the Army of Silesia in France to be supplied; that his army corps consisted mainly of Landwehr, without any battle experience and badly officered, as well as lacking equipment and cartridges; and the lack of cavalry and artillery; and of course the continuing inactiveness of Bernadotte. Finally, Blücher was convinced that the Duke of Saxe-Weimar was correct in his actions, but held up his orders regarding Maubeuge:

> After the circumstances indicated by Your Highness to me from Tournay of the 16th of the month, I cannot but approve of the fact that Your Highness has proceeded to the blockade and siege of Maubeuge, and retain Borstel's Division until the decision of this operation, as was my earlier intention. I am sorry that by the delay of the arrival of His Royal Highness the Crown Prince of Sweden, such an important corps is being held back, which could now take very decisive steps by operating on the right bank of the Oyse. However, I realize that Brabant cannot be left before the Crown Prince of Sweden has arrived, at least in Brussels. Your Excellency will, however, after the reinforcement by General Thielmann, be strong enough to keep Maubeuge blockaded as well, in case the attempt on it should fail, so that our communication is secure. My communication over Chalons and Vitry with Nancy is reopened, but as over the next days major battles have to happen with the great army, so far I cannot make any use of it. I ask Your Highness to send me reports, one day after the other, kindly informing me of the events at Your Highness' Army Corps, and the advance of the Crown Prince of Sweden.[13]

---

11 Letter of 26 March 1814 from the Duke of Saxe-Weimar to his wife, in Egloffstein, *Carl August*, pp.45, 153.

12 Letter of 22 March 1814 from Müffling to the Duke of Saxe-Weimar, in Egloffstein, *Carl August*, pp.45-46.

13 Letter of 21 March 1814 from Blücher to the Duke of Saxe-Weimar, in Egloffstein, *Carl August*, pp.76, 152.

It is probable that the British as well exerted pressure to keep the Duke of Saxe-Weimar in the southern Netherlands, shown by a letter from Lord Clancarthy: 'But, in this case, it would be necessary for us *vue* the nature and amount of our troops, to keep the Duke of Saxe-Weimar, with his force, in Flanders, to cover our siege towards France, and prevent interruptions by the neighbouring garrisons; and upon this subject I have written last night to Lord Castlereagh.'[14]

Maubeuge

As has been described, the French in Maubeuge were blocking the main line of communications for Blücher's Army of Silesia, all transports having to make detours along secondary roads and having to be protected from sallies from the fortress. There was, however, another reason why the place needed to be secured for the allies. The Army of Silesia was now operating far from its main ammunition depot, so it was decided to form two ammunition stores closer to the army. The Prussians decided that on the eastern line of communication the store would be placed at Coblenz, on the northern line of communication in Mons. Mons was chosen because of its advantageous location to receive the ammunition received from Great Britain, as well as the close vicinity of the weapons factories and iron foundries around Liège.[15] Of course, French presence in Maubeuge close by was a threat which could not be ignored, probably also explaining Graham's willingness to let the Duke of Saxe-Weimar borrow his siege train.

With the city being such a hindrance as well as Blücher's orders to try capture the city, the Duke had no other choice than at least to make the effort. Which however would not be an easy task to accomplish: the fortress was small and relatively strong with high walls, and if the governor would not capitulate, storming the walls could become a very costly affair with probably heavy casualties. To be able to execute the siege, III German Corps was reorganised.[16] *Generalleutnant* von Le Coq received command of the troops that would execute the attack on Maubeuge. In addition, the Duke had requested General Graham if he could borrow the siege artillery that had been previously used before Antwerp, which was granted. On 6 March, *Oberstleutnant* Raabe took over the siege artillery including the necessary ammunition from the British in Herenthals, transporting them with requisitioned wagons and 300 horses. This siege train moved over Louvain to Brussels, escorted by a detachment of Gablenz' blockade corps.

Sources differ much about the strength of the French garrison of Maubeuge, from 1,000 to 3,000 men with 80 to a 100 heavy guns. At best estimate strength was about 1,000 men (reportedly composed of a battalion of the Gardes Nationales du Pas-de-Calais (c. 500), a battalion of Douaniers (c. 500), 30 cavalry of the depot of the 1er Régiment de Chasseurs à Cheval, and a company of gunners composed of citizens) to which the 400 prisoners were added that had been freed from the prisoner transport near Rouveroy; a

---

14 Letter of 23 March from Lord Clancarthy in The Hague to Lord Bathurst, in Vane, *Correspondence of Viscount Castlereach*, pp.388-392.

15 Crusius, *Der Winterfeldzug*, p.234.

16 See Appendix III for the composition and dispositions of III German Corps.

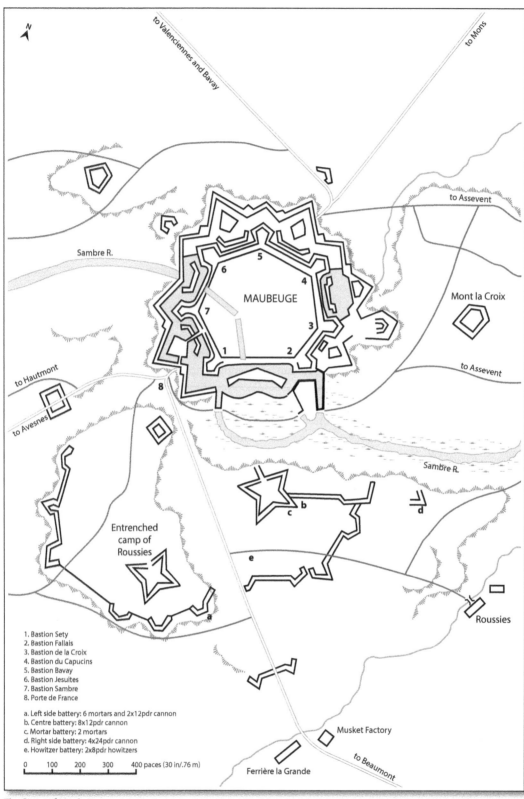

to Valenciennes and Bavay

to Mons

to Assevent

Sambre R.

MAUBEUGE

Mont la Croix

6

5

4

7

3

1

2

to Assevent

8

to Hautmont

to Avesnes

Sambre R.

Entrenched
camp of
Roussies

b

c

d

e

a

f

Roussies

1. Bastion Sety
2. Bastion Fallais
3. Bastion de la Croix
4. Bastion du Capucins
5. Bastion Bavay
6. Bastion Jesuites
7. Bastion Sambre
8. Porte de France

a. Left side battery: 6 mortars and 2x12pdr cannon
b. Centre battery: 8x12pdr cannon
c. Mortar battery: 2 mortars
d. Right side battery: 4x24pdr cannon
e. Howitzer battery: 2x8pdr howitzers

0   100   200   300   400 paces (30 in/.76 m)

Musket Factory

Ferrière la Grande

to Beaumont

The Siege of Maubeuge.

total of nearly 1,500 men. Maubeuge was a small fortress, although still in good condition. It was positioned very strategically: on the east bank of the Sambre, it blocked all shipping, and it lay on the crossroads of the roads leading from Mons to Laon and from Valenciennes to Beaumont. On the southeast side the fortress was protected by a wet ditch, filled with water from the Sambre. To the southeast lay the entrenched camp of Rousies; east of that the heights of Assevent were also occupied by the French. These heights as well as the entrenched camp offered positions favouring any attacker, also providing the necessary cover to approach the fortress. The French were commanded by *Colonel* Schouller. With such strong opposition before him and the presence of French troops in a number of neighbouring fortresses, the Duke of Saxe-Weimar again requested the Prussian *Major* Graf von Klinkowström, on his way to join Bülow's III Prussian Corps), to aid in the siege of Maubeuge. On 12 March the British siege artillery arrived, the British 24-pdr cannon and Dutch mortars mentioned in Appendix III, including the necessary ammunition. They were accompanied by a British artillery officer Captain Gardiner with some British gunners and these would join the Saxons to assist them during the siege of Maubeuge. However, the ammunition was scarce and would only suffice for 48 hours of bombardment: 750 roundshot for the 24-pdr cannon, 112 bombs for the 12-inch Gomer mortar, 391 bombs for the 11-inch and 361 bombs for the 7½-inch mortars with the necessary powder. It was therefore hoped that the governor of Maubeuge would capitulate before the guns ran out of ammunition. If not, Maubeuge would have to be stormed and the walls scaled with ladders. Although preparations were made for this, it was also clear that this could lead to heavy loss. With the siege artillery also six 9-pdr field cannon were received, which were sent to Tournay were a Saxon artillery officer was ordered to train the 'Belgian' crew of 60 men for these. As it proved difficult to find these immediately, initially they were augmented with 20 volunteers of the Infanterie-Bataillons 'Anhalt-Bernburg' and 'Schwarzburg'. Command was given to the Belgian *Souslieutenant* Verwaert.

On 17 and 18 March the besieging units marched to their assigned positions. In the evening of the 17th, the bridge across the Sambre at Jeumont was secured. Marching further next day, a second bridge was built across this river to connect Requignies and Boussois. During the following night, III./2. Provisorischen Linien-Regiment (*Major* Moritz) was pushed forward to Assevent, constructing a crude walking bridge across the river made from farmer's carts. On the 21st at 8:00 a.m., the French made a sortie with 300 infantry and 30 cavalry, directed at Assevent. The outposts of the III./2. Provisorischen Linien-Regiment pulled back in some nearby houses, barricading themselves, buying time for the commander of the battalion to form his troops. Supported by two companies of the II. Grenadier-Bataillon which crossed the Sambre over the crude walking bridge, the French were thrown back into Maubeuge, leaving behind a few men killed. The Saxons had six wounded. That same afternoon at 3:00 p.m., the besieging troops advanced on Maubeuge in five columns to reach their final positions. Supported by *Major* Graf von Klinkowström's Prussians, on the 21st, the entrenched camp of Rousies was captured. Saxon grenadiers opened communications with *Generalleutnant* von Borstell's Prussian division at Bavay. The following night, near the road to Beaumont, the construction of three siege batteries started, difficult enough in the still-frozen ground.

On the left side, just to the left of the road to Beaumont, a battery was constructed for six mortars (3x Dutch 7½-inch, 2x Dutch 11-inch, 1x French 12-inch Gomer) and two 12-pdr cannon of the 1. 12-Pfünder Fußbatterie, commanded by *Premierlieutenant* Krinitz. The battery was positioned behind the corner of the entrenched camp of Rousies, protecting it against fire from the fortress. On the right side of the battery, embrasures were cut out for both 12-pdr cannon. On the right side of the road to Beaumont and closer to Maubeuge, the centre battery was constructed behind the corner of a huge square redoubt. It was armed with 8 12-pdr cannon; four of the Prussian ½ 12-Pfünder Fußbatterie (*Premierlieutenant* Lent) and four of the 1. 12-Pfünder Fußbatterie (*Lieutenant* Schulze). It was commanded by *Hauptmann* Rouvroy I. Close to this centre battery, behind the redoubt, the remaining two Dutch mortars (2x Dutch 7½-inch) were positioned also commanded by *Hauptmann* Rouvroy I. Behind these, in the deep ditch, came the bomb magazine for both centre positions. On the right side a third battery was constructed inside the ditch of an old defence work. It was armed with the four British 24-pdr cannon, commanded by *Hauptmann* Birnbaum. With the embrasures cut out in the old defence work itself, the battery had excellent cover against gunfire from Maubeuge.

The construction of these batteries provoked intense artillery fire from Maubeuge and in the morning of the 22nd, using the Porte de France gate, the French undertook another sortie of 600 men directed at the centre battery, supported by cannon fire from the fortress. They were immediately engaged by the 3rd company of the I. Gardebataillon and the 3rd company of the III. Grenadier-Bataillon which held the forward positions. Despite being outnumbered, these managed to maintain their positions until support came up from the II. Grenadier-Bataillon, after which the French retreated back to the fortress. Unfortunately, both mentioned grenadier companies pursued them too far and came under canister fire from the fortress, suffering an officer and five others dead and two officers and 34 others wounded.[17] To defend against future sorties, both 8-pdr howitzers of the 1. 12-Pfünder Fußbatterie, commanded by *Souslieutenant* Zimmermann, were placed in a battery between the left and centre battery, covering the Porte de France gate as well as the road to Beaumont.

On the 23rd between 4:00 and 5:00 a.m the siege batteries opened fire at Maubeuge, which was again replied to by the French cannon which concentrated their fire on the centre battery – the closest and most vulnerable target – causing considerable damage. Around 9:00 a.m. an even more unfortunate event happened when a French shell hit the bomb magazine near the centre battery, which exploded with 140 bombs, killing three grenadiers and a few gunners in the explosion and wounding the

---

17 Bucher, *Der Feldzug*, p.122; Hans von Schimpf, *Geschichte der beiden Königlich Sächsischen Grenadier-Regimenter: Erstes (Leib-) Grenadier-Regiment Nr. 100 und Zweites Grenadier-Regiment Nr. 101, Kaiser Wilhelm, König von Preussen* (Dresden: Carl Höckner, 1877), pp.169-170.

commander *Hauptmann* Rouvroy I. Unable to operate effectively under this intense bombardment, the gunners were pulled back from the centre battery. The French now diverted their attention to both remaining batteries, but, despite the intense fire, these commenced firing, the 24-pdr battery ably assisted by the British Captain Gardiner and his gunners. It was however clear, even more after the bomb magazine had blown up, that the siege artillery was insufficient to reduce Maubeuge. Realising that storming the fortress was still impractical as well, the Duke of Saxe-Weimar as a last effort offered the French governor a honourable capitulation. Not surprisingly this was in vain, as predicted by *Generalmajor* von Müffling in a letter to the Duke of Saxe-Weimar: 'May heaven grant your Highness Maubeuge, but unless the defence works are bombarded and taken by storm, I do not count on it. Carnot's laws do not allow any commandant to capitulate to other conditions.'[18] It seems that in addition an effort was made to bribe the commander of Maubeuge, *Colonel* Schouller, offering him 100,000 Francs if he would capitulate: this offer was also turned down.[19] So the bombardment continued. However, the allies soon ran out of ammunition for their heavy guns and the bombardment ended around 6:00 p.m. During the night from the 23rd to the 24th, with much trouble the mortars and guns were pulled back again from the batteries. As it had rained heavily the whole night making moving the guns through the mud very difficult.

When the French became aware of the allied retreat, they immediately made another sortie, around 8:00 a.m., with 500 infantry and 40 cavalry. Following the road to Beaumont, near Ferrier la Grande they were engaged by a battalion of the Prussian 3. Ostpreußische Landwehr Infanterie Regiment (*Major* von Klinkowström) and its Fußjäger-Detachement. In support, a 12-pdr cannon deployed on the paved road and the French were repulsed. Reinforced with more infantry the French attacked a second time. While they tried to storm the Prussian position they were attacked in the left flank by a company of the II./2. Leichten Regiment led by *Haupmann* von Zeschau. After over two hours of fighting the French ended their attacks and retreated to Maubeuge. The Prussians lost eight men wounded, the French lost beside some deserters two dead, two officers and 12 others wounded, as well as one wounded cavalryman taken prisoner. After all guns finally had reached the paved road the allied siege train returned to Mons. The siege turned into a tight blockade and later to close observation. This at least prevented the French garrison to disturb allied communications along the road from Solre-le-Château to Avesnes. Many French historians celebrate *Colonel* Schouller as the heroic defender of Maubeuge for three whole months, against overwhelming odds. As described, this is a bit exaggerated.

With the attempt to capture of Maubeuge having failed, on 25 March, *Major* von Klinkowström finally continued his march to Laon to join III Prussian Corps. The Duke would also lose Borstell's trusted Prussian division by explicit order of Blücher, which left also to join Bülow's Prussian III Corps in two columns, on 29 and 30 March respectively. On his departure,

---

18 Letter of 20 March 1814 from *Generalmajor* von Müffling to the Duke of Saxe-Weimar, quoted in Egloffstein, *Carl August*, p.221; Fabricius, *Der Parteigänger*, p.325.

19 Von Wolzogen, *Memoiren*, pp.261-262.

Von Borstell wrote to *Generalleutnant* Le Coq: 'The officers and men of my division have learned to respect your troops as companion in arms and are reluctant to part with them. I ask of Your Excellency to announce this in my and my division's name to your Saxons and to recommend us to their memory.'[20] Only the Pommersches Husaren-Regiment with two cannon of the 6-Pfünder Reitende Batterie No. 11 under *Oberstleutnant* von Thümen would remain with the Duke to remedy the lack of cavalry. In addition, the Duke learned that Colonel Rebrejev's Cossack Regiment, of Wintzingerode's corps, raided between Beaumont and Philippeville. According to the Duke they moved aimlessly and misbehaved themselves, and as a result he did not hesitate to order its commander to join his corps immediately – much to the disapproval of Blücher when he learned about this act! It was fortunate that on 24 March, *Oberst* von Seydewitz arrived in Brussels with additional troops for III German Corps: 149 officers, 6,141 men and 778 horses:

I./1. Provisorischen Linien-Regiment (*Major* von Larisch) (14/508)
3. Landwehr-Infanterieregiment (3 battalions) (53/2,433)
4. Landwehr-Infanterieregiment (3 battalions) (48/2,301)
4th Squadron of the Husaren-Regiment (*Major* Stunzner) (9/172)
Reinforcements for the cavalry:
    Kürassier-Regiment (2/8)
    Uhlanen-Regiment (½ IV. squadron and complements) (3/100)
    Husaren-Regiment (-/23)
2. 12-Pfünder Fußbatterie (6 cannon, 2x 8pdr howitzers, *Hauptmann* Zandt) (4/200)
Main Artillery Park (*Major* von Großmann) (16/396)

---

20 Bucher, *Der Feldzug*, p.151; Larraß, *Geschichte des 6. Infanterie-Regiments*, p.199.

7

The Combat of Sweweghem (or Courtray)

While the siege of Maubeuge took place there was activity on the right wing of III German Corps. *Generalleutnant* von Thielmann had decided to act aggressively, to prevent Maison to come to the aid of Maubeuge during its siege. Besides sending several patrols into French-held territory he made a strong demonstration in front of Lille on 21 March as well as foraging around Saint-Amand, taking with him a hundred empty wagons for this purpose. He formed three columns:

1st (right) column (*Oberst* Fürst von Schönburg)
    III./1. Provisorischen Linien-Regiment
    Husaren-Regiment (1½ squadron, *Rittmeister* von Seebach)
    3. 6-Pfünder Fußbatterie (3 French 6-pdr cannon, *Premierlieutenant* Hirsch)
2nd (centre) column (*Major* von François)
    II./1. Landwehr-Infanterieregiment
    Husaren-Regiment (½ squadron, *Rittmeister* von Gordon)
    1. 6-Pfünder Fußbatterie (1 cannon, *Korporal* Schwidom)
3rd (left) column (*Generalmajor* von Brause)
    II./1. Provisorischen Linien-Regiment
    I. and III/1. Landwehr-Infanterieregiment
    Infanterie-Bataillon 'Anhalt-Dessau-Köthen'
    Landwehr-Bataillon 'Anhalt-Dessau-Köthen'
    Kürassier-Regiment (2 squadrons)
    1. 6-Pfünder Fußbatterie (5 cannon, 2x 8-pdr howitzers, *Hauptmann* Rouvroy II.)
    'Belgian' 9-pdr battery (2 guns)

The 1st column would have to march to Cheraing, repair the bridge across the Marque and then provide infantry cover for it, and to demonstrate with its cavalry in front of Lille. The 2nd column would march to Bouvines and provide support for the 1st column. Cheraing was occupied without opposition and the bridge repaired, the cavalry continuing their advance.

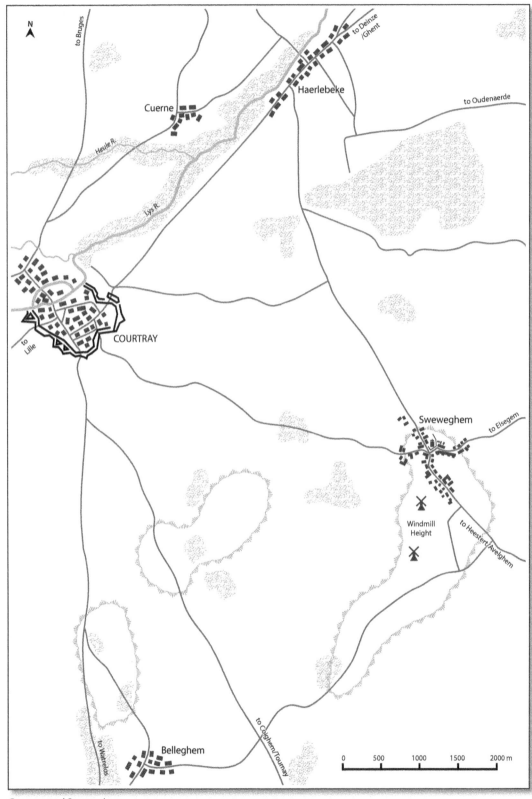

N

to Bruges

Cuerne

Haerlebeke

to Deinze /Ghent

to Oudenaerde

Heule R.

Lys R.

COURTRAY

to Lille

Sweweghem

to Elsegem

Windmill Height

to Heestert/Avelghem

to Watrelos

Belleghem

to Coighem/Tournay

0   500   1000   1500   2000 m

Courtray and Sweweghem.

Soon the hussars were engaged by French cavalry and despite being outnumbered defeated them completely. Elated by this success, *Oberst* Fürst von Schönburg continued his advance to Lille, pushing back the outposts of Barrois' division and again defeated the opposing French cavalry, including *Mameluks* of the Imperial Guard. These were pursued by the hussars into the Fives suburb of Lille. The pursuit continued too far though and the hussars lost two dead and some horses by the fire of the guns on the walls, after which they fell back. The French in Lille immediately reacted and sent out a strong force of four infantry battalions of the divisions of Barrois and Solignac, five cavalry squadrons and six guns, about 3,000 men. Against such odds the Saxon hussars had no other choice than to fall back on their infantry in Cheraing. The French deployed their troops against Cheraing as well as against the 2nd column in Bouvines, an artillery battery opening fire at the Saxon infantry defending the village. *Oberst* Fürst von Schönburg defended Cheraing until nightfall and retreated then to Baisieux.

At Bouvines, *Major* von François had occupied the village, then positioned the 1st division of his infantry as well as the 6-pdr cannon on a height in front of the village while a bridge was built across the brook. Then skirmishers supported by hussars were sent forward, wading through the three-foot-deep water of the Marque. The French infantry battalion deployed here formed square but was hit by a well-aimed shot of the 6-pdr cannon, whereupon it broke and fled back to the houses of Péronne village, pursued by the skirmishers and hussars. *Major* von François reformed his troops and now turned his attention to Sainghin village, also occupied by the French. Supported by the hussars and shouting 'Hurrah!', one-and-a-half companies of raw Landwehr charged into the village and captured it, while the remainder of the II./1. Landwehr-Infanterieregiment and the 6-pdr cannon deployed at the bridge build across the Marque.

Around 5.30 p.m. the French advanced in force and *Major* von François retreated back across the Marque, demolishing the bridge behind him. Behind the brook, three Landwehr companies led by *Hauptmann* Zwicker were deployed while the 6-pdr cannon fired at the advancing cavalry. In front of the brook, a French infantry battalion formed up in attack column, another one did the same on its right. Then an artillery battery with 6 guns deployed and although the fire of the Saxon 6-pdr cannon demolished one of these, the remainder opened fire on the Landwehr with canister. Then the French infantry attacked Bouvines but several attacks were defeated. The village was set on fire at three different places and finally the Landwehr was ordered to retreat, covered by *Hauptmann* Zwicker's skirmishers. French skirmishers penetrated into the village, cavalry crossed the Marque and tried to capture the retreating 6-pdr cannon but failed. The Landwehr formed a rough square and retreated fighting. Supported by canister fire from the 6-pdr cannon, they managed to survive several cavalry attacks until Cysoing was reached, were darkness made an end to the fighting.

Generalmajor von Brause's 3rd column, accompanied by *Generalleutnant* von Thielmann, started its advance to Pont à Marque via Orchies at 10:00 a.m. to cover the foraging at Saint-Amand. Arriving at Pont à Marque they found the village occupied by the French, about 400 infantry with 50 cavalry. *Generalmajor* von Brause deployed his artillery and sent forward a skirmisher line; after a few cannon shots the greatly outnumbered French retreated. The column remained in Orchies for the night and returned to its previous positions near Tournay on the 22nd. Another small incident took place at Saint-Amand. A patrol of the Kürassier-Regiment, commanded by *Lieutenant* von Schönberg, occupied at this place a drawing bridge across the Scarpe, while at the same moment, on the other side of the bridge, eight French lancers advanced to engage them. An exchange of pistol shots followed, without any loss on either side, after which both sides retreated again.[1] Saxon loss of the 1st and 2nd column together was nine men dead, two officers and 30 others wounded and two men missing. French loss was estimated at 40-50 dead and around 80 wounded. It was clear that the French troops the Saxons were up against were mostly raw as otherwise the outnumbered Saxon would have been defeated easily. On the other hand, the Saxons, and especially the raw Landwehr fighting for the first time, behaved very well, *Generalleutnant* von Thielmann writing in his after-action report:

> ... that in these combats the III. Battalion of the 1st Line Regiment, the Hussars and the foot artillery attached to the column of Major von Francois fought with great courage, hardly needs a special mentioning, as the bravery of the Saxon troops is recognized. But that the II. or Wittenberger battalion of the 1st Landwehr Regiment – here for the first time under enemy fire – was not inferior in bravery and discipline to all the troops served must not go unnoticed and must be presented to others as a glorious example for emulation.[2]

Général de Division Maison advances again

Despite the fact that Napoleon had lost the Battle of Laon (9-10 March), *Général de Division* Maison had lost nothing of his fighting spirit. Learning about the allied siege and subsequent blockade of Maubeuge and not deceived by *Generalleutnant* von Thielmann's activity, he calculated that the concentration of forces must have weakened the allied right flank seriously. His previous effort failing, he again planned to reinforce himself with a substantial part of the garrison in Antwerp, reaching a numerical superiority which would enable him to go over to the offensive. He had drawn as much men from the fortresses as possible. On 14 March he had about 6,000 men at his disposal: Barrois' division (95/2,742); Solignac's division (1,404) and Castex' cavalry brigade (48/832).[3] Maison advanced on 25 March to Menin with four of Solignac's infantry battalions, two cavalry squadrons and two guns. *Major* Hellwig was easily pushed out of Menin and retreated to Courtray. Following up their success the French attacked Courtray as well, aided by simultaneous sorties out of Condé and movements from the garrison of Antwerp in the direction of Ghent. Hellwig also abandoned Courtray and retreated east to Oudenaerde, followed by Penne's brigade of Solignac's division, with some cavalry and a few light artillery guns. Which halted for

---

1 Bucher, *Der Feldzug*, p.152; Von Schimpff, *Geschichte des Garde-Reiter-Regiments*, pp. 361-362.
2 Quoted in Bucher, *Der Feldzug*, p.144.
3 Weil, *La Campagne*, Vol. 4, p.312.

the night in Peteghem close to this city. Next day, Maison left Courtray again and now turned his attention on Ghent, while Penne's brigade retreated again to form Maison's advance guard.

Receiving news of the approaching French, in Ghent Colonel Bikhalov called to the citizens to arm themselves and to defend their city. Some Cossacks ventured out of the city and engaged the French but were quickly defeated by *Général de Brigade* Lalaing d'Audenarde's 2e Régiment de Chevau-Légers Lanciers de la Garde. The effort was futile, the citizens and the Cossacks with two guns were no match for the French. When Penne's brigade charged the gate, Colonel Bikhalov and his Cossacks were driven out of the city easily and hotly pursued by the guard lancers, with Bikhalov nearly captured. Bikhalov also lost his self-made mobile artillery, two light naval cannon that had been fixed on the front part of wagons to accompany his Cossacks: 'The pain of losing these two guns, for which he had been practicing his Cossacks for weeks, was very deep.'[4] About 30 men of the 2e Régiment 'de Flandre' of the *Légion Belge* that was raised in Ghent and had participated in the defence, including its commander *Colonel* de Polis, were taken prisoner. Maison regarded them as traitors and threatened to deliver them to a court martial to be shot. Learning about Maison's threat, the Duke of Saxe-Weimar immediately send a letter to Maison, threatening with retaliation by executing French generals and senior officers in the event that citizens of Ghent or members of the 2e Régiment 'de Flandre' came to any harm.[5] In the end, these Belgians would be exchanged against French soldiers after the ceasefire. Nevertheless, again the city would suffer, this time from the French who behaved even worse than the Cossacks had done, thieving and plundering. Maison had to take harsh measures to restore order, but he himself did not hesitate to draw a half million francs from the city coffers to pay the arrears of wages of his soldiers. He placed his advanced posts in St. Nicolas, Waesmünster and on the road to Alost to where Bikhalov had retreated.

Generalleutnant von Thielmann decided to cut off the retreat route of Maison's corps and occupied Courtray with seven infantry battalions, four squadrons and 13 field guns, about 5,000 men in all. To secure Tournay, *Oberst* von Egloffstein remained behind with three battalions of the Anhalt-Thuringian Division (Infanterie-Bataillon 'Gotha' and both battalions of the Infanterie-Regiment 'Anhalt-Dessau-Köthen'), 30 hussars of IV. Squadron, the nucleus of the 4e Régiment 'de Namur' of the *Légion Belge* and four 9-pdr cannon of the 'Belgian' battery, about 2,100 men in all). To be able to support him, the Prussian *Oberstleutnant* von Thümen was ordered to march from St. Ghislain to Leuze with the units under his command; two battalions, the Prussian Pommersches Husaren-Regiment (3 squadrons) and two cannon of the 6-Pfünder Reitende Batterie No. 11.

Thielmann soon received reliable information about the French superior strength, deciding that his presence in Courtray served no purpose and

---

4   J.C. Kretzschmer, *Soldaten-, Kriegs- ind Lager-Leben. Blüthen der Erinnerung aus dem Befreiungskriege* (Danzig: L.G. Homann, 1838), Vol. 2, pp.213-214.

5   Letter of 28 March 1814 from the Duke of Saxe-Weimar to *Général de Division* Maison, in *Journal Officiel*, p.144.

taking in account that a French march to Brussels would be a possibility as well, on 27 March he returned to Tournay. From there he marched to Oudenaerde, where he was reinforced by the I./1. Provisorischen Linien-Regiment and 3. Landwehr-Infanterieregiment that had just arrived from Saxony. This gave Thielmann's corps (excluding Hellwig's *Streifcorps* and Colonel Bikhalov's Cossack Regiment) a strength of 8,000 infantry, 700 cavalry and 13 field guns. Hellwig's *Streifcorps* was reinforced with IV./ Husaren-Regiment. The next day followed by a Landwehr battalion and two field guns, placing outposts in Courtray, Haerlebeke and Deinze. *Major* Graf Pückler managed to leave Bruges with about 400 men of the 1er Régiment d'Infanterie Légère that had been raised there, marching around the rear of Maison's French corps to Courtray and Tournay.

Although the intentions of *Général de Division* Maison were still unclear to the Duke of Saxe-Weimar, he could not ignore the threat created by his advance. With French strength estimated at 14,000 or even 15,000 men, a French march to capture Brussels again seemed a possibility –as was believed before, when Maison appeared before Oudenaerde. Losing this capital city would have to be prevented whenever possible as a French occupation, beside political consequences, could have an undesirable effect on the population, which until now was supporting the allied cause reluctantly at the best. Indeed, the news of the French advance, spread by Bikhalov's dispersed Cossacks and fugitives, of course greatly exaggerated, was already the cause for panic. Lacking a proper garrison, many citizens believed that Brussels would be lost: wagons were packed with belongings. A. van Bylandt, a Dutch citizen residing in Brussels, wrote to the Prince of Orange:

> On the 27th, the official news arrived here that the French had made a diversion and that the garrison of Antwerp had attacked the Walem bridge near Mechelen, so that we are surrounded by enemies, and without sufficient strength if the Prince of Sweden continues not wanting to move. The English here had an unauthorized diplomatic commissioner, who fled with all the English. Assisted by Prince Ernest d'Aremberg, who is raising a Belgian regiment, I proposed the mass levy of the inhabitants of Flanders to put an end to these attempts of the enemy; but General Murray, who commands the Belgian troops, discourages this, under the pretext that we should not give such a bad example to France. I admit that if we like to listen to such arguments, we will not go far.[6]

The British also believed that Brussels could be Maison's real target, Lord Clancarty writing to Lord Liverpool:

> By an intercepted letter from Antwerp of the 26th inst., it appears that a considerable part of the garrison of that place had marched to join the force under General Maison at Ghent, and that the object of this movement is to attack

---

6   Letter of 27 March 1814 from A. Van Bylandt to the Prince of Orange, in French in Colenbrander, *Gedenkstukken*, p.527.

whatever force might be at Brussels, and clear the route of Flanders, so as to open the whole of that province to the garrison.[7]

In addition, many supplies had been gathered in Brussels which should be prevented to fall into French hands. On 29 March the French reconnoitred in the direction of Termonde and although their patrols were turned back in some insignificant fighting, it sufficed to convince the Duke of Saxe-Weimar, as well as Thielmann, that Brussels could be Maison's real target. Measures had to be taken to prevent this in any case. However, at the same time, the Duke was not prepared to give up the blockade of Maubeuge because of its threat to allied communications. In Brussels the hospitals were emptied for men able to handle a musket and together with non-combatants of the army they were formed into provisional battalions: 'It was touching how many brave fellows, holding the stick in their right hand, and the musket in their left hand, or the officers with bandaged heads, his arm in a bandage, or limping with a staff, but having the sword in the fist.'[8] To assure the citizens that Brussels was safe, its governor *Generalmajor* Graf von Lottum stated on 28 March: 'I inform the public that the enemy has succeeded in occupying Ghent. The brave Colonel Bikhalov offers him the point at Alost. I will leave with considerable forces. He was driven back at Antwerp. We pursue him from all sides, and there is nothing to fear for Brussels.'[9] On 31 March this was followed by a publication from the Duke of Saxe-Weimar: 'The inhabitants of Brussels can be reassured about the operations of General Maison. All measures have been taken to make his undertakings fail. A reconnaissance which General Maison undertook this morning with a thousand men was, as we have just learned, beaten back.'[10] Naturally additional and substantial means to cope with Maison's threat had to be found. On the 27th the Duke again had sent an urgent message to Field Marshal Stedingk – commanding the Swedish forces in the absence of Bernadotte who was still at the headquarters of allied sovereigns – pleading for aid. Fortunately, this time support would come!

The Russo-German Legion

Part of Bernadotte's Army of the North was *Generalleutnant* von Wallmoden's Russo-German Army Corps. It consisted of a Cossack Brigade (Major General Tettenborn), a brigade consisting of Hanoverian and Hanseatic units (Major General Lyon) and the Russisch-Deutschen Legion (Russo-German Legion, commanded by *Generalmajor* von Arentschildt). This corps had fought some minor battles, especially at Göhrde (18 September 1813) against the French and at Sehestedt (10 December 1813) against the Danes. After the convention had been closed with Denmark the corps was used in the blockade of Hamburg, especially Harburg, together with Bennigsen's Russian troops. In January 1814, Tettenborn's Cossack brigade was transferred to the Russian army in France and marched on 24 January, arriving in Rheims on 25

---

7   Letter of 2 April 1814 from Lord Clancarty to Lord Liverpool, in English in Colenbrander, *Gedenkstukken*, pp.101-102.
8   Kretzschmer, *Soldaten-Leben*, p.215.
9   *Allgemeine Zeitung*, 5 April 1814.
10   *Allgemeine Zeitung*, 8 April 1814.

February. That same month, Wallmoden received orders from Bernadotte to march to the Southern Netherlands with all the troops that could be spared in the blockade. Together with Bennigsen it was decided that Major General Lyon's brigade would remain, while *Generalleutnant* von Wallmoden would leave with the Russo-German Legion. From 16 to 20 February the units left their positions in the blockade, marching to Bremen where the last units arrived on the 23rd. Except for the units of the Russo-German Legion, the only other unit to accompany them was the Hanoverian Kielmanseggesche Jäger-Korps.

The Russo-German Legion had been raised in Russia end 1812, mainly formed out of soldiers from Napoleon's army that marched into Russia: a mix of nearly all European nations, especially German (Rhine Confederation), Prussian and Dutch. On 6 July 1813 a treaty had been closed by which the Legion came into British pay, on the condition that it would be used on the European mainland. This changed in February 1814 when the Legion came into Hanoverian pay.[11] The first five infantry battalions contained mainly veteran soldiers, having fought at least in the Russian campaign, some of the men four campaigns or more. The 6. Infanterie-Bataillon was formed of men from the captured Saxon Regiment 'Maximilian' with one year's service (still wearing their Saxon uniforms), while the 7. Infanterie-Bataillon was formed from young men from Saxony and Saxe-Coburg with only basic training. To these, Dutch deserters of the 147e and 148e Ligne had been added. Both raw battalions were brigaded with two more experienced battalions, forming two infantry brigades to which the cavalry and artillery were added.[12]

On 27 and 28 February the Legion left in three columns, with a strength of 124 officers and 4,965 others (except for the staff). From 14-16 March the Rhine was crossed at Dusseldorf. *Generalleutnant* von Wallmoden as well as the whole Legion had high hopes that they would see action in battle now, sharing the glory of Napoleon's defeat. Still in Hannover, Wallmoden had already travelled in advance of the Legion to Bernadotte in Liège, to receive further orders. To his disappointment, he was assigned to observe the French-held fortresses of Venlo and Maastricht. He also found to his astonishment that the Swedish army was not stirring a bit. Despite all this he had no choice as to follow orders and on 17 and 18 March, the 1. Brigade deployed with the front against Maastricht, the 2. Brigade against Venlo. *Generalleutnant* von Wallmoden however did not consent, next trying to use British influence to be ordered to join General Graham in the blockade of Antwerp, using the argument that although the Legion was in Hanoverian pay, de facto it was Great Britain paying the bill. This worked and finally Bernadotte agreed, and on 23 March the Legion resumed its march. Led by *Generalmajor* von Arentschildt, the Legion reached Louvain on 27 March, were it was joined the next day by Wallmoden himself who resumed command in person.[13]

---

11 Barthold von Quistorp, *Die Kaiserlich Russisch-Deutsche Legion. Ein Beitrag zur Preußischen Armee-Geschichte*, p.217, 234.

12 See Appendix VI for the composition of the Russo-German Legion as it would join the Duke of Saxe-Coburg.

13 Von Quistorp, *Die Kaiserlich Russisch-Deutsche Legion*, pp.226-227.

At Louvain, urgent requests were received. The first one on the 27th, *Generalmajor* von Arentschildt receiving a letter from the mayor of Brussels, Baron van der Linden d'Hooghvorst, to come to the aid of the city. Some moments later *Oberst* von Zeschwitz arrived, sent by the Duke of Saxe-Weimar with the same request. Arentschildt responded immediately, sending his 1. Brigade to Brussels, while the 2. Brigade continued to Antwerp. Approved by Wallmoden on his arrival, the 1. Brigade entered Brussels on the 28th, hailed by its citizens. Wallmoden also informed Field Marshal Stedingk about the decision to come to the aid of the Duke of Saxe-Weimar instead of Graham. Stedingk agreed, taking in account the gloomy impression that it would make if Brussels were lost with 25,000 Swedes idle spectators only a few marches away. Therefore, he also he marched a Swedish division to Louvain to be close to Brussels in case of an emergency. It took more courage for Stedingk to take this decision than one would imagine: when in 1813 Lieutenant General von Döbeln decided to send a Swedish division to the aid of Hamburg he was immediately relieved of his command by Bernadotte, court-martialled and sentenced to be executed, but pardoned later. Luckily the situation was different now, and when Bernadotte returned from the headquarters of the allied sovereigns he confirmed the decisions that had been made and marched his whole army to Brussels.[14]

On the arrival of the Russo-German Legion the governor of Brussels, *Generalmajor* Graf von Lottum, left Brussels and marched to Alost on the 27th with all troops at his disposal; units already present, augmented with units that had just arrived from Germany. I./4. Landwehr-Infanterieregiment remained in Brussels to guard the Main Artillery Park as well as the 2. 12-Pfünder Fußbatterie which was not ready to take the field. With the above troops, Lottum occupied Alost with a post in Termonde. He was reinforced with the 1. Husaren-Regiment and the 9-Pfünder Fußbatterie of the Russo-German Legion. On the 29th the remaining troops of the 1. Brigade of the Legion also left Brussels again, on 30 March arriving in Alost as well. The 2. Brigade of the Legion in the meantime had relieved the Saxon troops of *Generalmajor* von Gablenz' blockading corps before Antwerp while the Prussian units remained in place. Gablenz arrived also in Alost on 30 March, were he was reinforced with I./4. Landwehr-Infanterieregiment and 2. 12-Pfünder Fußbatterie just arriving from Brussels. The allies had now concentrated a force of 7,450 infantry, 1,500 cavalry and 30 guns at Alost of which command was given to *Generalleutnant* von Wallmoden. It was composed as follows:

Russo-German Legion
    4 infantry battalions, 4 cavalry squadrons, 16 guns[15]
Corps of *Generalmajor* von Gablenz
    Jäger Bataillon
    1. Leichten Infanterie-Regiment (2 battalions)

---

14 Anon., *Der Feldzug des Corps des Generals Grafen Ludwig von Wallmoden-Gimborn an der Nieder-Elbe und in Belgien, in den Jahren 1813 und 1814* (Altenburg: H.A. Pierer, 1848), pp.5, 74.

15 See Appendix VI for details.

I./4. Landwehr-Infanterieregiment

Uhlanen-Regiment (2½ squadron)

2. 6-Pfünder Reitende Batterie (2 cannon, 2x 8-pdr howitzers, *Hauptmann* Probsthain)

2. 12-Pfünder Fußbatterie (6 cannon, 2x 8pdr howitzers, *Hauptmann* Zandt)

Detachment of *Generalmajor* Graf von Lottum

II. and III./4. Landwehr-Infanterieregiment

Landwehr-Bataillon 'Weimar'

Landwehr-Bataillon 'Gotha'

Freiwillige Jäger zu Fuß 'Schwarzburg'

Freiwillige Fußjäger/1. Westphälische Landwehr-Infanterie-Regiment (Prussian)[16]

Brandenburgschen Dragoner-Regiment (Prussian, 3 squadrons)

2. 6-Pfünder Reitende Batterie (2 cannon)

Unattached

Colonel Bikhalov's Cossack Regiment

After the arrival of *Generalleutnant* von Thielmann with his corps, strength would be raised to 14,000 infantry, 2,500 cavalry and 43 guns. The Duke of Saxe-Weimar went to Alost to take over command. *Général de Division* Maison in the meantime, as described, had no plans to capture Brussels, but was making an effort to unite his corps with part of the garrison of Antwerp. From Ghent, Maison's *sous-chef d'état-major, Colonel* Villatte, was despatched to Antwerp escorted by a voltigeur company and 50 cavalry, with orders for Roguet to join Maison's I Corps. On 27 March *Général de Division* Roguet's Young Guard division left Antwerp and joined Maison; about 4,000 to 4,500 infantry, 260 cavalry and 14 guns, raising his strength to 9,700 infantry, 1,360 cavalry and 35 guns.[17] In exchange for Roguet's Division, about a thousand unarmed recruits were added to the garrison of Antwerp. For the time being, however, Maison remained in and around Ghent, forming a threat for the blockading troops around Antwerp as well as for the positions of III German Corps, and Brussels. Therefore, the Duke of Saxe-Weimar decided to attack him on the 31st, although Maison's strength was estimated now at 12-15,000 infantry, 1,100 cavalry and 36 guns.[18] To be able to support the attacking troops, *Generalleutnant* von Wallmoden and *Generalmajor* von Gablenz were ordered to advance from Alost to Oudenaerde. Before reaching Ghent, the advance guard of the Duke of Saxe-Weimar's corps near Alost, formed of *Generalmajor* Graf von Lottum's detachment reinforced with the 1. Husaren-Regiment of the Russo-German Legion, as well as the outposts of

---

16 *Oberstleutnant* Rüchel had arrived from 's Hertogenbosch already some time ago with the Prussian 1. Westphälische Landwehr-Infanterie-Regiment (3 battalions and a Fußjäger detachment) and I./2. Westphälische Landwehr-Infanterie-Regiment, but refused to join the Duke of Saxe-Weimar's III Army Corps until having received formal orders. Only the Fußjäger detachment (*Hauptmann* von Wulffen) would take part in the operations (Bucher, *Der Feldzug*, pp.167, 213).

17 Calmon-Maison, 'Le Général Maison', p.198.

18 Bucher, *Der Feldzug*, pp.147-148, 164.

Generalleutnant von Thielmann's corps, confirmed that the French had left Ghent during the night of 29 to 30 March.

Leaving behind his wounded, Maison had brushed away *Major* Hellwig's posts of Deinze and Sweweghem and marched to Courtray, away from Brussels, and as such an attack on Brussels became less probable. At the same time, aided by a thick fog, allied outposts in front of Lille were surprised and driven back to Tournay, after which the arrival of allied reinforcements forced the French to retreat on their turn. Together with Lottum, Colonel Bikhalow entered Ghent again on the 30th, his Cossacks pursuing the retreating French taking a few prisoners. *Major* Hellwig retreated to Oudenaerde with his *Streifcorps* and joined Thielmann. When Thielmann received news of the French retreat, he immediately called in his posts and marched to Avelghem, sending I/1. Provisorischen Linien-Regiment to Tournay to reinforce the troops present there and to secure it against a French attack. Sources differ on why Thielmann advanced; obviously with Maison retreating the direct threat had been removed. According to his prime biographer, von Hüttel, the reason was the following: not knowing the real strength of the French and in addition expecting that only the rearguard of Maison's corps would be present, he planned to be at Courtray on the 31st to be able to block the retreat path of Maison, or at least to be at hand to attack its rearguard. Thielmann had received a report stating that Maison had retreated to Bruges in two columns, with only a small detachment remaining at Courtray. He would try to pin down the French, until Wallmoden and Gablenz could move in for the main attack, as was agreed upon.[19]

The facts however tell another story:

- *Generalleutnant* von Thielmann had no orders to attack. On the contrary, he had received the directive to be very careful with his infantry, weak in numbers as well as raw, and not to engage in any serious fighting until Wallmoden had arrived;
- It was hardly probable that the experienced *Général de Division* Maison would have divided his corps so close to the allies, which could have exposed him to being defeated piecemeal;
- On 30 March a parliamentarian, send by Maison to Thielmann, had told him that 'he was not so weak anymore, as maybe was believed by the allies; he would proof that to *Général* Thielmann, if he would encounter him in the open'.[20]

According to some historians, the reason that Thielmann advanced without waiting for Wallmoden's troops to arrive, was that he wanted all

---

19 R. von Hüttel, *Der General der Kavallerie Freiherr von Thielmann* (Berlin: Verlag Laue, 1828), pp. 56-57; Bucher, *Der Feldzug*, p.203.

20 Anon., 'Der Feldzug des dritten deutschen Armee-korps in Flandern, im Jahre 1814 – Versuch eines Beitrages zur allgemeinen Kriegschichte der Alliirten (Aus dem Tagebuche eines deutschen Officiers)' in *Oestreichische militärische Zeitschrift* (Wien: Anton Strauß's sel. Witwe, 1831) , Vol. 3, pp.25-26; Bucher, *Der Feldzug*, pp.194, 203; Crusius, *Der Winterfeldzug*, p.256.

the honour for engaging the enemy independently.[21] It is also possible that after the successes on the 21st he overestimated the capabilities of his troops, especially the Landwehr, at the same time underestimating the quality of the French. Whatever the truth, fact remains that Thielmann's advance brought his corps into a very dangerous situation.

The Combat of Sweweghem (or Courtray)

In order to attack *Général de Division* Maison's rearguard, *Generalleutnant* von Thielmann organised the troops at his disposal in two brigades:

1st Brigade (right wing) (*Generalmajor* von Brause)
  II. and III./1. Provisorischen Linien-Regiment
  1. Landwehr-Infanterieregiment (3 battalions)
  Freiwillige Jäger zu Fuß 'Anhalt' (detachment)
  Husaren-Regiment (I., II. and IV. squadron)
  1. 6-Pfünder Fußbatterie (4 cannon, 2x 8-pdr howitzers, *Hauptmann* Rouvroy II.)

2nd Brigade (left wing) (*Generalmajor* Prinz Paul von Württemberg)
  3. Landwehr-Infanterieregiment (3 battalions)
  Infanterie-Bataillon 'Anhalt-Bernburg'
  Infanterie-Bataillon 'Schwarzburg'
  Kürassier-Regiment (2 squadrons)
  3. 6-Pfünder Fußbatterie (5x 6-pdr cannon, *Premierlieutenant* Hirsch)[22]
  'Belgian' 9-pdr battery (2 guns)

Major Hellwig's *Streifcorps* **(Prussian)**
  Fußjäger Bataillon (3 companies, *Hauptmann* Kamlah)
  Büchsenjager (c. 100)
  Freiwillige Reitende Jäger (1 squadron)
  Husaren (3 squadrons)

I/1. Provisorischen Linien-Regiment was ordered to march to Tournay in the morning of the 31st, to reinforce *Oberst* von Egloffstein commanding here. To support Thielmann, Egloffstein had to demonstrate in the direction of Courtray to divide French attention. On 31 March between 4:00 and 5:00 a.m., *Generalleutnant* von Thielmann started his advance following the road leading to Avelghem, via Sweweghem, directly to Courtray. The 1st Brigade formed the advance guard and had to capture Sweweghem. After its capture, the 2nd Brigade would join in the advance to Courtray. At the same time, *Major* Hellwig had to capture Belleghem, to the left of Sweweghem. The advance would initially lead through heavily intersected terrain, opening up to a plain about a kilometre from Courtray. Arriving at Avelghem without opposition, both Landwehr companies of the Infanterie-Bataillon 'Anhalt-Bernburg' were left behind to occupy the village and the 1st Brigade

---

21 Anon., 'Der Feldzug des dritten deutschen Armee-korps', Vol. 3, p.26; Bucher, *Der Feldzug*, p.204; Crusius, *Der Winterfeldzug*, p.256.

22 Initially armed with three French 6-pdr cannon, two Saxon 6-pdr cannon had been added from the 6-Pfünder Fußbatterie (*Hauptmann* Rouvroy II.).

continued its advance to Sweweghem. The village was occupied by a French infantry battalion of about 600 men and a few horse; the entrances of the village were lightly barricaded. The French gave way easily and Sweweghem was quickly captured without much loss, the French retreating along the road to Courtray. *Generalmajor* von Brause was only able to send a few cannon shots after them. To cover his right flank, he ordered I./1. Landwehr-Infanterieregiment to follow the road to Haerlebeke, but to remain in line with his force and to maintain communications with him.

After the capture of Sweweghem, *Generalmajor* von Brause divided his brigade in two echelons. As an advance guard he kept with him II. and III./1. Provisorischen Linien-Regiment, three hussar squadrons and four guns of the 1. 6-Pfünder Fußbatterie. As second echelon they were followed by II. and III./1. Landwehr-Infanterieregiment. From the rest of the troops, the remaining two guns of the 1st brigade deployed on the Windmill Height, just south of Sweweghem and close to the road. They were covered by both squadrons of the Kürassier-Regiment, forming a reserve. Prinz Paul von Württemberg followed the 1st Brigade to Courtray, at a distance of about 1,500 paces, with both line companies of the Infanterie-Bataillon 'Anhalt-Bernburg', I. and II./3. Landwehr-Infanterieregiment and the five 6-pdr cannon of the 3. 6-Pfünder Fußbatterie, the latter was some time later ordered to go back and to deploy on the Windmill Height as well. Both remaining battalions of his brigade (III./3. Landwehr-Infanterieregiment and the Infanterie-Bataillon 'Schwarzburg') as well as both cannon of the 'Belgian' 9-pdr battery remained in position between Prinz Paul von Württemberg and the reserve on the Windmill Height. Each brigade divided in two echelons this way with a central reserve further back. The 1st Brigade continued its march on to the plain in front of Courtray, which is completely open, providing a clear view of the whole city and its surroundings. Arriving before the city, the II. and III./1. Provisorischen Linien-Regiment deployed on both sides of the road, sending forward skirmishers to engage the French skirmishers. But then *Generalmajor* von Brause had an unpleasant surprise, when massive French forces debouched from all gates of the city, deploying in three directions.

Général de Division Maison wanted to prevent the allies from deploying their troops completely on the plain before Courtray, attacking them in the much more intersected terrain while they were still marching forward following the roads.[23] Courtray remained occupied by the Gendarmes d'Elite à Cheval, the artillery park, and part of Castex' cavalry near the Menin gate. Participating in the attack, *Général de Division* Barrois supported by the 2e Régiment de Chevau-Légers Lanciers de la Garde was ordered to take command of the left, to march through Haerlebeke straight for Sweweghem to attack the allied right flank and cut off their retreat to Oudenaerde. *Général de Division* Solignac supported by a squadron of the 2e Régiment de Chasseurs à Cheval de la Garde had to attack the allied left in the direction of Tournay. Maison himself accompanied the centre column, consisting of Roguet's Young Guard division advancing in close columns proceeded by a dense mass of tirailleurs, supported by the 2e Régiment de Chasseurs à

23 See Appendix VIII for the French order of battle.

Cheval de la Garde led by *Général de Brigade* Meuziau and the 1er Régiment de Gardes d'Honneur. The centre column had the task to contain Brause's 1st Brigade, while both outflanking divisions could cut the Allies in two. It was however perfectly clear to Brause that the allies had not engaged Maison's rearguard but his complete I Corps, and that they were in no position to hold their ground against these overwhelming odds. He also recognised that it would not be easy to break of the fight and to retreat. Deploying the four guns of the 1. 6-Pfünder Fußbatterie, Brause had his cannon opened fire on the French troops marching to their assigned positions, sending at the same time an urgent message to Thielmann about his observations.

Prinz Paul von Württemberg noticed the French advance as well, and to cover the left flank he ordered both line companies of the Infanterie-Bataillon 'Anhalt-Bernburg' to advance and to engage the French. Before they had advanced a thousand paces, heavily outnumbered, they were engaged by much more experienced French tirailleurs. To support them Prinz Paul von Württemberg ordered I. and II./3. Landwehr-Infanterieregiment forward as well. They were ordered to advance in close column, sending forward skirmishers. This was still not enough to stop the French, despite that the Landwehr was reinforced by their 3rd ranks dispersing as skirmishers also. The first and second rank had to act as support but by mistake these were also dispersed in skirmish order. With all the infantry of his first echelon committed, Prinz Paul von Württemberg ordered two companies of the Infanterie-Bataillon 'Schwarzburg' from his second echelon to deploy in skirmish order as well, to the left of those of his first echelon.

While the allied left flank and centre were engaged in fierce skirmisher fighting, the third French column led by Barrois was marching through Haerlebeke. The advance guard consisting of the brigade of d'Arriule (four battalions with artillery and cavalry), in the face of which the I./1. Landwehr-Infanterieregiment was forced to retreat against the overwhelming odds. At that moment *Generalleutnant* von Thielmann arrived at Brause's position. It was clear that his corps was heavily outnumbered by the French who were turning his left flank; Hellwig's *Streifcorps* that ought to be at Belleghem would be much too weak to prevent him from being cut off. With French cavalry squadrons closing in, and as the troops from *Generalleutnant* von Wallmoden and *Generalmajor* von Gablenz were much too far away to provide aid, the only option was an immediate retreat. Brause was ordered to fall back to the position where Prinz Paul von Württemberg had been ordered to deploy, was the artillery sent back to the Windmill Height while two hussar squadrons, led by *Oberst* von Leyser, were sent to the aid of I./1. Landwehr-Infanterieregiment at Haerlebeke. Despite that the French were pressing the 1st Brigade hard, its retreat was executed in an orderly way. First, the II. and III./1. Landwehr-Infanterieregiment forming the second echelon were ordered to fall back to a position left of Sweweghem, to provide cover for the retreat of the skirmishers of Prinz Paul's 2nd Brigade, which by now was completely dispersed as skirmishers. Because of the cavalry threat both Landwehr battalions retreated in *Bataillonsmassen* as these raw men were too untrained to form square and to retreat in that formation. Brause's II. and III./1. Provisorischen Linien-Regiment were much too experienced to panic in the situation they found themselves in. To oppose the numerous French tirailleurs more and more companies were dispersed as skirmishers, until seven companies had been deployed this way. Protected by these skirmishers the Saxons slowly retreated. The French cavalry, including the Mameluks, noticing the retrograde movement, immediately tried to exploit the situation and charged into the skirmish line, taking a number of them prisoner. A brave counterattack by a hussar squadron, led by its leader *Major* von Taubenheim as well as the commander *Oberst* Fürst zu Schönburg in person, threw back the French cavalry, freeing many prisoners. On the right near Haerlebeke the I./1. Landwehr-Infanterieregiment was also in trouble. Most of the Landwehr had now been dispersed in skirmish order to occupy a ditch, in a desperate effort to stop the French. Nearly overwhelmed, its commander *Oberstleutnant* von der Mosel and the other officers were unable to re-form to conduct an orderly retreat. They were saved by the timely arrival of *Oberst* von Leyser, who executed some brilliant charges with his hussars to throw back the French, providing the Landwehr the chance to extricate themselves and to retreat to Sweweghem.

The II. and III./1. Landwehr-Infanterieregiment, retreating in *Bataillonsmassen*, had reached their assigned positions to the left of Sweweghem safely. But when the French closed in they gradually received more and more fire from the French tirailleurs. When the commander of the III./1. Landwehr-Infanterieregiment, *Major* von Könneritz, fell seriously wounded, their courage was put to the test but the battalion held. Finally, they were pulled back from this vulnerable position and deployed again on the other side of Sweweghem, providing cover for the 3. 6-Pfünder Fußbatterie on the Windmill Height. On the other side of the village, the II. and III./1. Provisorischen Linien-Regiment still executed their fighting retreat, slowly falling back. The French skirmishers and artillery directed their attention to a more vulnerable target, the artillery and cuirassiers deployed on the Windmill Height.

In the meantime, *Generalleutnant* von Thielmann had sent several orders to Prinz Paul von Württemberg ordering him to retreat, but he refused, stating that he saw no danger in remaining in his previous position. Despite the odds he continued the unequal skirmisher fight. When he finally realised that he was in real trouble, it was already too late. Dispersing the last men of his close-column Landwehr battalions in skirmishing order his troops fell back through the intersected terrain, trying to keep pace with the French column turning the left flank. At that moment, Prinz Paul von Württemberg was ordered to report in person on the right wing; apparently a polite way to relieve him of his command. The Prinz handed over command to the commander of the 3. Landwehr-Infanterieregiment, *Oberst* von Dierschen, ordering him to continue the fight and to 'maintain the achieved advantages'. Dierschen and the Landwehr officers did their best to maintain order, but after many officers had been wounded or taken prisoner they started to run trying to reach safety in small groups or individually. A vigorous charge by the French 2e Régiment de Chasseurs à Cheval de la Garde led by the *Généraux* Castex and Meuziau did the rest. The remaining officers did their best to rally their troops but in vain as the rout became general and after all three battalion commanders had been wounded or captured by the French the whole infantry of the 2nd Brigade broke and ran. *Oberst* von Dierschen was taken prisoner.

In the centre, Brause had reached the outskirts of Sweweghem where he found the commanding officer of the Infanterie-Bataillon 'Anhalt-Bernburg' with one *Zug* of his battalion only: apparently the only infantry of the 2nd Brigade that had rallied. Collecting his skirmishers again, of which most had completely depleted their cartridges, he left the village to the French and continued his retreat in good order, covered by the cannon of the 3. 6-Pfünder Fußbatterie on the Windmill Height with both cuirassier squadrons in support; all the remaining artillery had already been ordered to retreat as well. After Sweweghem had been captured by the French, they deployed their artillery against this position, concentrating their fire on the Saxon artillery, and sent forward their tirailleurs again. One horse team lost three horses, immobilising the cannon, and at that moment a cavalry attack followed. The Saxon cuirassiers counterattacked and enabled their artillery to retreat, except for the immobilised cannon. With the French cavalry disordered while trying to bring back the captured cannon, the Saxon cuirassiers again attacked, this time supported by a hussar squadron. Close combat followed with the French cavalry, reportedly including some Mameluks of the Imperial Guard, and the gun was recaptured again but not without serious loss: *Oberst* von Thümmel, leading the attack, was badly wounded and would die of his wounds later. The capture of the gun was in vain: without means to bring it away it had to be abandoned again.[24]

The cavalry attacks did buy time though for *Generalmajor* von Brause to reform his brigade and to continue his retreat, covered by the remaining cannon of the 3. 6-Pfünder Fußbatterie, the II. and III./1. Provisorischen Linien-Regiment, the cuirassiers and IV./Husaren-Regiment. The French stopped their attacks and followed at a distance, firing at the rearguard with their artillery. Between Sweweghem and Avelghem, the retreating troops were joined by *Major* Hellwig's *Streifcorps*, returning from Belleghem. Following his orders, Hellwig had tried to capture this village, but before he arrived there he was already engaged by substantial French forces. After his troops had used up all their cartridges, at that same moment he became aware of the retrograde movement of Thielmann's corps, and so ordered the retreat as well:

> We succeeded in pushing back the enemy over Sweweghem. From here I was detached to Belleghem, on the road to Tournay, to push back the enemy from this side as well. Before I arrived here though, the Saxon corps had already been thrown back … Therefore I would, because the enemy now also pushed forward at Belleghem as well, be cut off, and had found no way out for my cavalry in the intersected terrain, if I had not been so vigilant in observing their movements.[25]

---

24 Von Schimpff, *Geschichte des Garde-Reiter-Regiments*, p.363.
25 Quoted in Anon., 'Ueber das Gefecht von Sweweghem am 31. März 1814', in *Militair-Wochenblatt*, Vol. 14 (Berlin: Ernst Siegfried Mittler, 1829), p.4136.

Hellwig managed to retreat safely and joined the Saxons covering their retreat, his Fußjäger Bataillon (*Hauptmann* Kamlah) fighting off the pursuing French. According to Hellwig's diary, *Lieutenant* von Plotho with 70 men executed a bayonet attack against French cavalry which had surrounded some Saxon cavalry. By this bold act, two officers and 30 troopers were set free.[26] *Hauptmann* Kretzschmer further relates: 'It was said that Thielmann had the Hellwig Hussars cut into the fleeing [Saxon Landwehr] battalions to bring them to a halt, but I did not see it myself, but I saw that they ran away in the greatest confusion and suffered a tremendous loss.'[27] Together, the units still formed retreated to Avelghem, to where Prinz Paul von Württemberg also had managed to find his way. Arriving here, he ordered both Landwehr companies of the Infanterie-Bataillon 'Anhalt-Bernburg' that had been left behind here, to collect the numerous fugitives of his brigade. Not surprisingly, these fugitives had no heart for another fight and stayed well clear of the village, continuing their rout partially in the direction of Oudenaerde, a part crossing the Scheldt and running further, some of them not to be stopped before they had reached the Rhine. When Thielmann arrived, he concluded that under the circumstances it was impossible to make a stand here and he ordered to continue the retreat to Oudenaerde.

Some hours before, *Generalleutnant* von Wallmoden had arrived at Oudenaerde with the 1st Brigade of the Russo-German Legion, as well as *Generalmajor* von Gablenz with his troops except for the 2. 12-Pfünder Fußbatterie which had much trouble moving the heavy cannon along the muddy roads. At Oudenaerde the troops were allowed a short rest, waiting for the expected arrival of *Generalleutnant* von Thielmann with his troops to unite for the planned joint attack against the French. At that moment they were alarmed by a Saxon officer, his horse covered with foam, reporting that Thielmann's corps had been completely defeated at Sweweghem and was retiring to Oudenaerde in total disorder. Immediately the troops were mustered and resumed their march. Soon they encountered fleeing Landwehr, carts and wagons blocking the road. About a kilometre in front of Oudenaerde, near Elsegem, the troops deployed: the 1st Brigade of the Legion to the left of the road with an artillery battery deployed in front to receive the French; Gablenz to the right of the road:

> Now the eye was offered a very unpleasant spectacle. The troops of Thielmann's corps consisted almost exclusively of Landwehr, most of whom had not yet fired a shot, when in the morning they came in contact with the veterans of General Maison; they were soon overrun, and the disorder in which they found themselves is hardly to be described. Only a few squadrons of cavalry and one line battalion were still formed; everything else ran in heaps of 10 to 20 men on and beside the road, and only in Oudenaerde and behind the Scheldt they managed to collect them again. They gave the striking proof of how dangerous it

---

26 (F.W. von Mauvillon), 'Tagebuch des Hellwigschen Partisanen-Corps, von dessen Entstehung bis zu seiner Auflösung, mit einigen Bruchstücken aus dem Leben des Anführers', in *Militairische Blätter*, Vol. 1 (Essen and Duisburg: G.D. Bädeker, 1820), p.147.
27 Kretzschmer, *Soldaten-Leben*, p.218.

is to expose raw troops, which have good will but not the habit of discipline, in the open field to a serious attack, where a firm attitude must give the protection against a penetration, which should provide wall and ditch.[28]

28 Von Quistorp, *Die Kaiserlich Russisch-Deutsche Legion*, p.229.

8

Tournay

Another allied detachment had been on the march this day to join the Allied concentration at Oudenaerde. After the recapture of Ghent, *Generalmajor* Graf von Lottum's detachment with some Cossacks had marched over Deinze along the road to Courtray. Arriving at Haerlebeke in the afternoon, fighting here was already long over and they found the place occupied by a French detachment of about three hundred men. Supported by *Rittmeister* von Simolin's squadron, the 1st squadron (*Premierlieutenant Graf* zu Dohna II.) of the 1. Husaren-Regiment of the Russo-German Legion charged the French, pushing them back under the walls of Courtray. At that moment Lottum's jäger companies arrived, which after some skirmishing pushed the French back into Courtray itself. With darkness falling, outposts were placed in front of the gates, but during the night the French evacuated Courtray and returned to Lille, pursued by the Cossacks.

The French, which had lost about 300 killed or wounded during the engagement, had ended their pursuit of *Generalleutnant* von Thielmann's corps at Avelghem, so the troops deployed at Elsegem were not engaged. *Général de Division* Maison had ordered *Général de Division* Barrois to pursue the retreating allies with his division. Leaving behind an infantry regiment, the Gendarmes d'Elite à Cheval and the 2e Régiment de Chevau-Légers Lanciers de la Garde to occupy Courtray, he advanced with the remainder of I Corps along the road to Tournay: Solignac's division forming the advance guard, followed by Roguet's Young Guard division. Expecting that most allied troops had been in the field and were beaten, he believed he had a good chance of capturing the now weakly held place with a *coup de main*.

Thielmann's corps had not been completely broken by the fighting but he suffered a major defeat and heavy losses as a result, totalling about 1,900 men. The losses of the infantry and cavalry are of interest as it shows the fierceness of the fighting as well as the disintegration of the 2nd Brigade. Loss of *Generalmajor* von Brause's 1st Brigade was:

> II. and III./1. Provisorischen Linien-Regiment: 10 men killed; battalion commander *Major* von Eychelberg and 69 others wounded; battalion commander *Major* von Wittern, 1 officer and 99 others prisoner/ missing.

1. Landwehr-Infanterieregiment: 58 men killed; battalion commander *Major* von Könneritz, 4 officers and 103 others wounded; 1 officer and 232 others prisoner/missing.

Freiwillige Jäger zu Fuß 'Anhalt'; 1 officer and 2 others wounded.

Husaren-Regiment: 2 men killed; 9 men wounded; 2 officers and 4 others prisoner/missing.

The loss of *Generalmajor Prinz* Paul von Württemberg's 2nd Brigade:

3. Landwehr-Infanterieregiment: 2 officers and 146 others killed; all 3 battalion commanders (*Major* von Zimmermann, *Major* von Elterlein and *Major* von Kommerstaedt), 5 officers and 210 others wounded; its commander *Oberst* Dierschen, 12 officers and 794 others prisoner/missing. As a result of the losses suffered, 3. Landwehr-Infanterieregiment was reduced to two battalions.

Infanterie-Bataillon 'Anhalt-Bernburg': 9 men killed; 1 officer and 9 others wounded; 8 men prisoner/missing.

Infanterie-Bataillon 'Schwarzburg': 22 men killed; 8 men wounded; 1 officer and 56 others prisoner/missing.

Kürassier-Regiment: 1 officer and 4 others killed; the commander *Oberst* von Thümmel and 11 others wounded; 1 men missing.

Oberst von Thümmel would die on 8 April from the wounds suffered this day. In addition, the 3. 6-Pfünder Fußbatterie had to abandon one of its cannon as described in the previous chapter.

The biographer of *Generalleutnant* von Thielmann, von Hüttel, states that the peril that Thielmann found himself in was caused by the early retreat of *Major* Hellwig. He relates about this event that 'the Division Barrois etc. turned the left flank totally uncovered by the 'unexpected' retreat of Hellwig's Corps to Oudenaerde, attacking the brigade of *Generalmajor* Prinz Paul von Württemberg successfully.'[1] This representation of facts is not in accordance with the various reports. *Major* Hellwig's retreat, as described, did not go further than the road between Sweweghem and Avelghem were he joined Thielmann's rearguard. The retreat of Thielmann's corps was already in progress when *Major* Hellwig retreated from Belleghem. So it seems that von Hüttel is covering up the mistake made by Thielmann of attacking the French with his corps without waiting for support. Thielmann himself was clearer about the causes of his defeat in his after action report (1) and an additional report (2), although not prepared to take the whole responsibility for his defeat, also blaming the Prinz Paul von Württemberg:

(1) As I am terrified myself about the magnitude of the loss, I only plea Your Highness to believe that half of the missing people are on their way home … With the Landwehr, the mistake is that several battalions are completely without officers who have served. With such troops one risks his whole honour … The cavalry has done more than one can expect: I am not in the position of proposing to Your Highness some officers to distinguish, for the affair was unfortunate.

---

1 Anon., 'Ueber das Gefecht von Sweweghem', pp.4136-4137.

(2) The striking disproportion of the loss of *Generalmajor* von Brause, who commanded the vanguard, and was thus in fact fighting the enemy, to that of Prinz Paul on my left wing, is the key to the narrative of the day, noting that the vanguard would have lost scarcely the third part of what it really lost, if it had not been obliged to engage itself more seriously than planned, to protect that left wing from being wiped out … This day I have to thank only to the inexperienced bravura and ill-considered use of the new battalions, of course, the wretchedness of the troops has also contributed much to this.[2]

So, Thielmann was not satisfied about the behaviour of the 3. Landwehr-Infanterieregiment and the German battalions of his 2nd Brigade. His judgment of the Landwehr is not fair. These men were newly raised and untrained, marching straight into battle on their arrival. Their ranks counted only few experienced officers and despite the fact that the men were willing enough, they were badly clothed and armed, without any necessary training and discipline. It was a mistake to disperse them in skirmishing order, as is illustrated by the disastrous result. Their subsequent rout contrasts with the behaviour of their fellow Landwehr men in the 1st Brigade, which were held together in *Bataillonsmassen*, supported by line skirmishers, artillery, and cavalry, and remained steady under fire and while facing cavalry attacks. Thielmann himself was involved in raising these troops in Saxony, and so knew about their lack of training, equipment, cartridges and so forth.

Generalmajor von Brause's after action report gives the hussars their well-deserved praise:

> The Husaren-Regiment behaved consistently well and worthy of its old fame, and the squadron of *Major* von Taubenheim, and especially the company of *Rittmeister* von Lindemann, owes the line infantry – and perhaps the whole – that there was no greater loss; for the enemy cavalry, after the retreat had begun, charged into the mentioned infantry with much impudence, and was thrown back only by the resolute turning about and charge of the squadron Taubenheim, at the head of which the *Fürst* von Schönburg had placed himself. This attack was decisive, and by it many infantrymen that had been taken prisoner were freed.[3]

Prinz Paul von Württemberg

Although there were grounds for blaming Prinz Paul von Württemberg for the debacle, it was Thielmann who was in command and who made the decision to engage the French. As it was, the way Prinz Paul von Württemberg had handled his troops at Sweweghem was the last act sealing his fate as a commander in III German Corps. Prinz Paul was a relative of Emperor Alexander. During the armistice mid 1813 he had left his family, his father still a fervent ally of Napoleon, and had entered Russian service. By

---

2   After action report of 3 April 1814 (1) and additional report of 3 April 1814 (2) from *Generalleutnant* von Thielmann to the Duke of Saxe-Weimar, quoted in Bucher, *Der Feldzug*, pp.204-205; Albrecht Graf von Holtzendorff, *Beiträge zu der Biographie des Generals Freiherrn von Thielmann und zur Geschichte der jüngst vergangenen Zeit* (Leipzig: Wilhelm Rauck, 1830), p.148.

3   After action report from *Generalmajor* von Brause to *Generalleutnant* von Thielmann, in Holtzendorff, *Beiträge zu der Biographie*, pp.148-149.

his own request the prince had received command of the Anhalt-Thuringian Division. There were problems with the young and inexperienced prince from the start, although not surprisingly most contemporary sources refrain from mentioning his mistakes at all or do not mention the Prinz by name. Nevertheless, the amount of evidence is substantial. On his march to the Low Countries he ordered much too long and fatiguing marches, resulting in the loss of 250 men out of 3,500 who could not keep up. Arriving at Lippstadt, the men of the Infanterie-Bataillon 'Gotha' were ordered to cross the swollen Lippe river at night, having to wade through the ice cold and swollen water up to their breast. Not surprisingly, next morning several men were missing, apparently drowned during the crossing during darkness. Others fell sick. Then there was the incident at the French-held fortress-city Venlo:

> … which, as at least in the brigade was the general belief, Prinz Paul wanted to try to capture by a *coup de main* or even by a fierce storm. In fact, the battalions were placed in such tight quarters around the fortress that they could be concentrated quickly, and that circumstance, as well as a puzzling brigade order, increased the belief in the impending storming of the fortress. But the night before, the Prinz was ordered by the Duke of Weimar to march as quickly as possible over Hasselt, St. Tron, Tirlemont and Louvain to Brussels, to where he set off without delay and which was reached on the 26th of February.[4]

After his arrival, several serious incidents occurred of various kinds, with Prinz Paul failing to maintain order amongst his troops, stating that he treated the region as enemy territory and making requisitions as such. On 8 March, the cause unknown, a strong argument rose between de commanding officer of the Saxon Grenadiers, *Oberst* Prinz Bernhard von Sachsen-Weimar and Prinz Paul:

> And here it seems to have come to a very violent scene between Prince Bernhard and Prince Paul of Württemberg. The latter, by his presumptuous conduct, had given rise to all sorts of complaints in the preceding days. The repugnance of the ineffective standing around had increased Bernhard's bad temper; it took only a spark to light the powder keg. A new encroachment by Prince Paul brought about the explosion, and the violence of our prince broke loose with all his terrible power. There was a very lively exchange of words, the end of which would have led without the mediation of others to the most blatant consequences. Finally, at midnight, Prince Bernhard in a letter to the General Command demanded a recall from the Thuringian-Anhalt Division.[5]

On 9 March, the Duke of Saxe-Weimar reprimanded Prinz Paul in a letter, apparently not with the expected result, as on the 15th it was followed by a second one:

---

4 Hauptmann Gustav Jacobs, *Geschichte der Feldzüge und Schicksale der Sachsen-Gotha-Altenburgischen Krieger in den Jahren 1807-1815* (Altenburg: Expedition des Eremiten, 1835), p.314.
5 Starkloff, *Das Leben des Herzogs Bernhard*, pp.146-147.

Let me remind Your Royal Highness, in view of the inconveniences that have already occurred, coupled with the bad reports about your military conduct, that I, as commanding General in Russian Service, have the right, according to the Imperial supreme regulation, to remove every subordinate general, whose conduct may contribute to the disadvantage of the Army Corps, immediately from the Army Corps subordinated to him. *Generalleutnant* von Thielmann is instructed to report to me about Your Royal Highness's behaviour in the service.[6]

On 13 March, the Duke of Saxe-Weimar had written to his wife about the prince: 'Prince Paul behaves so infamously, that I will drive him out of the army on the first day (sic!), he has no shadow of military knowledge, and behaves like a beggar letting his people steal for his own.'[7] On the 26th, he wrote: 'Prince Paul is with Thielmann, so I do not see him anymore.'[8] About the debacle at Sweweghem, the Duke would write to his wife: 'Then the brave Schwarzburg contingent and a few Saxon Landwehr battalions, who to be honest, had lost their commanders, threw away their arms and packs, and fled in utter confusion, even without shoes … '.[9] So the fact that the young prince was sent away after the engagement at Sweweghem is no surprise. He was succeeded by *Oberst* von Egloffstein, while Prinz Paul von Württemberg departed for the headquarters of the allied sovereigns. Unfortunately, it was not only Prinz Paul von Württemberg's troops who plundered, extorted and robbed the population. Already mentioned are Bikhalov's Cossacks, the citizens of Ghent even begging the Duke to replace these by other troops. There are however reports of many other units, for example of the Russo-German Legion, as well of the 4. Reserve- or Elb-Infanterie-Regiment which was in *Generalleutnant* von Borstell's Prussian 5th Division.[10]

Karl Bernhard of Sachsen-Weimar-Eisenach. (Rijksmuseum)

The Defence of Tournay

Général de Division Maison was elated about his victory at Sweweghem. He had inflicted heavy loss on the Allies and believed they were in no state to fight again for a while. With his hands free, he decided to try to capture Tournay by a *coup de main*. Tournay is situated on the Scheldt, which at that time divided the city exactly in two. That also gave it strategically importance, as an allied bridgehead on the left bank of the Scheldt. Also on the left bank

6   Letter of 15 March 1814 from the Duke of Saxe-Weimar to *Generalmajor Prinz* Paul von Württemberg, quoted in Egloffstein, *Carl August*, pp.64-65.
7   Letter of 13 March 1814 from the Duke of Saxe-Weimar to his wife, in Egloffstein, *Carl August*, pp.63, 146-148.
8   Letter of 26 March 1814 from the Duke of Saxe-Weimar to his wife, in Egloffstein, *Carl August*, pp.152-154.
9   Letter of 2 April 1814 from the Duke of Saxe-Weimar to his wife, quoted in Egloffstein, *Carl August*, p.93.
10   Egloffstein, *Carl August*, p.219.

a citadel was situated, consisting of five bastions, although nearly completely razed down. Although somewhat in decay it was still a formidable defence work, dominating the city. The defences of the city itself consisted of a medieval brick wall with half round turrets. This had later been changed in an earthen wall by throwing up ground on the inner side. In addition, modern earthen outer works had been added to the defences, but there was only a ditch at the lower parts of the terrain. The city had three gates on the right bank of the Scheldt, four on the left bank. The latter were Porte de Valenciennes; Porte de Martin; Porte de Lille; and Porte de Courtray or Sept Fontaines. All these gates were arched over, except for the Porte de Sept Fontaines, which had an open entrance protected by a small earthen traverse erected by the Saxons. The defences had further been repaired as well, under supervision of *Hauptmann* Blödterll of the *Generalstab*. Inside the city, a number of stone bridges across the Scheldt connected both sides of the city. To defend the city and citadel against a formal siege, an estimated 10,000 men with 100 guns would be necessary. It had been estimated however that three infantry battalions and a field artillery battery would suffice to protect the city against a *coup de main*. When pressed hard, these would retreat into the citadel.

The troops at Tournay were commanded by *Oberst* von Egloffstein and consisted of three battalions of the Anhalt-Thuringian Division (Infanterie-Bataillon 'Gotha' and both battalions of the Infanterie-Regiment 'Anhalt-Dessau-Köthen'), 30 hussars of IV. Squadron, the nucleus of the 4e Régiment 'de Namur' of the *Légion Belge* (*Colonel* Marquis de Trazegnies d'Ittre) and four 9-pdr cannon of the 'Belgian' battery (*Souslieutenant* Verwaert), about 2,100 men in all. They had just been reinforced by I/1. Provisorischen Linien-Regiment that had been sent by *Generalleutnant* von Thielmann just before the engagement at Sweweghem.

Oberst von Egloffstein had left Tournay with the greater part of the troops at his disposal, to demonstrate in the direction of Courtray as had been ordered by Thielmann. He had taken up positions near Marquain and Pecq during the morning of the 31st. When the French troops approached early in the afternoon, commanded by *Général de Division* Maison himself, Egloffstein found himself heavily outnumbered, especially by the French cavalry. He therefore had no other option then a hasty retreat back to the city. Arriving here, he took the necessary defensive measures with the troops at his disposal. Both battalions of the Infanterie-Regiment 'Anhalt-Dessau-Köthen' occupied the walls on the sides of the city an attack was to be expected. The 1st company of the 'Infanterie-Bataillon 'Gotha' occupied the citadel, while initially the remainder of this battalion remained in reserve on the market place along with I./1. Provisorischen Linien-Regiment, which would give heart to the raw soldiers of the other battalions by its steadiness. The four 9-pdr cannon of the 'Belgian' 9-pdr battery had been placed on several bastions.

Around 5:00 p.m. Maison arrived before the fortress. After a short reconnaissance the French advance guard commanded by *Général de Division* Solignac attacked in column immediately, their attack directed at the Porte de Sept Fontaines and Porte de Lille gates. Without having any ladders or other means to scale the wall or to force the gates, the French suffered severe losses from the infantry on the walls and the few cannon. After this attack had failed, the French deployed their artillery against the fortress. While howitzers threw their shells inside, two cannon specifically fired at the Porte de Lille to prepare for a second attack. In the meantime, their infantry collected ladders from the houses and nearby villages and prepared to storm the fortress a second time. Then they charged again, this time their attacks directed at all four gates on this side of the Scheldt. But again the attack was beaten off, and so was a third attack, by the defending Infanterie-Regiment 'Anhalt-Dessau-Köthen' ably commanded by *Oberst* Hoppe. After most companies had completely ran out of cartridges, during four hours of continuous fighting, they were relieved by the Infanterie-Bataillon 'Gotha' supported by a division of the I./1. Provisorischen Linien-Regiment, which continued the fight until night fell. During the fighting a young infantry officer of Saxe-Weimar arrived with a small command. He had been escorting some wagons when he heard the noise of the fighting and joined the fight with his men on the left flank. Next to arrive were four guns of the Prussian 6-Pfünder Reitende Batterie No. 11. This battery was on the march to *Generalleutnant* von Borstell's division on the right bank of the Scheldt, when it also heard the noise of the fighting. On his own account, its commander changed direction and marched to Tournay as well, but it arrived too late to take part in the fighting.

Until now only Solignac's division had attacked Tournay as Roguet's division, exhausted from the previous fighting, marched slowly and as a result arrived much later. By then it was clear to Maison that his efforts were in vain and he limited his attacks now to bombarding the city, causing much damage. During the night, even more Allied reinforcements arrived; around 9:00 p.m. a squadron of the Prussian Pommersches Husaren-Regiment and next morning around 4:00 a.m. the first units of *Generalmajor* von Gablenz' corps. Gablenz had set off at 10:00 p.m. and marched the whole night along the right bank of the Scheldt river, via Leuze, to come to the aid of Tournay. By then the French had already left. Maison had ended his bombardment around 11.30 p.m. and, receiving news about the imminent arrival of substantial allied reinforcements, around 3:00 a.m. he retreated to Lille, having lost about 300 men dead and wounded. Barrois was ordered to retreat to Lille as well, covering with his division the retreat of the Gendarmes d'Elite à Cheval guarding the prisoners, the park and baggage from Courtray. So Maison totally failed to take any advantage of his crushing victory over *Generalleutnant* von Thielmann's corps at Sweweghem. The allies lost only few men in Tournay.

The after-action report from *Oberst* von Egloffstein has more interesting details about the French attack:

> The commandant of the place *Hauptmann* von Hartitsch, on behalf of me, already reported to Your Excellency yesterday evening that the enemy had attacked the city of Tournay yesterday, as the 31st of March, in the afternoon on all points of the left bank of the Scheldt. After the battle was over, and after the troops under my command have been fortunate to repulse three fierce assaults, I feel obliged to report Your Excellency most obediently the details of this battle.
>
> Upon receiving Your order that I should make a strong sortie against Marquin, to position myself on the height on that side, and to restore the boat-bridge at

Raminies, I sent the hussar *Leutnant* von Ziegler to Your Excellency on the road to Courtray, with the message that the enemy had withdrawn from Marquin, and was no longer visible at the distance of a mile from the city; but scarcely had this officer left the city on the Courtray road for about 1 1/2 hour, when he saw significant columns of cavalry and infantry moving on this road towards Courtray. The report which I had received, I decided to march towards the enemy on the road from here to Courtray with the greater part of the garrison and 2 cannon. Very soon I met enemy cavalry, forcing me to return to the city both by the great superiority of the enemy as well as the poor horse teams and immobility of my cannon.

The enemy followed me closely, and I had barely reached the city when he already attacked the Sept Fontaines gate. About half-past five o'clock this attack had spread to all the gates on the left bank of the Scheldt, and the enemy set up batteries against the Lille and Sept Fontaines gates; and especially undertook against the Lille gate, with a bravura not to be denied him, three assaults, which however were beaten of every time by the bravery of our troops. The bombardment of the city lasted until about half-past eleven o'clock at night, and the town suffered much by several hundred entering cannon balls. Our loss in dead and wounded is very insignificant; the enemy, on the other hand, lost about 300 men; on his retreat he did not take so much time to take his wounded with him, and early this morning I had a large number of them, some of them in the moat, admitted to the hospital. Now, at seven o'clock in the morning, there is nothing at all to be seen of the enemy near the city, but I will undertake reconnaissance's at several points. According to the prisoners, *Général de Division* Maison has commanded the assaults in person; he had about 6,000 men, with six howitzers and two cannon.

The troops under my command have fought with great bravery. I recommend to Your Excellency, in particular, *Oberst* Hoppe and *Hauptmann* von Hartitsch, commandant of Tournay, who with great bravery and skill repulsed the attacks on the Sept Fontaines gate. In addition, the mere presence of the Royal Saxon Line Battalion of the 1st Regiment has greatly contributed to the lucky outcome of this battle, as our young people have put their complete faith in the support of these old and brave warriors.

I conclude, quite obediently, that part of the enemy column was provided with ladders, and that the newly-raised Belgian artillery displayed great proof of its courage and enthusiasm.[11]

Oberst Hoppe, commander of the Infanterie-Regiment 'Anhalt-Dessau-Köthen', would receive the Russian Order of St. Anna for his defence of Tournay. *Generalleutnant* von Thielmann issued a special order of the day, praising the brave behaviour of the troops at Tournay.

---

11 After action report of 1 April 1814 from *Oberst* Egloffstein to the Duke of Saxe-Weimar, in Egloffstein, *Carl August*, pp.156-158.

9

The End of the Campaign

After having occupied Courtray, on 1 April, *Generalmajor* Graf von Lottum returned to Ghent with his detachment and the Cossacks. The 1. Husaren-Regiment of the Russo-German Legion returned to Wallmoden's 1st. Brigade. Early on that same day Thielmann marched from Oudenaerde to Tournay with his whole corps. *Generalleutnant* von Wallmoden took up positions with the 1st Brigade of the Russo-German Legion between Alost and Oudenaerde. On 3 April *Oberstleutnant* von Thümen left to join *Generalleutnant* von Borstell's division with his Pommerschen Husaren-Regiment, but this was not such a big loss anymore since the arrival of the Russo-German Legion. The Duke however had to remain on his guard, as there was another important development. On 2 April he had received a letter from the commander of IV German Corps, Kurprinz Wilhelm von Hessen-Kassel, with very disturbing news. Simultaneous with Maison's advance to Ghent, *Général de Division* Durutte, although blockaded by the Russians, had managed to leave Metz with a strong column. Reinforced by part of the garrisons of Saarlouis and Thionville, he had forced the blockading corps of the latter fortress back to Luxembourg. Then he continued his march west via Longwy. The Kurprinz said that it was assumed that Durutte would try to join the French main army under Napoleon. The Duke of Saxe-Weimar and Wallmoden agreed with this opinion, believing that about 20,000 French were concentrating near Avesnes, south of Maubeuge.

To counter this threat the Duke of Saxe-Weimar concentrated his troops and also decided to keep Wallmoden's Russo-German Legion with him instead of sending it to General Graham, the Duke writing to Graham: 'This scheme inspired us to assemble between Mons and Tournay all the forces available in Belgium, in order to oppose the projects of the enemy and to thwart them by some enterprises.'[1] Graham replied that he completely agreed with this plan, also because with the departure of *Général de Division* Roguet's Young Guard division from Antwerp the threat from that side had diminished, and the 2. Brigade of the Russo-German Legion was relieved by the Prussian 1. Westphälische Landwehr-Infanterie-Regiment (three battalions and a Freiwillige Fußjäger detachment) and I./2. Westphälische

---

1   Letter in French of 2 April 1814 from the Duke of Saxe-Weimar to General Graham, quoted in Egloffstein, *Carl August*, p.97.

Landwehr-Infanterie-Regiment, all under the command of *Oberstleutnant* Rüchel with a strength of 65/2,796 and already idle at Lier for some time. On 3 April news was received that these troops finally would be placed under the orders of the Duke of Saxe-Weimar. Coming from the Prussian Reserve Corps in Westphalia, commanded by Prinz Ludwig von Hessen-Homburg, they would replace the three battalions of the 4. Reserve- or Elb-Infanterie-Regiment which would march to Mons via Brussels in order to re-join Bülow's Prussian III Corps. The troops blockading Antwerp had also been reinforced by a Dutch artillery battery which had left Breda on 22 March. To remedy the lack of cavalry, Graham added the 3rd Hussar Regiment of the King's German Legion to Rüchel's infantry. At the same time though, Graham wrote to Major General Taylor:

> [2 April] You will see by Walmoden's letter sent to Lord Clancarty what a bad hand General Thielman has made of his attack on Maison. It appears too that Maison will be at the head of a formidable corps which, well managed, will keep that frontier in a constant state of alarm. I am forced on this account to suspend the projected operation against Batz which I had settled should be conducted by Major General Gibbs; I foresee that it will be almost hopeless to expect any assistance in the blockade of Antwerp from Walmoden …
>
> [3 April] have letters from the Duke of Saxe Weimar and Wallmoden of which I send you copies which will all elucidate the subject on which you will have to report to Lord Bathurst. I shall write to Walmoden to say that, fully sensible of the superior importance of watching the enemy's movements, I approve of his remaining on the frontier. But I write at the same time to the Duke of Saxe Weimar to say that I cannot continue to furnish troops for the occupation of that post of Lier, which being for the purpose of their own communications they must make arrangements to protect and that in a few days I shall recall the two Dutch battalions sent there on the spur of this occasion. Meanwhile, the garrison of Antwerp, weak as it is, will have the command of the country almost entirely as far as the Nether, and entirely so of the rich country on the left of the Scheldt, so that the reduction of the place by blockade, now the numbers of the garrison is reduced, is very hopeless … [2]

Finally, there came the news that the Dutch efforts in raising an army made good progress and that they were forming a mobile army corps of 20,000, organised in two divisions of two brigades each, between Breda and 's Hertogenbosch: On 11 April the hereditary Prince of Orange would resume command of 20 infantry battalions (including a battalion from the Duchy of Nassau taken into Dutch pay), two dragon squadrons and one of hussars, and three artillery batteries.[3] Although not all of these units were ready to do battle and for the moment could only be used for auxiliary duties, at least about 11,500 men (six line, three *jager* and nine militia battalions) were ready for battle. For now, the Duke reorganised the troops at his disposal and shifted them east, with *Generalleutnant* Wallmoden resuming command

---

2 Letters of 2 and 3 April 1814 from General Graham to Major General Taylor, in Taylor, *The Taylor Papers*, p.159.
3 Koolemans Beijnen, *Historisch Gedenkboek*, Vol. 1, pp.222-223.

of the reserve consisting of his Russo-German Legion and *Generalmajor* von Gablenz' troops.[4]

Generalleutnant von Thielmann marched from Oudenaerde to Tournay with his corps. Hellwig remained at Oudenaerde with his *Streifcorps*, patrolling up to Courtray. *Generalmajor* von Lottum returned to Brussels, taking with him the 3rd squadron of the Brandenburgschen Dragoner-Regiment. The Landwehr-Bataillon 'Weimar' and Landwehr-Bataillon 'Gotha' remained in Ghent as garrison. While these movements took place, also on the 3rd, the Duke of Saxe-Weimar received a letter from Blücher (sent 31 March) about the capture of Paris by the allies and the hope for a swift end of the war. Of course, the news was received with joy and on the 4th a parade was held in Brussels to celebrate the event, but there still was no peace and French troops were still on the move. On the 4th it was reported that *Général de Division* Maison had marched south from Lille with his whole I Corps. The next day new intelligence was received, that Maison had turned southeast to Valenciennes, reportedly with a force of 8,000 infantry, 1,200 cavalry and 23 guns. This news was linked to the aforementioned report about *Général de Division* Durutte, maybe in connection with an effort from Napoleon to push north. During the evening of the 6th, cavalry patrols brought more news; that Maison had left Valenciennes and marched in the direction of Cambray or Douay. Based on these reports the Duke believed that Maison was marching to Paris: 'Just today it became clear that General Maison marches with about 13 to 14 thousand men and 60 pieces of cannon over Cambray and Douay to Paris.'[5] A few hours later a letter arrived from Emperor Alexander (sent 30 March, so just before the attack on Paris), ordering the Duke to attack Maison immediately:

> Our armies are before Paris, to-morrow we shall attack, with the hope of success. As our line of communications is now being established on the Soissons and Compiegne roads, it is of the greatest consequence that these should be kept open. General Bülow has been appointed to this service; but as the forces he has now under his orders are insufficient, it is His Majesty's pleasure that, without losing a moment, you should detach General Borstell to his aid, with all the troops which belong to Bülow's corps. It is likewise the Emperor's wish that you should begin to act vigorously on the offensive, as it is said in the reports of the minister-of-war to Napoleon, which have just been intercepted, that General Maison, having not more than 5,000 men under his command, is in great fear of being attacked by you.[6]

As already described the situation was totally different: *Generalleutnant* von Borstell had already left on the explicit order of Blücher, Maison was much stronger than stated in the Emperor's letter and Paris had already been captured. Nevertheless the threat was real and the Duke of Saxe-Weimar

---

4   See Appendix IV.

5   Letter of 7 April 1814 from the Duke of Saxe-Weimar to General Volkonsky, quoted in Egloffstein, *Carl August*, p.224.

6   Letter of 30 March 1814 from General Volkonsky to the Duke of Saxe-Weimar, in English in Mikhailofsky-Danilefsky, A., *History of the Campaign in France, in the Year 1814* (London: Smith, Elder, and Co. Cornhill, 1839), pp.342-343.

immediately started his preparations to march south. His quick decision was being aided by Bernadotte who, returning to Liège, totally unexpectedly had announced the dispatch of a Swedish corps to join the Duke. It would consist of two infantry brigades, a cavalry division and a battery of 6 guns, commanded by *Generallöjtnant* Baron de Boye. The first measure the Duke took was sending Colonel Rebejev's Cossack Regiment after Maison to shadow his movements at least to Douay. Then the various parts of III German Corps were put in motion for an advance south:

- Leaving behind the Anhalt-Thuringian Brigade (except the Infanterie-Regiment 'Anhalt-Dessau-Köthen') and the 'Belgian' 9-pdr battery to garrison Tournay until the Swedish troops would arrive, *Generalleutnant* von Thielmann marched to a new position near Bury, north of Condé;
- *Generalmajor* von Gablenz marched with his troops from Ath to Beloeil;
- *Generalleutnant* von Wallmoden with the Russo-German Legion marched from Lessines to Ath;
- *Generalleutnant* von Le Coq marched from Mons to Bavay.

No fighting however would follow: after receiving the news of the allied capture of Paris, *Général de Division* Maison returned to Lille. Here he received on 9 April news about Napoleon's abdication. The Duke of Saxe-Weimar had received through General Volkonsky an order to be forwarded to Maison, from the minister of war of the new French government, to stop all hostilities immediately and to treat his opponents as allies. Also on the 9th at 2:00 p.m. a meeting took place at the village Pont-a-Treffin, between Maison and *Generalleutnant* von Thielmann. At the start of this meeting, the above order was forwarded to Maison. A temporary truce was agreed upon, over the following days followed by additional truces with the French garrisons in the various fortresses. On the 13th the British General Graham would also close a truce with Carnot in Antwerp. On 12 April, a demarcation line was agreed upon. This line started at Landrecies, following the Sambre to Maubeuge and then along the border of the French *Département du Nord* via Menin, to the sea between Ostend and Blankenberghe. The next day prisoners were exchanged: 19 Allied officers and 463 others returned, the latter mostly from the 3. Landwehr-Infanterieregiment which has suffered so much during the battle of Sweweghem. For the time being, III German Corps moved to cantonments in the southern Netherlands. The four Freiwillige Jäger zu Fuß companies of the Saxon Duchies were also allowed to return home: as these consisted mostly of young students, according to the Duke it was more profitable if they could continue their studies as soon as possible. For III German Corps the war had ended, but not without cost. During the fighting of the previous weeks it had lost 4 officers and 294 others killed; 28 officers and 519 others wounded.

Aftermath

Although the fighting had ended, still more reinforcements were on their way to join III German Corps, a column commanded by *Generalmajor* von Bose:

I./3. Provisorischen Linien-Regiment
I./2. Leichten Infanterie-Regiment
5. Landwehr-Infanterieregiment
6. Landwehr-Infanterieregiment
Uhlans (½ 4th squadron) (85)
Hussars (½ 4th squadron and 5th squadron) (173)
2. 6-Pfünder Fußbatterie (6 cannon, 2x 8-pdr howitzers, *Hauptmann* Knauth)
2nd Mobile Park
Reinforcements for the infantry and cavalry

Around this time they had reached Coblenz, were their march was halted regarding the circumstances. It was decided to let I./3. Provisorischen Linien-Regiment and both Landwehr regiments remain in Coblenz, while the remaining troops would continue their march to the southern Netherlands to join III German Corps. On 21 April, the Duke of Saxe-Weimar handed over command to *Generalleutnant* von Thielmann and left for Paris. Early May, *Generalmajor* von Gablenz marched home with all Landwehr units, Saxon as well as those of the Saxon Duchies, as well as the volunteers. As the future of Saxony still had to be decided, it was believed advisable not to let the line troops of III German Corps return to Saxony for now so they marched mid-June to the Aachen region. These troops would make history again when they revolted on their partition when part of Saxony was ceded to Prussia.

Appendix I

Composition and Strength III German Corps, 3 January 1814[1]

Generalstab (19/7):

Commander in Chief: General of Cavalry Herzog von Sachsen-Weimar-
   Eisenach

Aide de Camp: *Oberst* Ziegler von Kliphausen

Chef of the General Staff: *Generalmajor Freiherr* von Wolzogen

Chef of the General Quartermaster Staff: *Oberstleutnant* von Aster

Generalleutnant von Le Coq

Staff officer 'du jour': *Oberst* von Zeschwitz

Intendant of the Mobile Corps: *Hauptmann* von Nostitz

Stabsdragoner (squadron, *Leutnant* von Rechenberg) (-/69)

Commander of the artillery: *Oberstleutnant* Raabe

Commander of the foot artillery brigade: *Major* Gau

Commander of the horse artillery brigade: *Major* von Roth

1. Infanterie-Brigade (*Generalmajor* von Ryssel)

1. Provisorischen Linien-Regiment (*Major* von Wittern, later *Oberst* von
   Einsiedel)
   II. Bataillon (*Major* von Eychelberg) (14/487)
   III. Bataillon (18/665)

Bataillon Füsiliere des Herzogs zu Sachsen-Weimar (*Major* von Linker)
   (14/729)[2]

II./2. Leichten Infanterie-Regiment (*Major* von Selmitz) (12/523)[3]

1. 6-Pfünder Fußbatterie (6 cannon, 2x 8-pdr howitzers, *Hauptmann*
   Rouvroy II.) (4/170)

1. Mobile Park (4/138)

2. Infanterie-Brigade (vacant)

2. Provisorischen Linien-Regiment (*Major* von Brand, 24 March *Oberst*
   von Seydewitz)

---

1   Strengths given are combatants present, divided in officers/others.
2   For the time being attached to the 2. Leichten Infanterie-Regiment.
3   The Leichten Infanterie-Regiment is also referred to as Schützen Regiment

II. Bataillon (14/584)

III. Bataillon (*Major* Moritz) (14/578)

1. Leichten Infanterie-Regiment (*Major* von Rade, later *Oberstleutnant* von Bose)

    I. Bataillon (12/436)

    II. Bataillon (9/435)

Jäger Bataillon (*Major* von Jeschki) (10/396)

1. 12-Pfünder Fußbatterie (6 cannon, 2x 8-pdr howitzers, *Hauptmann* Rouvroy I.) (4/200)

Infanterie-Reserve

Provisorisches Garde-Regiment (*Oberst* Prinz Karl Bernhard von Sachsen-Weimar)

    I. Gardebataillon (*Hauptmann* von Jeschki, later *Major* von Römer) (18/672)

    II. Grenadier-Bataillon (*Major* von Wolframsdorf) (20/692)

    III. Grenadier-Bataillon (*Oberstleutnant* von Anger) (15/657)

Cavalry-Brigade (9 squadrons) (*Generalmajor* von Gablenz)

Kürassier-Regiment (3 squadrons, *Oberst* von Berge/*Oberst* von Thümmel) (31/469)

Uhlanen-Regiment (3 squadrons, volunteer *Oberstleutnant* von Niesemeuschel) (31/398)

Husaren-Regiment (3 squadrons, volunteer *Oberst Fürst* zu Schönburg) (30/428)

1. 6-Pfünder Reitende Batterie (4 cannon, 2x 8-pdr howitzers, *Hauptmann* Birnbaum) (4/141)

2. 6-Pfünder Reitende Batterie (4 cannon, 2x 8-pdr howitzers, *Hauptmann* Probsthain) (4/141)

Sappeur und Pontonnier Kompagnie (Saxon, *Ingenieur-Hauptmann* Claus) (1/52)[4]

---

4   *Haupmann* Claus with two officers and fifty others had been attached to Bernadotte's Swedish Army Corps following Leipzig, serving at the siege of Glückstadt. It would rejoin III German Army Corps not before 16 March.

Appendix II

Composition, Strength and Dispositions of III German Corps 20 February 1814[1]

Headquarters of the Duke of Saxe-Weimar (at Ath)
Generalstab (24/7):
Commander in Chief: General of Cavalry *Herzog von Sachsen-Weimar-Eisenach*
Aide de Camp: *Oberst* von Ziegler
Chef of the General Staff: *Generalmajor Freiherr* von Wolzogen
Chef of the General Quartermaster Staff: *Oberstleutnant* von Aster
Staff officer 'du jour': *Oberst* von Zeschwitz
Intendant of the Mobile Corps: *Hauptmann* von Nostitz
Stabsdragoner (squadron, *Leutnant* von Rechenberg) (1/59)
I. Gardebataillon (*Oberst Prinz* Bernhard von Weimar) (15/619)

Posts of Mons (*Generalmajor* von Ryssel)[2]
II/2. Leichten Regiment (*Major* von Selmitz) (12/520)
2. Provisorischen Linien-Regiment (*Major* von Brand, later *Oberst* von Seydewitz)
    II. Bataillon (14/506)
    III. Bataillon (*Major* Moritz) (16/535)
Füs/2. Reserve-Infanterie-Regiment (Prussian) (10/610)
Kürassier-Regiment (3 squadrons, *Oberst* von Berge) (27/442)
Pommersches Husaren-Regiment (Prussian, 2 sq., *Oberstleutnant* von Thümen) (20/437)[3]

---

1   Including attached units. Strengths are of 20 February (Prussians) and 24 February 1814 (Saxons). Two Saxon cavalry squadrons, one each of the uhlans and the hussars with a total of 260 men, had become part of *Oberst* von Geismar's *Streifcorps*. Strengths given are combatants present, divided in officers/others.
2   This corps had outposts and communication posts at Beaumont, Solre sur Sambre, Givry, Quaregnon, Ciply, Cuesmes, Jemappes and Hautraye, commanded by the commanding officer of the Prussian hussars, *Oberstleutnant* von Thümen.
3   Strength include both squadrons that were with *Generalleutnant* von Le Coq.

Freiwillige Jäger-Schwadron (Prussian, 1 sq., *Rittmeister* Tilemann von Schenck) (3/79)

1. 6-Pfünder Reitende Batterie (4 cannon, 2x 8pdr howitzers, *Hauptmann* Birnbaum) (4/130)

Reserve for Mons and Tournay and Leuze (*Generalleutnant* von Le Coq)[4]

II. Grenadier-Bataillon (*Major* von Wolframsdorf) (18/638)

III. Grenadier-Bataillon (*Oberstleutnant* von Anger) (14/645)

1. Provisorischen Linien-Regiment (*Major* von Wittern, later *Oberst* von Einsiedel)
   II. Bataillon (13/439)
   III. Bataillon (17/577)

Husaren-Regiment (Saxon, 2 sq., Saxon volunteer *Oberst* Fürst von Schönburg) (28/422)[5]

1. 12-Pfünder Fußbatterie (Saxon, ½ battery, 4 guns) (3/170 battery total)

1. 6-Pfünder Fußbatterie (6 cannon, 2x 8-pdr howitzers, *Hauptmann* Rouvroy II.) (4/147)

Pommersches Husaren-Regiment (Prussian, 2 sq., *Major* von Arnim)

Posts of Tournay (5th Prussian Division, *Generalleutnant* von Borstell)[6]

1. Pommersches Infanterie-Regiment (*Oberstleutnant* von Schon)
   Grenadier-Bataillon (*Major* von Romberg) (16/638)
   Freiwillige Fußjäger-Detachement (4/124)
   I. Bataillon (*Major* von Donop) (19/729)
   Freiwillige Fußjäger-Detachement (3/111)
   II. Bataillon (*Major* von Reitzenstein) (15/760)
   Füsilier-Bataillon (*Major* von Cardell) (13/608)
   Freiwillige Fußjäger-Detachement (1/66)

2. Reserve-Infanterie-Regiment (*Major* von Mirbach)
   I. Bataillon (*Major* von Massow) (13/463)
   II. Bataillon (*Major* von Hövel) (13/522)

2. Churmärkisches Landwehr-Infanterie-Regiment (*Major* von Bekendorf)
   I. Bataillon (*Major* von Massow) (13/510)
   II. Bataillon (15/569)
   III. Bataillon (19/519)

Westpreußisches Uhlanen-Regiment (4 sq., *Major* von Beyer) (22/507)
   Freiwillige Jäger-Schwadron (1 squadron) (1/40)

Pommersches National-Kavallerie-Regiment (4 sq., *Major* von Zastrow) (15/323)

---

4 This corps had outposts and communication posts at Harchies, Bonsecour, Blaton, Basecle, Reruwels, Bury, Villers and Vilaupin.

5 Strength include the squadron (*Major* von Fabrice) that was with *Oberst* von Geismar's *Streifcorps*.

6 This corps had its outposts and communication posts at Froidemont, Bruielle, Antoing, etc.

12-Pfünder Fußbatterie (Prussian, ½ battery, 4 guns)[7]
1. 12-Pfünder Fußbatterie (Saxon ½ battery, 4 guns)
6-Pfünder Fußbatterie No. 10 (8 guns, *Hauptmann* Magenhöfer) (3/124)
6-Pfünder Reitende Batterie No. 11 (8 guns, *Lieutenant* Borchardt) (4/129)
Sappeur und Pontonnier Kompagnie (Saxon, *Ingenieur-Hauptmann* Claus) (2/51)[8]

Major Hellwig's *Streifcorps* (Prussian)[9]
Fußjäger Bataillon (3 companies, *Lieutenant* Walther) (c. 300)
Büchsenjager (c. 100)
Freiwillige Reitende Jäger (1 squadron) (c. 160)
Husaren (3 squadrons) (c. 400)

Colonel Bikhalov's Cossack Regiment (*Bikhalov I Danskoi Kazachii Polki*) at Ghent[10]

Blockade detachment of Antwerp at Lier (*Generalmajor* von Gablenz)
Jäger Bataillon (*Major* von Jeschki) (10/363)
1. Leichten Regiment (*Major* von Rade, later *Oberstleutnant* von Bose)
    I. Bataillon (9/436)
    II. Bataillon (8/434)
Uhlanen-Regiment (I. and III. sq., Saxon volunteer *Oberstleutnant* von Niesemeuschel) (27/367)[11]
2. 6-Pfünder Reitende Batterie (4 cannon, 2x 8pdr howitzers, *Hauptmann* Probsthain) (4/129)
4. Reserve- or Elb-Infanterie-Regiment (Prussian, 3 battalions, *Oberstleutnant* von Reuß) (c. 1,400)
    I. Bataillon (*Oberstleutnant* von Hanstein)
    II. Bataillon (*Oberstleutnant* von Stutterheim)
    Füsilier-Bataillon (*Major* Le Blanc)
    Freiwillige Fußjäger-Detachement (*Hauptmann* von Liebhaber)
Brandenburgschen Dragoner-Regiment (Prussian, I. Squadron, *Major* von Osten)
Freiwillige Jäger-Schwadron (Prussian, squadron, *Rittmeister* Massow)

Garrison of Brussels
Bataillon Füsiliere des Herzogs zu Sachsen-Weimar (*Major* von Linker) (13/609)

---

7 This battery was not from the 5th Division itself. It was composed of men of the 12-Pfünder Fußbatterie No. 5 of *Hauptmann* Conradi, as well as the reserve artillery of Prussian III Corps.
8 Attached to Bernadotte's Swedish Army Corps. It would join III German Corps on 16 March.
9 Hellwig was at Courtray, to cover the right flank and to observe Lille, Yper and Ostend.
10 To observe Ostend, Sas-van-Gent, and Antwerp, and to hamper communications of Antwerp and the French troops south of it by patrolling the left bank of the Scheldt.
11 Strength include II. Squadron (*Major* von Berge) that was with *Oberst* von Geismar's *Streifcorps*.

Brandenburgschen Dragoner-Regiment (3rd squadron)
1. Artillery Park (3/92)

Composition and Dispositions of III German Corps, 18 March 1814

HAUPTCORPS (Duke of Saxe-Weimar, HQ in Mons):

Command of *Generalmajor* von Ryssel[1]
I. and II./2. Provisorischen Linien-Regiment
III./2. Landwehr-Infanterieregiment
Bataillon Füsiliere des Herzogs zu Sachsen-Weimar
1. 6-Pfünder Reitende Batterie (4 cannon, 2x 8-pdr howitzers, *Hauptmann* Birnbaum)
Pommersches Husaren-Regiment (4 squadrons and Freiwillige Jäger-Schwadron)

Prussian Division of *Generalleutnant* von Borstell[2]
1. Pommersches Infanterie-Regiment (4 battalions and 3 Fußjäger-Detachements)
2. Reserve-Infanterie-Regiment (2 battalions)
2. Churmärkisches Landwehr-Infanterie-Regiment (3 battalions)
Westpreußisches Uhlanen-Regiment (4 squadrons and Freiwillige Jäger-Schwadron)
Pommersches National-Kavallerie-Regiment (4 squadrons)
6-Pfünder Fußbatterie No. 10 (8 guns, *Hauptmann* Magenhöfer)
6-Pfünder Reitende Batterie No. 11 (6 cannon, 2 howitzers, *Leutnant* Borchardt)

Besieging corps of *Generalleutnant* von Le Coq[3]
I. Gardebataillon

---

1   Main Corps at Mons. Detachment of *Oberstleutnant* von Thümen near St. Ghislain, to observe Condé and Valenciennes; garrison of Mons commanded by *Major* von Cerrini (III./2. Landwehr-Infanterieregiment).
2   At Bavay, acting as covering and observation force against Valenciennes and Le Quesnoy.
3   Besieging force of Maubeuge. *Generalleutnant* von Le Coq would execute the siege of Maubeuge itself. A Landwehr battalion, as well is the Prussian Freiwillige Jäger-

II. Grenadier-Bataillon

III. Grenadier-Bataillon

III./2. Provisorischen Linien-Regiment

II./2. Leichten Regiment

I. and II./2. Landwehr-Infanterieregiment

Freiwillige Jäger zu Fuß Kompagnie 'Weimar'

Freiwillige Jäger zu Fuß Kompagnie 'Gotha'

Kürassier-Regiment (2 squadrons)

Freiwillige Jäger zu Pferde 'Weimar und Gotha' (1 squadron)

Freiwillige Jäger-Schwadron/Pommersches Husaren-Regiment

1. 12-Pfünder Fußbatterie (6 cannon, 2x 8-pdr howitzers, *Hauptmann* Rouvroy I.)

12-Pfünder Fußbatterie (Prussian, ½ battery, 4 guns, *Premierleutnant* Lent)

4 British 24-pdr cannon

8 Dutch mortars (1x French 12-inch Gomer, 2x Dutch 11-inch, 5x Dutch 7½-inch)

DETACHED CORPS (*Generalleutnant* von Thielmann) at Tournay and posts

1. Provisorischen Linien-Regiment (2 battalions)

1. Landwehr-Infanterieregiment (3 battalions)

Infanterie-Bataillon 'Gotha'

Infanterie-Regiment 'Anhalt-Dessau-Köthen'

    Infanterie-Bataillon 'Anhalt-Dessau-Köthen' (line infantry)

    Landwehr-Bataillon 'Anhalt-Dessau-Köthen' (Landwehr)

    Freiwillige Jäger zu Fuß 'Anhalt' (detachment)

Infanterie-Bataillon 'Anhalt-Bernburg' (2 line, 2 Landwehr coys)

Infanterie-Bataillon 'Schwarzburg'

Kürassier-Regiment (2 squadrons)

Husaren-Regiment (2 squadrons)

1. 6-Pfünder Fußbatterie (6 cannon, 2x 8-pdr howitzers, *Hauptmann* Rouvroy II.)

3. 6-Pfünder Fußbatterie (3 French 6-pdr cannon, *Premierleutnant* Hirsch)

'Belgian' 9-pdr battery (6 guns) (*Souslieutenant* Verwaert)

Major Hellwig's *Streifcorps* (also under Thielmann) at Menin and Courtray.

    Fußjäger Bataillon (4 companies, *Hauptmann* Kamlah) (c. 450)

    Büchsenjager (c. 100)

    Freiwillige Reitende Jäger (1 squadron)

    Husaren (3 squadrons)

Colonel Bikhalov's Cossack Regiment (*Bikhalov I Danskoi Kazachii Polki*) at Ghent.

Schwadron, would occupy Beaumont to observe Philippeville.

BLOCKADE DETACHMENT OF ANTWERP (*Generalmajor* von Gablenz)

Jäger Bataillon
1. Leichten Infanterie-Regiment (2 battalions)
Uhlanen-Regiment (2 squadrons)[4]
2. 6-Pfünder Reitende Batterie (4 cannon, 2x 8-pdr howitzers, *Hauptmann* Probsthain)
4. Reserve- or Elb-Infanterie-Regiment (3 battalions)
Brandenburgschen Dragoner-Regiment (1st squadron)
    Freiwillige Jäger-Schwadron (1 squadron)

GARRISON OF BRUSSELS (*Generalmajor* Reichsgraf von Lottum)

Landwehr-Bataillon 'Gotha'
Landwehr-Bataillon 'Weimar'
Landwehr-Bataillon 'Schwarzburg'
Brandenburgschen Dragoner-Regiment (III. Squadron)

---

4   On 27 March joined by IV./Uhlanen-Regiment.

Appendix IV

Organisation and Dispositions of III German Corps 3 April 1814

Generalleutnant von Thielmann's corps at Tournay:

Saxon Infantry Brigade (*Generalmajor* von Brause)
1. Provisorischen Linien-Regiment (3 battalions)
1. Landwehr-Infanterieregiment (3 battalions)

Anhalt-Thuringian Brigade (*Oberst* von Egloffstein)
Infanterie-Bataillon 'Gotha'
Infanterie-Regiment 'Anhalt-Dessau-Köthen' (1 line, 1 Landwehr battalion, jäger detachment)
Infanterie-Bataillon 'Anhalt-Bernburg'
Infanterie-Bataillon 'Schwarzburg'

Cavalry
Uhlanen-Regiment (2½ squadron)
Brandenburgschen Dragoner-Regiment (Prussian, 2 squadrons)

Artillery
1. 6-Pfünder Fußbatterie (6 cannon, 2x 8-pdr howitzers, *Hauptmann* Rouvroy II.)
3. 6-Pfünder Fußbatterie (Saxon, 2 French 6-pdr cannon, *Premierlieutenant* Hirsch)
'Belgian' 9-pdr battery (6 guns) (*Souslieutenant* Verwaert)

Attached: *Major* Hellwig's *Freicorps*, occupying Ghent with a post in Oudenaerde
Fußjäger Bataillon (4 companies, *Hauptmann* Kamlah) (c. 450)
Büchsenjager (c. 100)
Freiwillige Reitende Jäger (1 squadron)
Husaren (3 squadrons)

Generalleutnant von Le Coq's corps at Mons:

Saxon Infantry Brigade (*Generalleutnant* von Le Coq)
I. Gardebataillon
II. Grenadier-Bataillon
III. Grenadier-Bataillon
2. Landwehr-Infanterieregiment (3 battalions)
II./2. Leichten Regiment
Freiwillige Jäger zu Fuß Kompagnie 'Weimar'
Freiwillige Jäger zu Fuß Kompagnie 'Gotha'
Freiwillige Jäger zu Fuß Kompagnie 'Schwarzburg'

Saxon Infanterie Brigade (*Generalmajor* von Ryssel)
2. Provisorischen Linien-Regiment (3 battalions)
Bataillon Füsiliere des Herzogs zu Sachsen-Weimar
3. Landwehr-Infanterieregiment (2 battalions)[1]

Cavalry
Husaren-Regiment (3 squadrons)
Freiwillige Jäger zu Pferde 'Weimar und Gotha' (1 squadron)
2 Cossack regiments (Bikhalov & Rebrejev)

Artillery
1. 12-Pfünder Fußbatterie (6 cannon, 2x 8-pdr howitzers, *Hauptmann* Rouvroy I.)
1. 6-Pfünder Reitende Batterie (4 cannon, 2x 8-pdr howitzers, *Hauptmann* Birnbaum)
1st Mobile Park

British siege train (in Mons)
4 British 24-pdr cannon
8 Dutch mortars (1x French 12-inch Gomer, 2x Dutch 11-inch, 5x Dutch 7½-inch)

Reserve: *Generalleutnant* von Wallmoden:

***Generalmajor* von Gablenz near Ath**
Jäger Bataillon
1. Leichten Infanterie-Regiment (2 battalions)
4. Landwehr-Infanterieregiment (3 battalions)
Kürassier-Regiment (4 squadrons)
2. 12-Pfünder Fußbatterie (6 cannon, 2x 8pdr howitzers, *Hauptmann* Zandt)
2. 6-Pfünder Reitende Batterie (4 cannon, 2x 8-pdr howitzers, *Hauptmann* Probsthain)

---

1   After the engagement at Sweweghem, because of the heavy loss sustained the regiment was reduced to two battalions.

Generalleutnant von Wallmoden's Russo-German Legion at Grammont
6 infantry battalions, Kielmanseggesche Jäger-Korps, 8 cavalry squadrons
and 24 field guns (see Appendix VI for details).

Enghien, HQ (Duke of Saxe-Weimar)
Landwehr-Bataillon 'Weimar'

Garrison of Brussels (*Generalmajor* Reichsgraf von Lottum)
Landwehr-Bataillon 'Gotha'
Landwehr-Bataillon 'Schwarzburg'
Brandenburgschen Dragoner-Regiment (Prussian, 3rd squadron)
Main Artillery Park

Blockading detachment before Antwerp
4. Reserve- or Elb-Infanterie-Regiment (3 battalions)[2]
1. Westphälische Landwehr-Infanterie-Regiment (3 battalions and a
Fußjäger detachment)
I./2. Westphälische Landwehr-Infanterie-Regiment
3rd Hussar Regiment, King's German Legion

---

2 Would depart to join Bülow's Prussian III Corps.

Appendix V

Organisation of the Saxon Landwehr

Seven regiments of three battalions each, with each a reserve depot of a half battalion. The Saxon regions would raise these battalions with a nominal strength of 810 men:

1. Landwehr-Infanterieregiment (*Oberstleutnant* von Arnsdorf)
I. (Dresdener) Bataillon (*Oberstleutnant* von der Mosel)
II. (1. Wittenberger) Bataillon (*Major* von François)
III. (1. Niederlausitzer) Bataillon (*Major* von Könneritz)

2. Landwehr-Infanterieregiment (*Major* von Wolan)
I. (1. Thüringer) Bataillon (*Major* von Taucher)
II. (2. Thüringer) Bataillon (*Major* von Planitz)
III. (1. Voigtländer-Neustädter) Bataillon (*Major* von Römer)

3. Landwehr-Infanterieregiment (*Oberst* von Dierschen)
I. (1. Leipziger) Bataillon (*Hauptmann* von Zimmermann)
II. (1. Erzgebirgisches) Bataillon (*Major* von Elterlein)
III. (Schönburgisches) Bataillon (*Major* von Kommerstaedt)

4. Landwehr-Infanterieregiment (interim: *Major* von Selmnitz)
I. (1. Meißener) Bataillon (*Major* von Selmnitz)
II. (2. Leipziger) Bataillon (*Major* von Bünau)
III. (1. Oberlausitzer) Bataillon (*Major* von Buchner)

5. Landwehr-Infanterieregiment
I. (2. Meißener) Bataillon (*Hauptmann* von Sahr)
II. (2. Wittenberger) Bataillon (*Hauptmann* von Roos)
III. (2. Niederlausitzer) Bataillon (*Major* von Köckritz)

6. Landwehr-Infanterieregiment
I. (2. Oberlausitzer) Bataillon (*Hauptmann* von Unwerth)
II. (2. Erzgebirgisches) Bataillon (*Hauptmann* von Einsiedel)

III. (2. Voigtländer-Neustädter) Bataillon (*Hauptmann* von Lindemann)

7. Landwehr-Infanterieregiment[1]
I. (3. Oberlausitzer) Bataillon (*Hauptmann* von Steindel)
II. (3. Leipziger) Bataillon (*Hauptmann* von Schreibershofen)
III. (3. Erzgebirgisches) Bataillon (*Major* von Boxberg)

Two reserve companies (Thüringer Kreis) of 218 men each.

---

1   The 7. Landwehr-Infanterieregiment would never march because of lack of experienced officers and NCOs.

Composition of *Generalleutnant* von Wallmoden's Russo-German Legion, March 1814

Staff:

Commander in Chief and Chef: *Generalleutnant* von Wallmoden-Gimborn

Chef of the General Quartermaster Staff: *Oberstleutnant* von Clausewitz

General Quartermaster Staff: *Rittmeister* Graf von Wartensleben

General Adjutant: *Oberstleutnant* von Stülpnagel

Commander Russo-German Legion: *Generalmajor* von Arentschildt

Commander of the artillery of the Russo-German Legion: *Oberstleutnant* von Monhaupt

1. Brigade (*Major* von Natzmer I.)

1. Infanterie-Bataillon (*Hauptmann* von Schaper) (18/450)

2. Infanterie-Bataillon (*Hauptmann* von Köller) (18/450)

7. Infanterie-Bataillon (*Hauptmann* von Gregersdorf) (18/450)

Kielmanseggesche Jäger-Korps (*Oberst* Graf von Kielmansegg) (16/600)

1. Husaren-Regiment (4 squadrons, *Oberst* Freiherr von der Goltz) (24/600)

9-Pfünder Fußbatterie (8 British 9-pdr, *Hauptmann* Maghino) (5/200)

2. Reitende Batterie (Russian: 6x 6-pdr cannon, 2x ¼-pud licorne), *Premierleutnant* von Tiedemann II.) (5/188)

Park-Kolonne (*Premierleutnant* Hoyer) (4/74)

2. Brigade (*Oberst* Wardenburg)

3. Infanterie-Bataillon (*Hauptmann* von Tiedemann I.) (18/450)

4. Infanterie-Bataillon (*Hauptmann* von Horn) (18/450)

6. Infanterie-Bataillon (*Hauptmann* von Natzmer II.) (18/450)[1]

2. Husaren-Regiment (4 squadrons, *Major* Graf zu Dohna) (26/600)

1. Reitende Batterie (Russian: 6x 6-pdr cannon, 2x ¼-pud licorne, *Premierleutnant* Ramaer) (5/188)

---

1   At the Battle of Sehested (10 December 1813) the 5. Infanterie-Bataillon suffered such heavy loss that the battalion was disbanded, therefore it is not listed here. Except for the men of the 6. and 7. Infanterie-Bataillon, nearly all were veteran soldiers of several campaigns, therefore both battalions were brigaded with two experienced battalions. The infantry were armed with British muskets, the foot artillery with worn-out British iron cannon (probably old naval cannon), the horse artillery with Russian cannon and licornes (howitzers). There are indications that after the Battle of Göhrde the Fußbatterie had been provided with French 6-pdr cannon but this is not definite.

Appendix VII

Projected Final Order of Battle of III German Corps

Paper strength: (officers/other)

Stabsdragoner (2/62)

1. Infanterie-Brigade
1. Leichten Infanterie-Regiment (2 battalions) (46/1,440)
1. Provisorischen Linien-Regiment (3 battalions) (57/2,166)
1. Landwehr-Infanterieregiment (3 battalions) (59/2,430)
1. 12-Pfünder Fußbatterie (6 cannon, 2x 8-pdr howitzers) (4/200)
2. 6-Pfünder Fußbatterie (6 cannon, 2x 8-pdr howitzers) (4/181)

2. Infanterie-Brigade
2. Leichten Infanterie-Regiment (2 battalions) (46/1,440)
2. Provisorischen Linien-Regiment (3 battalions) (57/2,166)
2. Landwehr-Infanterieregiment (3 battalions) (59/2,430)
1. 6-Pfünder Fußbatterie (6 cannon, 2x 8-pdr howitzers) (4/181)

3. Infanterie-Brigade
Jäger Bataillon (21/662)
3. Provisorischen Linien-Regiment (3 battalions) (57/2,166)
3. Landwehr-Infanterieregiment (3 battalions) (59/2,430)
2. 12-Pfünder Fußbatterie (6 cannon, 2x 8-pdr howitzers) (4/200)

4. Infanterie-Brigade (Anhalt-Thuringian Division)
Bataillon Füsiliere des Herzogs zu Sachsen-Weimar (20/776)
Freiwillige Jäger zu Fuß Kompagnie 'Weimar' (5/99)
Freiwillige Jäger zu Fuß Kompagnie 'Gotha' (5/99)
Freiwillige Jäger zu Fuß Kompagnie 'Schwarzburg' (4/154)
Infanterie-Bataillon 'Gotha' (31/1,057)
Infanterie-Bataillon 'Anhalt-Dessau-Köthen' (16/576)
Infanterie-Bataillon 'Schwarzburg' (15/629)

Infanterie-Bataillon 'Anhalt-Bernburg' (2 line, 2 *Landwehr* companies)
   (15/494)
Landwehr-Bataillon 'Weimar' (16/592)
Landwehr-Bataillon 'Gotha' (20/697)
Landwehr-Bataillon 'Anhalt-Dessau-Köthen' (16/576)
Landwehr-Bataillon 'Schwarzburg' (12/462)
3. 6-Pfünder Fußbatterie (6 cannon, 2x 8-pdr howitzers) (4/181)

Reserve Brigade
Banner der freiwilligen Sachsen: Fußjäger (2 battalions)[1]
Line foot artillery company of the Banner (6 cannon, 2x 8-pdr howitzers)
   (4/181)
I. Gardebataillon (21/736)
II. Grenadier-Bataillon (21/714)
III. Grenadier-Bataillon (21/714)
4. Landwehr-Infanterieregiment (3 battalions) (59/2,430)

Cavallerie
Kürassier-Regiment (4 squadrons) (31/472)
Husaren-Regiment (6 squadrons) (32/588)
Uhlanen-Regiment (4 squadrons) (31/589)
Landdragoner (2 squadrons)
Banner der freiwilligen Sachsen: Husaren (2 squadrons)
Banner der freiwilligen Sachsen: Reitender Jäger (3 squadrons)
Freiwillige Jäger zu Pferde 'Weimar und Gotha' (1 squadron) (5/108)
1. 6-Pfünder Reitende Batterie (4 cannon, 2 howitzers) (4/159)
2. 6-Pfünder Reitende Batterie (4 cannon, 2 howitzers) (4/159)

Hauptpark (16/633)
1. Reserve Park (4/122)
2. Reserve Park (4/122)
Sappeur- und Pontonnier-Detachement (5/103)

---

1   Total strength of the Banner (infantry and cavalry, including the Landdragoner):
    (98/2,800)

Order of Battle of 1st French Army Corps (bis) (Maison), end of March 1814[1]

4e Division de Tirailleurs de la Jeune Garde (*Général de Division* Barrois)

1er Brigade
2e Régiment de Tirailleurs (2 battalions, *Colonel* Vionnet de Maringoné)
3e Régiment de Tirailleurs (2 battalions, *Colonel* Masson)

2e Brigade (*Général de Brigade* d'Arriule)
4e Régiment de Tirailleurs (2 battallions, *Colonel* Carré)
12e Régiment de Voltigeurs (2 battalions, *Colonel* Gromety)

Artillerie à Pied de la Garde

6e Division de Tirailleurs de la Jeune Garde (*Général de Division* Roguet)

1er Brigade (*Général de Brigade* Aymard)
9e Régiment de Tirailleurs (2 battalions, *Colonel* Bardin)
10e Régiment de Tirailleurs (2 battalions, *Colonel* Vézu)
11e Régiment de Tirailleurs (2 battalions, *Colonel* Vautrin)

2e Brigade (*Général de Brigade* Flamand)
12e Régiment de Tirailleurs (2 battalions, *Colonel* Mosnier)
13e Régiment de Tirailleurs (2 battalions, *Colonel* Laurede)

---

1 This corps was still incomplete, information is scarce and the formation changed quickly over time, with units still forming, and units and men drawn from or added to various garrisons. The battalions were weak and mainly composed of fresh conscripts. Order of battle composed of various sources.

Artillerie à Pied de la Garde

Division d'Infanterie Solignac (*Général de Division* Solignac)

1er Brigade (*Général de Brigade* Penne)
17e Régiment de Ligne (incomplete battalion)
28e Régiment de Ligne (incomplete battalion)
27e Régiment d'Infanterie Légère (incomplete battalion)

2e Brigade
51e Régiment de Ligne (incomplete battalion)
55e Régiment de Ligne (incomplete battalion)
65e Régiment de Ligne (incomplete battalion)
75e Régiment de Ligne (incomplete battalion)

Artillerie à Pied

Division de Cavalerie de la Garde (*Général de Division* Castex)
2e Régiment de Chasseurs à Cheval de la Garde (4 squadrons and a company of Jeune Garde Mameluks, *Général de Brigade* Meuziau)[2]
2e Régiment de Chevau-Légers Lanciers de la Garde (5 squadrons, *Général de Brigade* Lalaing d'Audenarde)
1er Régiment de Gardes d'Honneur (*Colonel* Randon de Pully)
3e Régiment de Gardes d'Honneur (detachment)
Gendarmes d'Elite à Cheval (300)
3e Comp. Artillerie à Cheval de la Garde

---

2 Consisting of the 6th, 7th, 8th and 9th squadron of the 1er Régiment de Chasseurs à Cheval de la Garde.

Bibliography

Books and Articles

Anon., 'Briefe eines zur Armee reisenden Sachsen', in *Deutsche Blätter* (Leipzig und Altenburg: Friedr. Arn. Brockhaus, 1814), Vol. 2, pp.441-445, 509-515: Vol. 3, pp.57-64, 353-358, 395-400, 410-416, 529-542.

Anon., 'Das Gefecht bei Courtray am 31. März 1814' in *Denkwürdigkeiten für die Kriegskunst und Kriegsgeschichte* (Berlin: G. Reimer, 1820), Vol. VI, pp.134-142.

Anon., *Der Feldzug des Corps des Generals Grafen Ludwig von Wallmoden-Gimborn an der Nieder-Elbe und in Belgien, in den Jahren 1813 und 1814* (Altenburg: H.A. Pierer, 1848).

Anon., 'Der Feldzug des dritten deutschen Armee-korps in Flandern, im Jahre 1814 – Versuch eines Beitrages zur allgemeinen Kriegschichte der Alliirten (Aus dem Tagebuche eines deutschen Officiers)' in *Oestreichische militärische Zeitschrift* (Wien: Anton Strauß's sel. Witwe, 1831), Vol.II, pp.186-214, 310-322; Vol.III, pp.19-38.

Anon., 'Die Vertheidigung von Tournay am 31. März 1814', in *Militair-Wochenblatt* (Berlin: Ernst Siegfried Mittler, 1829), Vol. 14, pp.4188-4189. With an addition in *Militair-Wochenblatt* (Berlin: Ernst Siegfried Mittler, 1830), Vol. 15, p.4225.

Anon., 'Geschichte des dritten deutschen Armee-Corps unter dem Befehle des Herzogs von Sachsen-Weimar im Feldzuge von 1814', in *Militärisches Taschenbuch* (Leipzig: Baumgärtnerschen Buchhandlung, 1824), Vol. 5, pp.1-32.

Anon., 'Über die Haltung Bernadotte's im Feldzuge 1814', in *Jahrbücher für die deutsche Armee und Marine* (Berlin: Verlag von A. Bath, 1895), Vol. 97, pp.335-337.

Anon., 'Ueber das Gefecht von Sweweghem am 31. März 1814', in *Militair-Wochenblatt*, (Berlin: Ernst Siegfried Mittler, 1829), Vol. 14, pp.4136-4137.

Anon., 'Ueber das glorreiche Gefecht bei Courtrai (Aus dem Briefe eines freiwilligen reitenden Jägers der Schaar von Sachsen-Weimar an einen Freund in Thüringen', in *Deutsche Blätter* (Leipzig und Altenburg: Friedr. Arn. Brockhaus, 1814), Vol. 3, pp.436-438.

Aerde, Roger van, 'Kozakken te Gent – De Geschiedenis van Peetje Kozak', in *Ghendtsche Tydinghen*, Vol. 11, Nr. 6 (Gent: Heemkundige en Historische Kring Gent v.z.w., 1982), pp.296-309.

Amoudru, 'Blocus d'Anvers en 1814. Carnot Gouverneur', in *Journal de l Ármée* (Paris, Bureau de Journal, 1834), pp.7-13.

Bamford, Andrew, *A Bold and Ambitious Enterprise – The British Army in the Low Countries, 1813-1814* (London: Frontline Books, 2013).

Bas,, F. de, *Prins Frederik der Nederlanden en zijn Tijd* (Schiedam: H.A.M. Roelandts, 1891).

Böttiger, C.W., *Geschichte des Kurstaates und Königreiches Sachsen* (Hamburg: Friedrich Perthes, 1831).

Bucher, Ludwig Ferdinand, *Der Feldzug des dritten deutschen Armee-Corps in Flandern, im Befreiungskriege des Jahres 1814* (Leipzig: Hermann Costenoble, 1854).

Bülau, Professor Friedrich (continued), *Geschichte des Sächsischen Volkes und Staates von Dr. C. Gretschel* (Leipzig: J.C. Hinrichs'sche Buchhandlung, 1853), Vol. 3.

Calmon-Maison, Jean Joseph Robert, 'Le Général Maison et le 1er Corps de la Grande Armée', in *Revue des Deux Mondes* (Paris: Bureau de La Revue des Deux Mondes , 1914) , Vol. 19, pp.168-204.

Cartellieri, Professor Dr. Otto, 'Der Einzug Karl August in Belgien', in *Belgischer Kurier – Brüsseler Tageszeitung* (Brussels, 30 October 1916), p.2.

Cartellieri, Professor Dr. Otto, 'Karl August von Sachsen-Weimar in Belgien – die Anfänge der provisorischen Regierung im Jahre 1814', in *Die Grenzboten, Zeitschrift für Politik, Literatur und Kunst*, Vol. 76, 1st quarter (Berlin: Verlag der Grenzboten G.m.b.h.), pp.92-96.

Colenbrander, Dr. H.T., *Gedenkstukken der Algemeene Geschiedenis van Nederland van 1795 tot 1840*, Vol. 7, *Vestiging van het Koninkrijk 1813-1815* ('s-Gravenhage: Martinus Nijhoff, 1914).

Coremans, Docteur, *Éphémérides Belges de 1814 (Février-Juillet), D'après les Archives du Gouvernement provisoire de Cette Époque* (Bruxelles: M. Hayez, 1847).

Crusius, A., *Der Winterfeldzug in Holland, Brabant und Flandern, eine Episode aus dem Befreiungskriege 1813 und 1814* (Luxemburg: B. Bückt, 1865).

(Damitz, Karl von), *Geschichte des Feldzuges von 1814 in dem östlichen und nördlichen Frankreich bis zur Einnahme von Paris* (Berlin, Posen und Bromberg: Ernst Siegfried Mittler, 1842-1843).

Egloffstein, Hermann Freihernn von, *Carl August im niederländische Feldzug 1814* (Weimar: Verlag der Goethe-Gesellschaft, 1927).

Egloffstein, Hermann Freihernn von, 'Carl Augusts Reise nach Paris und England 1814', in *Deutsche Rundschau*, Vol. 136 (Berlin: Gebrüder Paetel, 1908), pp.199-221, 406-418.

Etzel, Anton von, 'Das Kaiser Alexander Grenadier-Regiment', in *Zeitschrift für Kunst, Wissenschaft und Geschichte des Krieges*, Vol. 87 (Berlin: E.G. Mittler und Sohn, 1853), pp.197-225.

Fabricius, Hans, 'Der Parteigänger Friedrich von Hellwig und seine Streifzüge, im kriegsgeschichtlichen Zusammenhange betrachtet. Ein Beitrag zur Geschichte des kleinen Krieges in den Jahren 1792 bis 1814', in *Jahrbücher für die deutsche Armee und Marine*, (Berlin: Verlag von A. Bath, 1895) Vol. 97, pp.1-15, 131-147: Vol. 98 (1896) pp.53-73, 166-184, 313-327.

Flathe, Dr. Th., *Geschichte des Kurstaates und Königreiches Sachsen*, Vol. 3, *Neuere geschichte Sachsens von 1806-1865* (Gotha: Friedrich Andreas Perthes, 1873).

(Hasenkamp, Hugo von), *General Graf Bülow von Dennewitz in den Feldzügen von 1813 und 1814* (Berlin: F.A. Brockhaus, 1843).

Hauthal, Dr. Ferd., *Geschichte der Sächsischen Armee in Wort und Bild* (Leipzig: J.G. Bach, 1859).

Holtzendorff, Albrecht Graf von, *Beiträge zu der Biographie des Generals Freiherrn von Thielmann und zur Geschichte der jüngst vergangenen Zeit* (Leipzig: Wilhelm Rauck, 1830).

Hüttel, R. von, *Der General der Kavallerie Freiherr von Thielmann* (Berlin: Verlag Laue, 1828).

Jacobs, Hauptmann Gustav, *Geschichte der Feldzüge und Schicksale der Sachsen-Gotha-Altenburgischen Krieger in den Jahren 1807-1815* (Altenburg: Expedition des Eremiten, 1835).

Janson, Generalleutnant A. v., 'Der Herzog Karl August von Sachsen-Weimar und der Kronprinz Karl Johann von Schweden während des Feldzuges 1814 in den Niederlanden', in *Deutsche Rundschau*, Vol. CXXVIII (Berlin: Gebrüder Paetel, 1906), pp.40-54.

Koolemans Beijnen et al., G.J.W., *Historisch Gedenkboek der Herstelling van Neêrlands Onafhankelijkheid in 1813* (Haarlem: De Erven F. Bohn, 1912-1913).

Kretschmar, A. von, *Geschichte der Kurfürstlich und Königlich Sächsischen Feld-Artillerie von 1620-1820* (Berlin: Ernst Siegfried Mittler und Sohn, 1876).

Kretzschmer, J.C., *Soldaten-, Kriegs- ind Lager-Leben. Blüthen der Erinnerung aus dem Befreiungskriege* (Danzig: L.G. Homann, 1838), Vol. 2.

Larraß, Johannes Anton, *Geschichte des Königlich Sächsischen 6. Infanterie-Regiments Nr. 105 und seine Vorgeschichte 1701 bis 1887* (Straßburg i.E.: H.L. Kayser, 1887).

Meinecke, Friedrich, *Das Leben des Generalfeldmarschalls Hermann von Boyen* (Stuttgart: J.G. Cotta'schen Buchhandlung, 1896).

Merode-Westerloo, Comte de, *Souvenirs du Comte de Merode-Westerloo, Sénateur du Royaume* (Paris: E. Dentu & Bruxelles: Ch.-J.-A. Greuse, 1864).

Mikhailofsky-Danilefsky, A., *History of the Campaign in France, in the Year 1814* (London: Smith, Elder, and Co. Cornhill, 1839).

(Mauvillon, F.W. von), 'Tagebuch des Hellwigschen Partisanen-Corps, von dessen Entstehung bis zu seiner Auflösung, mit einigen Bruchstücken aus dem Leben des Anführers', in *Militairische Blätter* (Essen and Duisburg: G.D. Bädeker, 1820), Vol. 1, pp.97-152.

Ollech, (Karl Rudolf) von, *Carl Friederich Wilhelm von Reyher. General der Kavallerie und Chef des Generalstabes der Armee. Ein Beitrag zur Geschichte der Armee mit Bezug auf die Befreiungskriege von 1813, 1814 und 1815* (Berlin: Ernst Siegfried Mittler und Sohn, 1869), Vol.II.

Oppel, von, *Sammlung von Beiträgen zur Geschichte des Königl. Sächs. 1. Leichten Reiter-Regiments vacant Prinz Clemens. Zusammengetragen von dem Rittmeister und Adjutant von Oppel im Jahre 1829* (Freiberg: Gerlach'schen Buckdruckerei, 1857).

Plotho, Carl von, *Der Krieg in Deutschland und Frankreich in den Jahren 1813 und 1814* (Berlin: Carl Friedrich Amelang, 1817), Vol.III.

Poppe, Maximilian, *Chronologische Uebersicht der wichtigsten Begebenheiten aus den Kriegsjahren 1806-1815. Mit besonderer Beziehung auf Leipzigs Völkerschlacht und Beifügung der Original-Dokumente, Vol. 2, 1813-1815* (Leipzig: Theodor Thomas, 1848).

Poullet, Prosper, *La Belgique et la Chute de Napoleon 1er* (Bruxelles: Société Belge de Librairie, 1895).

Probst, F.P.von, *Geschichte des Königlich-Preußischen Zweiten Dragoner-Regiments* (Schwedt: J.C.W. Jantzen, 1829).

Quistorp, Barthold von, *Die Kaiserlich Russisch-Deutsche Legion. Ein Beitrag zur Preußischen Armee-Geschichte* (Berlin: Carl Heymann, 1860).

Schels, Major Joh. Bapt., 'Des Oberst Baron Geismar Streifzug in Belgien und Frankreich; im Februar und März 1814', in *Oestreichische militärische Zeitschrift* (Wien: Anton Strauß's sel. Witwe, 1838), Vol. 4, pp.115-135.

Schimpff, Georg von, *Geschichte des Kgl. Sächs. Garde-Reiter-Regiments* (Dresden: Wilhelm Baensch Verlagshandlung, 1880).

Schimpf, Hans von, *Geschichte der beiden Königlich Sächsischen Grenadier-Regimenter: Erstes (Leib-) Grenadier-Regiment Nr. 100 und Zweites Grenadier-Regiment Nr. 101, Kaiser Wilhelm, König von Preussen* (Dresden: Carl Höckner, 1877).

Sporschill, Johann, *Die grosse Chronik. Geschichte des Krieges des Verbündeten Europa's gegen Napoleon Bonaparte, in den Jahren 1813, 1814 und 1815* (Braunschweig: George Westermann, 1841), Vol. 1, Part 2.

Starkloff, R., *Das Leben des Herzogs Bernhard von Sachsen-Weimar-Eisenach, Königlich niederländischer General der Infanterie* (Gotha: E.F. Thienemann, 1865), Vol. 1.

Swederus, G. (transl. Frisch, Dr. C.F.), *Schwedens Politik und Kriege in den Jahren 1808 bis 1814 vorzüglich unter Leitung des Kronprinzen Carl Johan* (Leipzig: Fr. Fleischer, 1866, Vol. 2).

Taggesell, David August, *Tagebuch eines Dresdner Bürgers; oder Niederschreibung der Ereignisse eines jeden Tages, soweit solche vom Jahre 1806 bis 1851 für Dresden und dessen Bewohner von geschichtlichem, gewerblichem oder örtlichem Interesse waren* (Dresden: Hof-Buchhandlung von Rudolf Kuntze, 1854).

Taylor, Ernest (ed.), *The Taylor Papers, being a Record of Certain Reminiscences, Letters and Journals in the Life of Lieut.-Gen. Sir Herbert Taylor G.C.B., G.C.H.* (New York, Bombay & Calcutta: Longmans, Green, and Co., 1913).

Vane, Charles William, Marquess of Londonderry (ed.), *Correspondence, despatches, and Other Papers, of Viscount Castlereach, Second Marquess of Londonderry* (London: John Murray, 1853), Vol. IX.

Vane, Lieut.-General Charles William, Marquess of Londonderry, G.C.B. G.C.H., *Narrative of the War on Germany and France, in 1813 and 1814* (London: Henry Colburn and Richard Bentley, 1830).

Varnhagen von Ense, K.A., *Leben des generals Grafen Bülow von Dennewitz* (Berlin: Georg Reimer, 1853).

Wahl, Adelbert, *Geschichte des Europaïschen Staatensystems im Zeitalter der Französischen Revolution und der der Freiheitskriege (1789-1815)* (München & Berlin: R. Oldenbourg, 1912).

Weil, le Commandant, *La Campagne de 1814 d'Après les Documents des Archives Impériales et Royales de la Guerre à Vienne – La Cavalerie des Armées Alliées Pendant la Campagne de 1814* (Paris: Libraire Militaire de L. Baudoin, 1892 and 1896), Vols. 2 and 4.

Weltzien, Louis von, *Memoiren des königlich preußischen Generals der Infanterie Ludwig von Reiche* (Leipzig: F.A. Brockhaus, 1857), Vol. 2.

Werckmeister, G., *Tagebuch des Feldzuges von 1813 und 1814, geführt von Ferdinand Werckmeister, Oberjäger im Detachement der Freiwilligen des Dragoner-Regiments Prinz Wilhelm von Preußen*, http://www.georg-werckmeister.de/downloads/dragoner.pdf accessed 15 April 2019.

Wolzogen, Alfred Freiherrn von, *Memoiren des königlich preußischen Generals der Infanterie, Ludwig Freiherrn von Wolzogen* (Leipzig: Otto Wigand, 1851).

Zschokke, Heinrich (ed.), 'Denkschrift über den sächsischen Banner', in *Ueberlieferungen zur Geschichte unserer Zeit* (Aarau: Heinrich Remigius Sauerländer, 1817), pp.583-600.

Periodicals and Magazines

Allgemeine Zeitung. Mit allerhöchsten Privilegien (München, 1814).

National-Zeitung der Deutschen – Jahrgang 1814 (Gotha: Beckerschen Buchhandlung, 1814).

Archival Sources, Decrees and State Papers

Anon., *General-Gouvernements-Blatt für Sachsen*, Vol. 1-2 (Leipzig & Dresden: Redaction des General-Gouvernements-Blatts für Sachsen, 1813-1814) .

Anon., *Journal Officiel du Gouvernement de la Belgique*, Vol. 1 (Bruxelles: Chez Weissenbruch, 1814).

Moßdorf, Friedrich, *Drey Sammlungen der seit dem Monate Oktober 1813 bis zu Ende des Monats May 1815 zuerst in den Leipziger Zeitungen und sodann in den General-Gouvernementsblättern zerstreut erschienenen Landes-Gouvernements-Verfügungen für das Königreich Sachsen, nebst anderen Bekanntmachungen und Verordnungen, auch einigen gemeinnützlichen Aufsätzen* (Dresden: Königlich Sächsischen Hofbuchdruckerei, 1824).